HOW TO SET UP YOUR OWN
SMALL BUSINESS

MAX FALLEK

Published by
AMERICAN INSTITUTE OF SMALL BUSINESS
7515 Wayzata Boulevard, Suite 129
Minneapolis, Minnesota 55426
(952)- 545-7001

VOL. II

ISBN 0-939069-68-7
Library of Congress Catalog Number: 89-084218

TABLE OF CONTENTS

HOW TO SET UP YOUR OWN SMALL BUSINESS

VOLUME 1

VOLUME II

Chapter 13

Minding the store

How to handle those sticky problems

Operating your business can present you with a lot of surprises or, with careful planning, can present a smooth, efficient and pleasant environment for your customers.

To achieve the image you want to create involves careful planning — this will take time — well ahead of your grand opening. Successful businesses build first on their policies. They are written to become solid points of reference, from which operating procedures are developed. For example, if you know what your sales policy is, you can then set up the procedures to carry it out.

When you or your employees are 'minding the store,' you will be using established day-to-day procedures of inventory management, credit, security, what to do in emergencies, how to handle customers, and so on.

There will always be crises, but you can avoid most of them if you have anticipated the solutions before they occur.

In this chapter you will learn:

1. What business policies you should consider for your business, and how to apply them.

2. How to establish your own credit, as well as extend credit to your customers. How to apply for the major national charge card plans such as Visa, MasterCard and American Express.

3. How to collect past due accounts and how to write collection letters.

4. How to protect your business from fire, theft, pilferage and other threats.

5. How to provide for quality control, and then keep it working for you.

6. The principles of inventory management.

7. How to keep abreast of your industry through trade and/or professional organizations.

BUSINESS POLICIES

When you first start a small business, like most others, you will probably be your only employee. You are operating by yourself and making every business decision yourself — such as, where to locate, how to advertise, what merchandise and equipment to buy, what hours you are open.

As your business grows and you add employees, you will delegate some of these decisions to others, since you can no longer do everything yourself. When you delegate, you will want to make it very clear to your employee what area is to be his or her responsibility and how it should be managed. This will become your **Policy.**

Establish your policies with permanence in mind. Think them through carefully and write them down, so there can then be no question as to how you operate your business. Policies are not intended to help you through a crisis situation but to establish order and rules for running your business

As you write your policies, keep in mind "Consumerism" and "Customer Relations."

Consumerism is a word that has recently crept into the language. It's an "umbrella" term for several laws defining what you legally **have** to do in such areas as labeling, contract wording, safety warnings, truth-in-advertising, etc

Customer relations is what you **want** to do for your customer. It is your "goodwill." You can establish a written policy that says you and your company will be accommodating, helpful, courteous, reasonable, understanding, service oriented, efficient and all the other good things you might think of. But good customer relations is more than having the words written down — it is you and your employees putting them into practice.

Here are some examples of business policies you may want to consider:

1. Returns Policy

Customers today have learned to expect a cheerful return on just about anything. It's best to accept a return, or at least an exchange, if the merchandise is in saleable condition and, sometimes even if it isn't, for preserving goodwill. Budget a built-in loss figure for such situations. You can, however, explain your return policy with small, appropriate signs such as:

- Items for return or exchange will be accepted within 10 days of purchase when accompanied by sales receipt

- No Cash Refunds.

- We will repair or exchange any defective merchandise

2. Quality of Merchandise

As a retailer, your concern for quality merchandise starts with what you have accepted in the receiving room. After you've checked to be sure that the quantity you ordered has arrived on time, is fresh and in working condition, it's your responsibility to be sure it stays this way until the customer buys it. Make spot checks on the sales floor regularly.

The quality of merchandise (or service) you offer will quickly determine your reputation. If you can offer the ideal combination of high quality at a fair price, your customers will receive the **value** they expect for their money. And nothing will bring them back faster.

Because there is room in the marketplace for all levels of quality (good, better and best), look for the best opportunity for what you have to offer. Then be consistent. Build your reputation on consistency and value, then your customers will think of you, rather than your competition.

Your store's appearance will also reflect the quality of your merchandise. Clean floors, windows, restrooms are all important, as is the neat appearance of you and your employees. You will want the whole atmosphere of your store to reflect quality. If this is your intent (or demand), then your store appearance becomes part of your Business Policy.

3. **Sales Policy**

Other than offering the customer your fine product or merchandise, will you offer any discounts? Mark-downs? Many retailers promise customers such things as:

- Money-Back Guarantees

- Limited Warranties

- Free Home Trials

- Matching the Competition's Price, if Lower

Warranties from manufacturers vary and items usually must be taken to an authorized dealer for repairs. If that's you, what kind of reimbursement has the manufacturer agreed to give you?

Free home trials are a sales technique based on the assumption that if you can get a product into the home, chances are the customer will keep it. This can be risky, but the discretion is yours.

Will you offer product demonstrations? Some suppliers will do this for you free. Will you offer to teach customers, for instance, how to arrange flowers? Offer cooking classes? If you're renting boats, will you teach classes in boat safety?

If you guarantee the lowest prices, you must know your competition. Are they the specialty shops in your neighborhood? The mass merchant chain in town? The mail order house in New York? You'll have to be able to verify the prices, also, such as with a newspaper ad.

4. **Delivery Policy**

Very few merchants offer free deliveries, and you may not want to offer any at all. Should you choose to, figure the cost, add it to the purchase price and decide whether to use a local delivery service, UPS, mail or some other method. You may find free delivery gives you a competitive edge. Or, you must offer it to stay competitive. Whatever the case, count the cost before you take the plunge.

5. **Smoking Policy**

If there's a fire marshall's law against smoking, you'll be required to post it. You may also need to set aside areas for smoking and non-smoking. And if you simply don't want people to smoke, put up a courteous sign requesting that they not.

6. **Food and Pets**

If your decor or merchandise is easily damaged, you may not want to allow food or pets in your store. In the case of pets, a health ordinance may forbid them on the premises.

7. **Dress Codes**

About all you can require by law are shoes and modesty. Uniforms can be a good way to establish dress codes, but to achieve what you want in employee appearance, consider the appropriateness of the applicant's dress when hiring.

8. **Hours**

Your decision when establishing business hours should be based on the shopping habits of your customers, your competitor's hours and, in some cases, the agreement of other merchants in your area to fix certain business hours. After you've checked these out, your policy can be whatever you want. Important to you, however, will be your sales goals and the number of employees needed to staff your business properly when you are open.

9. **Gift Wrapping**

Many small merchants offer free gift wrapping to attract customers. This may be to your advantage, since most larger stores cannot afford to. Using paper, boxes or an emblem identifying your store is also good advertising.

10. **Contributions**

Establish this policy quickly, because you will soon be confronted by fund raisers. Initially, a commitment to the United Way in your area can be used as an umbrella approach. You may wish to add one more "favorite" charity; this contribution will give you the answer to use when asked for contributions from other organizations. Since contributions are tax deductible, it may be to your advantage to give more. People will understand if you can't contribute during your start-up phase, but they will be back later.

These are some of the policies you may want to consider when establishing yours. Once you have determined what policies you want, make sure your employees know and understand them. Also, ask them to keep you informed of comments or complaints made about your business. As the owner, you need to know.

CREDIT

How to Establish Your Own Credit

Having already obtained financing for your business will give you the base you need to establish operating credit. For perhaps three to six months, you will be referring creditors to your bank and personal charge accounts for verification of credit. Once this is established, build your business credit by paying your bills when due. If you've planned your cash-flow carefully, this should not be a problem.

You can check your current personal credit rating by requesting a report from your local credit bureau, listed under Credit Reporting Agencies in the yellow pages. If there are several agencies, ask your banker, or a store where you charge, which agency they use - and call them. Should you have any negative or incorrect reports, ask that agency what steps to take to correct them.

If you're operating your business with a loan from your bank, repaying your loan as scheduled will be the best credit rating you can establish.

How to Extend Credit

You may begin by offering no credit at all, but as you expand you'll learn that in order to increase your sales and keep up with the competition, you will need to offer this service to your customers. In dealing with other businesses, it is often a must.

If you have the inventory and financial means to extend your own credit, you can offer your customers a charge account from your store. Be sure to figure the costs of bookkeeping, accounting, collecting and interest if you provide this service. There will also be forms, statements to send, postage, credit returns and so on.

If you are not in a financial position to do this, you can offer one or more of the national charge account plans now widely used, including:

- American Express
- Visa
- MasterCard
- Diners Club
- Discover America

Accepting national charge cards is an essential service in order to keep up with the competition for certain types of retail businesses such as gift shops, clothing and furniture stores and restaurants, among others.

Verifying Credit

The most economical way to verify credit is to do it yourself. Ask for one or two credit cards the customer is presently using, or ask for a bank reference. If you feel it's necessary, call the accounts receivable departments of credit card companies and ask if this customer is current with his accounts. Or you can call the bank to ask if the customer's present balance will cover the cost of purchases just made.

One of the services your own bank may offer is to provide credit checks upon request. Tell the bank about your prospective account and they may be in a position to tell you whether or not to extend credit.

The Use of Credit Card Companies

Among the most popular consumer charge account services are Visa, MasterCard and American Express.

Visa/MasterCard

Visa/Mastercard sell their services to banks, not to the business owner, and both of these credit cards are handled in the same manner. The procedure is to call the bank in your community these companies do business with. (Your own bank will be able to tell you the name.)

You will sign an agreement with this bank to use their Visa/ MasterCard services, and their representative will tell you —

- How to handle charges and fill out forms.
- How to handle credits and returns.
- How to verify credit approval.
- How you will be reimbursed.

Usually, you deposit your sales slips in the bank as you would a normal bank deposit, and the amount is credited to your account. At the end of the month, you are billed a percentage of your gross sales for the use of their system. The amount is approximately 2-1/2 percent.

American Express

American Express is different from Visa/MasterCard in that you contact the company's representative in your community. If the number is not in your telephone directory, or if you live in a rural area, call the national WATS line information operator at 1-800-555-1212 to obtain the closest toll-free American Express number. Then call them and a representative will get in touch with you to explain their system. Unlike Visa/MasterCard, you will mail your sales receipts to an American Express office, which in turn sends you a check for the amount of your sales less a service charge.

Other charge companies include Diners Club, Shoppers Charge as well as regional plans which your own bank can tell you about. Service charges vary for each charge card company, from one community to another, and from one bank to another.

Examples of forms for Visa/MasterCard follow.

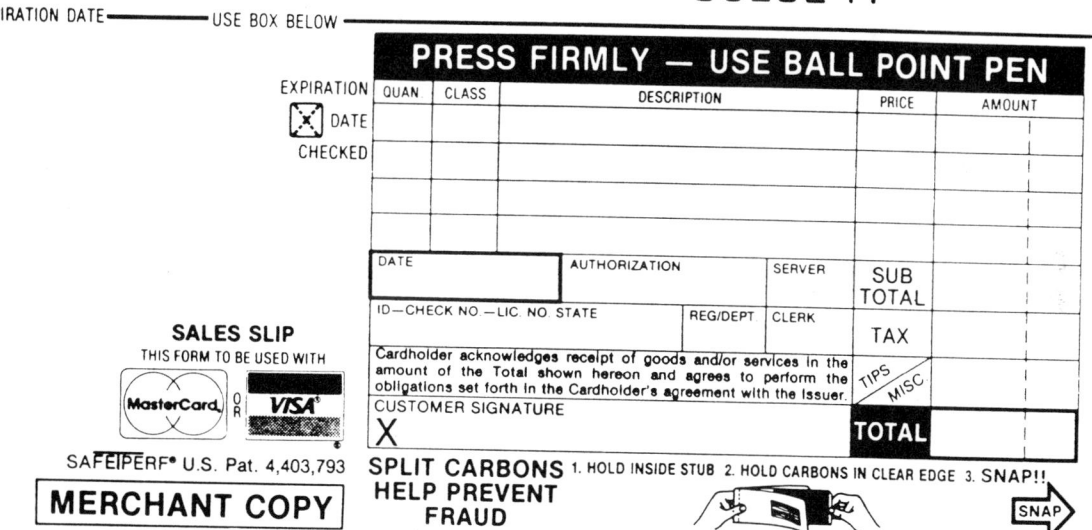

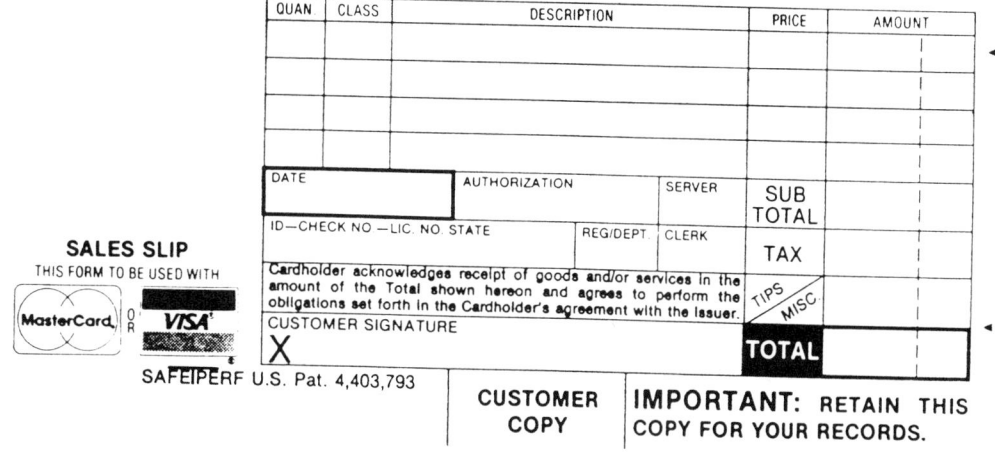

THIS COPY IS SENT TO THE
BANK WITH YOUR DEPOSIT.

CREDIT SLIP FORMS INCLUDE THREE COPIES

A. One copy for the merchant's records.

B. One copy to the customer.

C. One copy to the bank.

6711851

DATE	CLERK	DEPT.	REASON FOR RETURN		DATE OF SALE	
QUANTITY		DESCRIPTION		UNIT COST	AMOUNT	
CREDIT SLIP				SUB-TOTAL		
I request that the above cardholder account be credited with the amount shown as TOTAL because of the return of, or adjustments on, the goods, services and/or other items of value described, and authorize the bank to which this credit slip is delivered to charge my account in accordance with my agreement with such bank.				TAX		
MERCHANT SIGNATURE **X**				**TOTAL**		

THIS FORM TO BE USED WITH MasterCard OR VISA

MERCHANT COPY

MERCHANT: RETAIN THIS COPY FOR YOUR RECORDS

6711851

DATE	CLERK	DEPT.	REASON FOR RETURN		DATE OF SALE	
QUANTITY		DESCRIPTION		UNIT COST	AMOUNT	
CREDIT SLIP				SUB-TOTAL		
I request that the above cardholder account be credited with the amount shown as TOTAL because of the return of, or adjustments on, the goods, services and/or other items of value described, and authorize the bank to which this credit slip is delivered to charge my account in accordance with my agreement with such bank.				TAX		
MERCHANT SIGNATURE **X**				**TOTAL**		

THIS FORM TO BE USED WITH MasterCard OR VISA

CUSTOMER COPY

IMPORTANT: RETAIN THIS COPY FOR YOUR RECORDS

6711851

DATE	CLERK	DEPT.	REASON FOR RETURN		DATE OF SALE	
QUANTITY		DESCRIPTION		UNIT COST	AMOUNT	
CURRENCY CONVERSION RATE		RATE	AMOUNT		SUB-TOTAL	
I request that the above cardholder account be credited with the amount shown as TOTAL because of the return of, or adjustments on, the goods, services and/or other items of value described, and authorize the bank to which this credit slip is delivered to charge my account in accordance with my agreement with such bank				TAX		
MERCHANT SIGNATURE **X**						

THIS FORM TO BE USED WITH MasterCard OR VISA

CREDIT SLIP BANK COPY

The Abuse of Credit

There are simply no rules for spotting a deadbeat or slow payer on sight. Your best protection is to verify credit as suggested earlier, and review your experience in six months. At that time, you will have some history and be able to budget for minor losses.

If you operate on a 10% net profit level, it may take ten or more "good" sales of the same item to make up for one non-paying customer. So it pays to keep the bad apples in the right perspective.

Follow-Up and Collections

A slogan among creditors is: You Made Your Sale — or Did You? No sale is complete until the goods or services are paid for. To facilitate collections, here are some courteous prompts you might use in your initial billings:

- Please pay from this invoice — no statement will be sent.

- Second Billing — A reminder . . .

- Third Billing — We have not received your payment as of (date). Please remit.

- Fourth Billing — Past Due. Please remit.

Flag the accounts that have not been paid: keep them in your follow-up file, cross reference them to the customer's file, highlight them in your ledger — but keep very close track. You don't want them to slip by. Remember, your "good" and "fair" credit risks want to keep their books in order, too.

When you have used all these initial reminders, you are now into the fourth month of non-payment and some personal letters are in order. These can be very delicate, and if you are at all uncertain of the basics of good business letter writing, by all means get someone to do it for you. If they are familiar with the account, so much the better.

Collection letters should be spaced 2-4 weeks apart. Their language is friendly at first, then becomes more terse and demanding. Following are letters that will give you a feel of what you may want to say:

Letter #I - A Casual Reminder

Dear Mr. Lawrence:

Just a friendly reminder that your payment of $70.98 will be very much appreciated.

If your check is already in the mail, please disregard this notice and accept our thanks. If it is not, won't you take a moment to mail it today?

Cordially,

Letter #2 - A Strong Reminder

Dear Mr. Lawrence:

Another month has passed and your payment of $70.98 has not been received.

Since we have not heard from you, we assume the balance is correct and that your records agree with ours. Won't you therefore send us your check today or let us hear from you right away before the unpaid balance affects your credit standing?

Your cooperation will be appreciated very much, Mr. Lawrence.

Sincerely,

Letter #3 - The Discussion Letter

Dear Mr. Lawrence

We were disappointed that we did not hear from you in response to our last letter concerning your overdue account of $70.98. Perhaps you are experiencing problems that make it difficult for you to pay this amount all at once. If you are having difficulty making the full payment, and you'll tell me about it, I'm sure we can set up an easy payment plan for you.

Please let me hear from you right away. We'll both be happier when this matter is resolved to our mutual satisfaction.

Sincerely,

Letter #4 - An Urgent Message

Dear Mr. Lawrence:

For several months, we have been writing to you about your long overdue account of $70.98. We must know your intentions immediately.

We realize, of course, that many overdue accounts are the result of unexpected financial difficulties. In these cases we make every effort to help our customers find a better arrangement for making payment. However, we have not heard from you and cannot offer such help until we know your situation.

Please send us something today. Our company is no longer in a position to maintain your account under the present conditions. If we do not hear from you at once, we will have no choice but to pursue other collection procedures.

Sincerely,

The final step, of course, is the collection agency or small claims court. These are **not** recommended. The small claims court can decide in your favor, but you still may not get paid. If you use a collection agency, it will take one-third to one-half of the amount due. In both cases, you will have lost a customer permanently and he or she may strongly criticize you to others. When there are thousands of dollars at stake, this may be worth it; but certainly not for small amounts. If you have to write off the amount as a business loss, do so and simply do not extend credit again to this customer.

As you sort out situations which will determine your credit policy, hang on to your enthusiasm and optimism. You're starting a good business; it's exciting; it's going to work; and chances are, your trust and good faith in people will keep you floating far longer than playing the skeptical Scrooge.

SECURITY

Security is not a matter of trust; it's a matter of common sense. And you will need to provide for it in the areas of fire, theft, pilferage and looting.

1. **Fire**

In addition to insurance, plan to have a sufficient number of fire extinguishers on the premises. Required exit doors and escape routes should be posted. Check with other tenants in your building to coordinate safety procedures and follow the precautionary rules your local fire department will provide. In some locations, fire inspections are conducted periodically and you will want to avoid a violation tag.

2. **Theft**

Get a list of guidelines from your local police department on dealing with theft. In nearly all cases it is recommended that you not try to apprehend the thief. If your business area employs a security guard, leave the procedures to this professional.

Other than a security guard, you can subscribe to an outside security system, use TV surveillance cameras, convex mirrors or window sticker warnings. Police in many communities are increasing the number of foot patrol officers, and an occasional visit from your neighborhood policeman is a great deterrent to theft. However proud you may be, don't brag about your sales and inventory.

If you have a lot of walk-in traffic and your location attracts people of questionable character, here are a few suggestions:

a. Keep your cash register at the front near the door.

b. Use plenty of lighting in the checkout area as well as outside the door for high visibility.

c. If **possible**, use large windows in front to make the checkout area visible from the outside.

d. Keep a minimum of cash in the register. Large bills should be transferred to a safe.

e. Attach a tape measure at the side of the front door. It helps in describing the height of a thief.

f. Avoid having rear or side doors which could be used by thieves.

By far the cheapest and often the best security is the good eyes of your employees. Train them in observing people and let them know your policies on apprehending shoplifters. Proper store layout will help you do this. Keep your eye on "tumble tables." Review your experience after six months to a year, and then decide if you want to add more security.

3. **Pilferage**

Hopefully, you hired the right people in the first place and your employees are honest. If they are handling very valuable merchandise, such as furs, jewelry, art, or large amounts of cash, they may need to be bonded. In any case, you're dealing with human nature and, as disappointed as you might be if an employee does steal from you, there are some things you can do to avoid such a situation before it occurs:

- Checkout counter — use two people

- The perpetual inventory (see Inventory Management)

- Internal audits — your accountant's periodic review of the books.

- Your review of the accountant's review.

- Coat racks instead of employee lockers.

It's good to keep these things in mind, but try to avoid a Big Brother image.

4. **Looting**

The chances of your experiencing a major disaster are small. There are a number of steps you can take to prevent looting. Contact Civil Defense before something occurs to find out what plans have been set up for emergencies. Check with other tenants to see what their procedures are going to be. Know ahead of time who from your company can be called in and where they can be reached in an emergency. Good business managers also keep copies of their most important records in a safe location off the premises.

A word on confidentiality. While confidentiality is not necessarily security in the sense of dollar threats, it could become such in the case of trade secrets. Confidentiality is concerned with communication. When something is "top secret," don't put it in writing at all. This is the extreme and doesn't do a lot for your records. If it is in writing, you can mark it "Confidential", "Private", "Company Confidential", "Return to Me." Verbal confidentiality is casual — e.g., "Go ahead and use my car this afternoon ... I just don't want to make it a policy for everyone."

In between these extremes are the good, safe general rules: Need to Know versus Nice to Know. Some people need to know, for instance, about a sales promotion in order to get ready for it; it's nice for everybody else to know once you start promoting it. Discretion and common sense will tell you the degree of confidentiality you need to maintain.

QUALITY CONTROL IN MANUFACTURING

There are four aspects of quality control from which you can devise a system. They are:

• Supplies and use of materials.

• Employee assignments and supervision of operations.

• Quality of tools.

• Communications.

First, you will need to establish standards for your product and determine what your acceptable margin of error will be. For example, what shipping delays will you accept? How much overtime are you willing to pay to correct a problem? How much markdown will you offer for imperfect goods?

The methods for quality control are relatively simple and should begin in the receiving room.

1. Check every delivery for quantity and condition of items ordered.

2. After supplies and materials are turned over to production, use spot checks and final checks of finished goods before you approve for shipment.

3. Be sure employees are qualified for the tasks they're assigned to. Rotate employees, if possible, to relieve tedium.

4. Be sure tools are in proper working order and regularly maintained.

5. Develop a "final inspection" system for any product you make or sell. Check all shipments or deliveries against the order.

6. Discuss with your employees any suggestions they have for better methods of operation.

All of these methods are workable, but there is one more that covers everything. It's employee motivation. You're proud of your product, and when employees are proud of their own work, you'll get quality.

INVENTORY MANAGEMENT

It's All in the Timing

The Retailer's Motto — "The right item in the right place at the right time" — is the key to operating any kind of successful business and it's called Inventory Control. It can be tricky, but there are some principles to help you avoid disasters. **Stock Count** and **Perpetual Inventory** are the methods most widely used to determine how much inventory you have on hand.

1. **The Stock Count**

   The stock count can be obtained from the last preliminary visual "quick check" to an item-by-item count, recorded on a form and updated weekly or monthly.

   Following is an example of how a beauty shop kept track of shampoo weekly. A similar form is used for other items. The beginning and ending inventory is recorded, and the quantity sold and on order is recorded. In this instance, the manager has not indicated the quantity she plans to have on hand — but it would have been helpful to her.

DEPARTMENT: Shampoo   Week Ending _____

Item	Size	Begin Inv	Sold	Ending Inv	On Order
Apple Pectin	32 oz.	39	17	22	12
Apple Pectin	Tube	9	3	6	24
Quantum	32 oz.	8	2	6	
Botanical	16 oz.	12	4	8	

Another simple format, shown below, provides a weekly or monthly count of merchandise on hand and on order. Numbers in the left column are inventory control numbers assigned to items in inventory. A variety of forms are available from office supply firms.

SAMPLE FORM FOR WEEKLY STOCK COUNT

ITEM _____

Date		Date		Date		Date	
On Hand	Ordered	On Hand	Ordered	On Hand	Ordered	On Hand	Ordered
1							
2							
3							

It's time to reorder when the supply on hand will be used up or sold during the number of weeks it takes to receive reorders, plus a one-week cushion.

Let's assume from your experience that reordering will take four weeks for delivery. Your sales records show that you sell 10 units per week. Place your order when stock reaches 50 units (4 weeks + 1 week x 10 units per week). You may also have found that some vendors — particularly local ones — can give you faster delivery. If you can get next-day delivery, you may want to start using the second method — perpetual inventory.

2. **Perpetual Inventory**

This can be done manually by including it in your daily sales records. Tear off perforated price tags, indicating item number, size and color and put these in a box by the cash register. Subtract them from your stock on hand at the end of the day. Perpetual inventory is a simple matter of quantity on hand at the start of business, less the quantity sold, plus the number of returns equals the balance. Compare this total to your planned ending stock and the final figure will give you the quantity that needs to be ordered. In retail jargon, this is called "open to buy." It is the basis for ordering, and from this you can consider factors such as:

• Seasonal items
• Items to be featured in a future sale
• Dependability of vendor
• Holidays and closings
• What your competition is featuring

Arrange all the items to be ordered from one vendor on one form. List each item on one line on the form and if not ordering immediately, add items daily until you reach your deadline for ordering.

If you're hitting a crisis, you can always use "Rush" or "Special Attention," but find out what your vendor's policies and charges are for these services. A good relationship with your vendors can produce occasional miracles, but the best policy is to plan. So make periodic counts to verify your perpetual figures.

3. **Stock-Sales Ratio**

Some businesses prefer to work on a stock-sales ratio rather than the turnover formula described above. It may be wise to use both. The stock-sales ratio is arrived at by dividing the stock at the beginning of the month by the sales volume for the end of the previous month. If you're selling only one product, this is not a big task; but if you're selling a variety of items, the figures must be calculated for each item you carry or they won't tell you anything. This kind of clerical task should be delegated to an employee and can become part of a training program.

Knowing what your stock-sales ratios are won't tell you much unless you have standards to measure against. These standards will vary depending on the type of business you're in and the different products you sell.

As a general rule, try to keep the ratio as low as possible without continually running out of stock. Delivery times, seasons, styles, and other factors should all be considered.

The very nature of inventory management is not exact, but if you start with some of the basic principles, then experience - at **least** one year's - will give you a solid foundation. You will then be able to record "Last Year," "This Year," and "Plan" or:

12/31	YTD	TOTAL	PLAN
(Last Year)	(Current Year)	(Current Year)	(Next Year)

Your best resource in learning how to run a business is other people. Whenever people gather, they love to talk about their business; and you'll find that some of the mistakes you've made are not original. People will have tips for you and you'll be able to offer some of your own.

With this in mind, take a look at some organizations to which you can belong.

TRADE AND PROFESSIONAL ORGANIZATIONS

Join at least one association in your field. Dues are generally very reasonable in proportion to the education and training you will receive and the contacts you will make. It's a great way to keep up with your competition. Volunteer to serve on a committee if you have the time. You could become a well-known spokesperson in your field. It's a good form of advertising for your business.

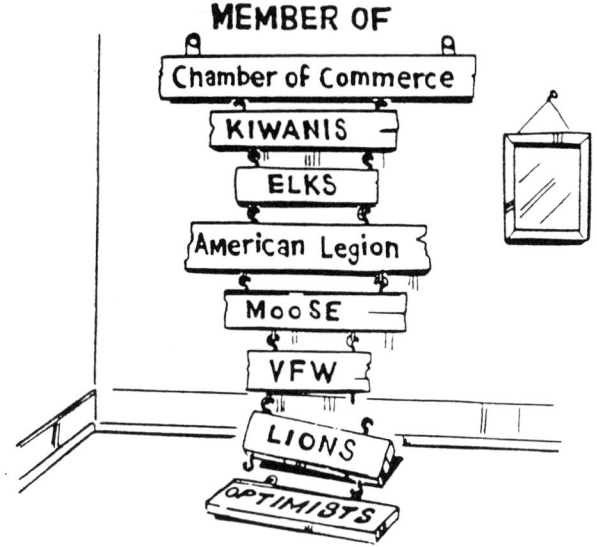

Other memberships to consider are:

1. **Business Associations**

    These are groups of businesses in a defined trade area which meet to exchange ideas, hold art fairs and sidewalk sales, plan cooperative advertising, etc. They often plan Christmas and holiday decorations for the area, hold kiddie carnivals, hire musicians and balloons for promotions. These are great business boosters, and you will want to participate.

2. **Chamber of Commerce**

    The Chamber is an organization of businesses from the national, regional, state and local levels. If you're in a metropolitan area, there may be subdivisions such as a "West Suburban Chamber of Commerce."

    Chambers operate with paid staffs and support both business development and total community development. Their staffs lobby in legislatures for bills of interest to members. They sponsor seminars and speakers on a number of topics. Sometimes the C of C will plan a community-wide festival, such as a winter carnival. They promote tourism. They also raise money and contribute to projects that will benefit an entire metropolitan area — such as downtown developments, athletic stadiums and so forth.

3. **Service Organizations**

    These are organizations such as the Jaycees, Kiwanis, Rotary or Optimist Clubs. Membership is generally open to everyone, whether business people or not, and the groups generally support some particular cause - such as raising money for seeing-eye dogs for the blind; building a group home for handicapped children; sending inner-city youth to camp. They schedule outside speakers for their meetings to present views on topics of interest to their members.

You may not have a great deal of time to be an active member in any of these organizations as you start your business, but it's wise to join one or two to exchange ideas and meet people.

You have just completed the chapter on Minding the Store. In this chapter you have learned:

1. The importance of establishing business policies before tackling procedures.

2. Procedures for establishing your own credit, extending credit to customers, and avoiding credit abuse.

3. The steps to take in security precautions for fire, theft, pilferage and looting.

4. Quality control can be achieved through good management of supplies and materials, good tools and good employee communications.

5. The principles of inventory control; effective methods for having the right item on hand to sell.

6. The value to your business of having membership in organizations.

Chapter 14

Ring up sales through salesmanship

Salesmen are made, not born

One of the most important factors in making your business venture a success is whether you can sell your product or service to those who need, want or desire it. The "best" product or service in the world is of little value if you can't persuade people to buy it.

You have already laid the groundwork for successful selling. Your market research in Chapter 3 has helped you determine: what you are trying to accomplish; who you could be selling to; who your competitors are; how you compare with them; how consumers behave; and, what the trends are in the marketplace. You have evaluated the problems and opportunities you will face in marketing your product. You have decided where you will concentrate your sales efforts. You have developed a pricing strategy and forecasted your sales. You have decided on a location for your business and a method of distributing your products or services. And you have planned an advertising and public relations campaign to create awareness and generate interest in your business.

Now, you are ready to sell your product or service. In this chapter you will learn:

1. What selling is.

2. What it takes to sell successfully.

3. How to "read" the buyer and adapt your sales presentation to his motives and personality.

4. The steps of successful prospecting.

5. How to prepare the sales presentation.

6. How to get off to a good start.

7. How to assess the prospect's needs, wants, problems and goals.

8. How to present your product or service to meet the buyer's needs.

9. How to work out the problems that keep him from buying.

10. How to close the sale.

You will learn how these basic principles apply to retail selling and to personal, telephone and direct mail selling.

SELLING: WHAT IS IT?

Selling is an Art

It takes more than a great product or service to build a business. It takes customers to buy that product or service. Customers buy only if you can show them they have needs your product or service can satisfy. They buy only if you can translate the features of your product into customer benefits.

Successful selling depends on your ability to:

1. Get the buyer's attention.

2. Uncover his needs, wants, problems and goals.

3. Show how your product or service will satisfy those needs.

4. Work out the problems that keep him from buying.

5. Ask for his business.

The future of your business depends on the art of selling. If you take advantage of the opportunity to serve people, to satisfy their needs and to solve their problems, you create satisfied customers. It is satisfied customers that continue doing business with you and recommend your products and services to others.

Selling is Communicating

When you sell, you communicate to your prospect something about yourself and the product you are selling. The process can be viewed as a series of steps, each involving a higher level of communication.

Let's start at the bottom step. First, you **approach** your prospect and introduce yourself and your company. Then you **specify** your reason for being there. Next, you **clarify** what your product or service will do and **explain** how these features will benefit the prospect. Then you **negotiate** terms and conditions that stand in the way of the buying decision.

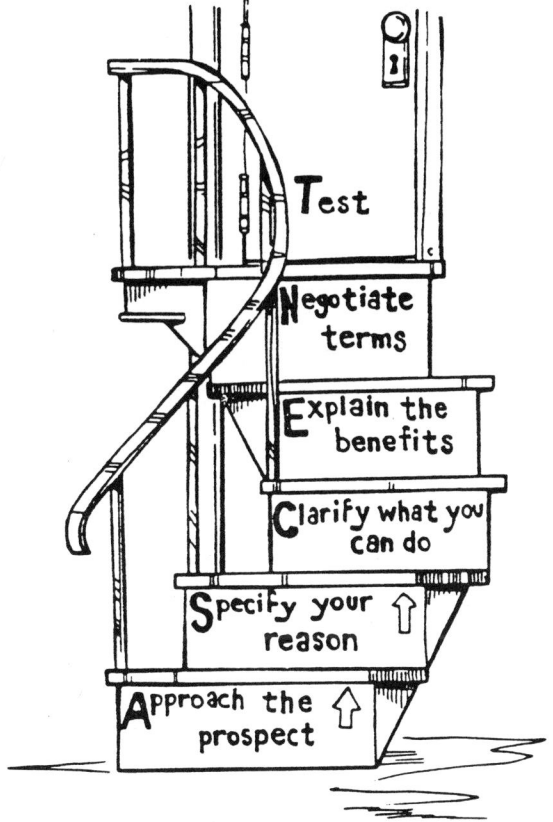

Source: The Education Group, Division of Human Development Systems, Inc., 1980.

Finally, you test the effectiveness of your communication by asking for the sale. NOTE: An easy way to remember these "steps" upward is that the first letters spell A S C E N T.

Like effective communication, selling isn't a monologue. It's a two-way process. A sale isn't in sight until the prospect becomes involved. You have to be skilled at asking questions and active listening to uncover his needs and interests. You have to "read" the prospect and adapt your message and communication style to his personality and buying motives. Through effective communication, you build a relationship with the customer based on trust and confidence. This forms the foundation for the sale and for future sales.

Selling is Giving the Customer a Reason to Buy

Selling is the art of persuading the prospect to buy. To be persuaded to buy, he must have a reason: he must be conscious of a need and believe that you and your product or service will satisfy that need. Selling is giving him a reason to buy. It's removing his doubts and reason for not buying.

Types of Selling

In selling your product or service, you can communicate your message to the prospective buyer personally, by telephone, or through direct mail. Depending on your business, any one or combination of the three types of selling will work best for you.

Personal selling involves face-to-face contact between the seller and the buyer. The sales presentation is made in person. In a face-to-face presentation, not only do you verbally communicate, but you can learn a lot about the prospect by observing expressions, behaviors, gestures and other nonverbal cues. The prospect can be directly involved in the selling process because he has the opportunity to touch and see your product. You can also involve him through the use of visual aids or sight-sellers.

Telephone selling saves time, money and energy. You can talk to a lot more prospects than personal selling would allow in the same amount of time, while eliminating the cost of travel. Because you lack visual cues, you have to rely more on your question asking and listening skills to get the information you need. It's also more difficult to "sell yourself" over the phone. Your smile, enthusiasm and personality must be projected totally through your voice. The telephone can be used to: get background information on a prospect; qualify him before a personal sales call; get an appointment; or, make the sale.

Direct mail continues to be an effective and profitable way to sell despite increases in the cost of postage, printing, paper, and mailing operations. Mailing lists cover every type of market and customer base and are available from a variety of sources. Direct mail may be used to: solicit inquiries about your product or service; pave the way for personal sales calls; and to sell products by mail order that are not usually available in stores or through other sources. Sales letters, brochures, order forms, catalogs, circulars, and other sales literature make up the direct mail package. To minimize the number of prospects who will toss your mail into the wastebasket without even reading it, a lot of care must go into putting a package together that will get the prospect's attention.

WHAT DOES IT TAKE TO SELL?

What Makes a Successful Salesperson?

It is often said that 20% of the salespeople get 80% of the sales. What do these top performers have that the rest don't? What makes them so successful?

To answer this question, let's first look at the reasons so many of them fail. A study by Dauner-Johnson in 1979 revealed the ten top problems leading to the termination of salespeople:

1. Poor work habits.

2. Lack of resourcefulness, initiative and fact-finding.

3. Inability to close the sale.

4. Unwillingness to canvass and establish new contacts.

5. Slow and unresponsive in overcoming objections.

6. Lack of self-evaluation and self-improvement.

7. Refusal to prepare and keep records.

8. Lack of creativity.

9. Lack of self-confidence and sustained enthusiasm.

10. Negative attitude and lack of sales interest.

So what does it take to be successful at selling? The answer is ability, skill, motivation and a "selling" personality.

To successfully sell your product or service, you and those who sell for you must have the ability to plan and organize a sales presentation. You must have extensive knowledge of the product or service you sell and personally believe in its value. You must be able to recognize the characteristics of a qualified buyer.

You must also be a skilled communicator. You must know what information to give and when to give it. You must know what questions to ask, when to ask them, and when to listen.

You must be perceptive to the motives and personality of the buyer. You must be able to anticipate common objections to your product or service and be skilled at overcoming them. You should be able to recognize buying signals, and know how and when to put on the close.

What about "personality"? Successful salespersons "sell themselves". This personal relationship is the foundation on which the sale—and possible repeat sales—is made. This means that the salesperson with the more desirable personality will get the order if the product or service has quality and is competitively priced.

Here are some personality characteristics salespersons should have, especially for building a repeat-sale type of business:

Reliability: If you make a statement, you mean it. If you make a promise, you keep it.

Honesty: Your sales pitch is made without false claims. You are personally sold on your product or service.

Sociability: You like people and are willing to accept them as they are. You enjoy the opportunity to meet new people.

Self-Confidence: You are sure of yourself and your abilities. When the prospect says "no", you don't take it personally.

Positive Attitude: You can go and sell, day after day, even if all your preceding days have been failures. You take your failures in stride. You learn from them to develop a successful selling technique.

Enthusiasm: You are excited about your product or service and project this excitement to your prospect.

Simplicity: You adhere to the KISS (Keep It Simple, Stupid!) principle. Your goal is to sell, not impress the prospect with your intelligence and vocabulary. You talk in language he understands.

Courtesy: You are polite, considerate, and treat the customer with respect.

Personal Appearance: The customer "buys" you as well as the product. From his point of view, if you take pride in your appearance, you take pride in your product. Your clothing and general appearance are appropriate for your type of business and your target market.

Product Knowledge

Successful selling requires extensive product knowledge. Half of your sales presentation is giving information about your product or service. The prospect's interest may have been aroused by your advertising, a friend, or your initial contact. His first motivation, at this point, is the need for more information. He expects you to be able to provide it.

You should be prepared to answer all of your prospect's questions with accuracy and confidence. When you show confidence in your product, your prospect is more likely to do so.

Product knowledge builds respect and respect leads to repeat sales. If your product isn't a repeat item. the respect you earn from a satisfied customer may lead to a word-of-mouth referral.

Knowing your product is essential to understanding what it can do for your prospective buyer. It puts you in a good position to overcome his reasons for not buying.

What should you know about your product or service? Before you try to sell it, you must understand its most important features. A **feature** is a characteristic of a product or service. Some examples of product features are: price; size; weight; color; finish; style; function; design; durability; guarantee; warranty; length of service; appearance; and reputation. Some examples of service features are: what the service does; where the service goes; price; how often the service is provided; and how long it takes to provide the service.

Here are some specific examples of how product features can be stated for the prospective buyer:

1. "Our vacuum cleaner comes with a 5-year warranty on all parts and labor."

2. "Our airline offers four non-stop flights to New York every business day."

3. "We have been manufacturing furniture for 52 years."

4. "These sweaters are 100% wool and are available in 6 colors and 3 styles."

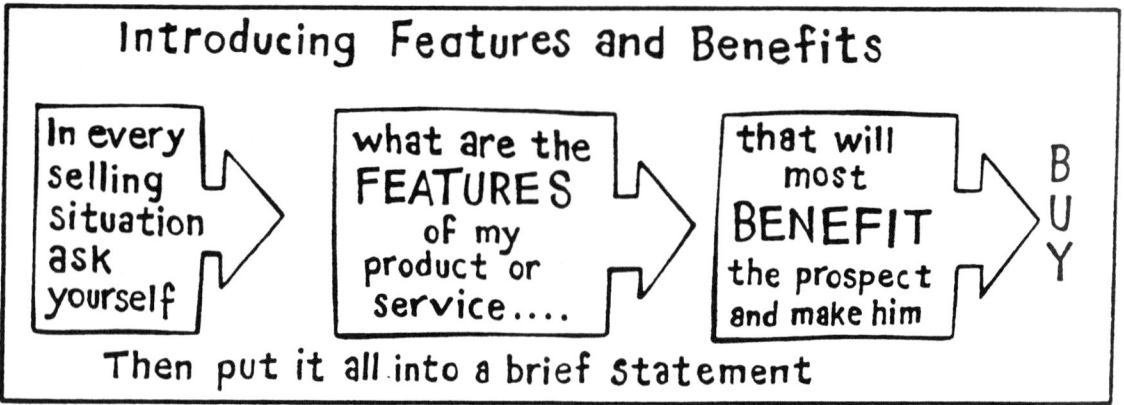

A **benefit** states what the product or service can do for the buyer in any of the following ways:

1. Saves the customer money.

2. Saves the customer time.

3. Solves the customer's problem.

4. Increases the customer's business.

5. Improves the health or safety of the customer, his family or his employees.

Some examples of benefits are:

1. "Because our vacuum cleaner is so lightweight, it is easier to carry up and down stairs."

2. "Our water conditioning system will make your cleaning easier because it prevents the build-up of lime deposits on your bathroom tile."

3. "Our secretarial service will save you money because you only pay for the services you actually use."

How do you and those who sell for you acquire this product knowledge so essential for successful selling? Depending on your business, any of the following may apply:

1. Being directly involved in researching and developing new products and services.

2. Formal training sessions and sales meetings.

3. Examining your product.

4. Reading all of the manufacturer's literature.

5. Visiting the manufacturer and understanding the manufacturing process.

6. Talking to other people who sell the same product or service.

7. Reading pertinent articles in magazines, journals and newspapers about your product line or type of service.

8. Talking to service or repair people whose job is product maintenance.

9. Getting "hands on" experience by using the product.

10. Listening to what customers have to say about the product or service.

11. Reading and studying about competing products or services. All selling situations call for a thorough knowledge of your competition in order to make accurate comparisons as to price, features and benefits.

UNDERSTANDING THE BUYER

We have said that selling is communicating. Just like effective communication, successful selling is related to your ability to understand people. Every customer is different. The sales approach that "sells" one customer may turn off the next. In selling, you must learn to be flexible in any situation. To develop a good working relationship, you need the ability to adapt your approach to the prospect.

Buying Motives

Why do customers buy? Different things motivate different people. A customer's reason for buying may be either subjective or objective. An objective buying motive is a result of reasoning. Most purchases of this nature are planned. Features such as price, economy, efficiency, durability, simplicity, low maintenance, good workmanship, and availability of parts and service enter into the buying decision. Some examples are:

1. A customer plans to insulate his house to reduce energy consumption and save money.

2. A customer plans to hire a lawn care service to save time.

Subjective buying motives stem from personal feelings. They may be associated with security, ego, self-satisfaction, entertainment, or pleasure. For example:

1. A customer buys a pin stripe suit to look more professional.

2. A customer buys lotion for smoother skin.

3. A customer buys from a certain salesperson because he likes and trusts him.

4. A customer buys new and innovative products because he likes to be among the first to recognize an opportunity.

5. A customer shops at a certain store because his friends do.

Reaching the Decision to Buy

The customer usually goes through a series of predictable steps in reaching a decision to buy a product or service. By understanding these steps, you are in an excellent position to assist the prospect in reaching a buying decision.

STEPS IN REACHING THE BUYING DECISION

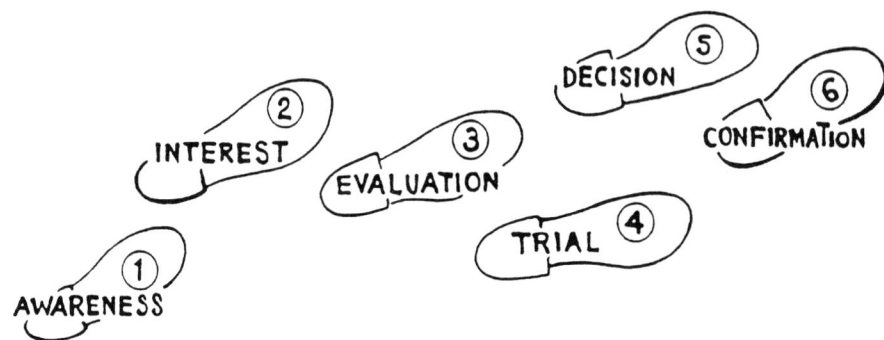

The first step is **awareness** of your product or service. This is usually created through advertising and publicity.

Next, he becomes **interested** as your product or service appeals to an identified need. Only when the prospect becomes conscious of a need will he move to satisfy it.

Next is **evaluation.** The customer evaluates the need to determine if it is important enough to do something about. He weighs the need against others he is conscious of, and assigns top priority to his need for your product or service. He also considers possible alternatives for solving his problem.

Next, in the trial step, he seeks proof that what you have told him is factual and your solution to his problem will work for him. He may talk to other users of your product or service or anyone else who may give an unbiased opinion. He may also "try out" the product.

Finally, he **decides** to buy. Frequently, the decision step is followed by a post-purchase phenomenon the customer goes through to **confirm** his buying decision. Even though he has made the mental decision to act, he may suffer a temporary case of "buyer's remorse".

Roles in Buying

Your time is valuable. Common sense tells you that in making contacts and sales presentations, it's the decision maker you want to talk to. What about the other people involved in buying the product? How will they influence the final decision?

There are five roles in buying. They may all be assumed by the same person but frequently more than one person is involved.

Initiator: The initiator first informs the prospect of your product or service. It may be a satisfied customer, it may be you, or it may be the prospect himself recognizing an unfulfilled need.

Influencer: The influencer is the person who influences the buying decision. It may be a spouse, a friend, or a co-worker.

Decider: The decider makes the ultimate decision to buy with input from the influencer.

Purchaser: The purchaser has control of the "purse strings".

User: The user is the person who will directly benefit from the product or service.

Successful selling requires you to understand buying roles and appeal to everyone involved in the buying decision.

Buying Personalities

You will find that in selling your product or service, you will consistently meet certain types of prospects. Here are some general buying personalities you may encounter and how to respond to them:

The **"Show Me How It Works"** buyer likes to analyze and understand everything about the product before buying. He expects a logical and detailed sales presentation and will ask a lot of specific questions. He will buy only after carefully considering prices and features of alternative products. He is slow to make a decision. You have to be patient, respond to all of his questions, and appeal to his logic.

The **"Let's Get On With It"** buyer is only concerned about what your product or service will do for him. He wants you to quickly solve his problems and deliver on your promises. Instead of a long, detailed presentation, he wants to get down to business. Give him important product information right away but don't bore him with great detail. He expects a fast-paced, hard-hitting presentation.

The **"I Know What I Want"** buyer is ready to buy. He is decisive and confident and has already decided on a specific brand or type of merchandise. Give him immediate, professional and personalized service. He understands the steps in making a sale and wants to be sold.

The **"I Want You To Like Me"** buyer buys when he feels comfortable with the seller. He is more interested in what others will think of his buying decision than the actual benefits of the product. He usually can't make the decision to buy alone and needs the approval of those affected by the decision. You can appeal to this type by showing how your product or service can benefit other people or improve relationships between peopie.

The **"What Do You Think"** buyer isn't sure about what he wants and doesn't trust his own judgement. He needs expert guidance in making a decision and constant reassurance that he isn't making a mistake. You must show confidence in your product to appeal to this type of buyer. Keep choices to a minimum. If he wants, make the decision for him.

The **"I Want To Be A Hero"** buyer has a strong, charismatic personality. He's a leader and feels others look up to him for new and innovative ideas. He wants his successes to be recognized. You can appeal to him by showing how your product can solve problems and make him look good. Be sure to applaud his decision to buy.

The **"I Dare You To Sell Me"** buyer is motivated by insecurity. He lacks self-confidence and feels a need to prove his worth to everyone. If you let him "toot his horn", the chip on his shoulder will gradually disappear and you can get down to business.

Other Buyer Characteristics

Age is another buyer characteristic that might affect your selling approach. Younger buyers are often searching for answers but aren't sure what to ask. They want you to tell them about your product or service: "You should use our service because it will save you money."

Middle aged buyers usually know what they want. They want you to show them what your product can give them: "Let me show you how our service will reduce your labor costs."

"Theres something I like about you... but I can't put my finger on it.."

Older buyers know what they want and have dealt with a lot of salespeople. They deserve respect for what they have learned through years of experience: "What service would work best for you?"

You can also adapt your presentation style to the buyer's speech pattern, mannerisms and behaviors. If he speaks rapidly, you should do the same. If his speech is slow and calculated, yours should be the same. If his behavior is rigid and formal, you should present yourself and your product as formally as possible. If he is informal, you can make a more relaxed presentation.

RETAIL SELLING

There are two principal forms of personal selling: **Retail Selling** and **Field Selling.** In retail selling the potential customer comes to the business establishment where the sale takes place. Field selling calls for the salesperson to seek out the potential customer by making calls at his place of business or home.

In field selling, which we will discuss later, the salesperson must **locate** prospects and convert them into customers. However, in retail selling the prospect **comes to** the salesman, thus making his job easier.

Many customers would submit that personal selling is a lost art in the retail store. In many cases, they would be correct. Many larger multi-unit retailers have stressed self-service, larger assortments, and lower prices at the expense of good personal selling.

Why would a customer shop in a small retail store when he can probably buy the same product for less at a large chain store? The answer lies in personal service. The success of the small retail store is directly related to how well its salespeople individualize their selling skills. By emphasizing good personal selling, the small retailer can gain a competitive edge over the bigger stores.

Store Appearance

The appearance of your store or office gives your customers an important first impression. You may not be able to afford elaborate, eye-catching displays. They might not even be appropriate for a small-engine shop, for example, or a hardware store. Whatever the nature of your business, be it blue collar or high fashion, you can be sure of one thing. Nothing puts a customer off more than sloppily displayed merchandise, dusty shelves and dirty floors. On the other hand, neatly arranged, easy to locate merchandise, and pleasant, clean surroundings reassure a customer. These things show that you're a professional. You care about your business, and you care enough about your customers to provide an attractive atmosphere to do business in.

Good Retail Selling

Personal selling at the retail level is the matching of customer needs with the retailer's merchandise. If the salesperson makes a good match, a satisfied customer is created and a long-term, profitable relationship can be established. To assure good personal selling in your retail store, you must:

1. Recruit and hire salespeople with a "selling" personality. The best way to build business and reduce turnover is to hire the right people in the first place. Write down what a sales job in your store would require a person to do. This "job specification" will provide a guide for appraising the capabilities of prospective employees.

2. Train and develop your salespeople. Include orientation, product knowledge, communication skills and sales training. Make use of regular and frequent sales meetings to update your employees on the features of new merchandise, store policies and sales strategies. Use the time to help them improve their selling skills.

You will, in most cases, be hiring and training sales help for your retail business. The key word here is training. Even the most promising new hires cannot perform unless they know and understand their job responsibilities. Develop a simple, but effective, training outline for each position from the assistant store manager on down to the part-time college student sales clerk. This outline should list the responsibilities of each position and **all** the information your employee will need to carry out those responsibilities.

For example, if you expect your assistant manager to schedule the other employees, be sure to include information on the shifts, length of lunch breaks, and number of people you want on the floor at all times. You should also include a copy of the scheduling form. This may sound obvious and elementary; however, unless you have all the information **written down** to the smallest detail, it's easy to forget, especially when you're in a hurry to train an employee.

The Buddy System

As your business grows you may not be able to do all the training yourself. The assistant manager could take over this responsibility. If, in your judgement, he or she already has too many responsibilities, you might consider the "Buddy System". Under the Buddy System you will assign a new hire to your most trusted, experienced employee. The senior buddy would then be accountable for the junior buddy's performance and job satisfaction.

Dressed to Sell

Besides job descriptions, the training materials provided to your employees should include a dress code. The standards you establish will depend on what type of product you are selling. The sales clerks in an upscale boutique would wear high fashion; the employees in a small engine shop would probably wear jeans. Also, you might want to consider how much handling and lifting your employees will be doing. If there is a lot of either involved, you might recommend slacks for the women and safe, sturdy shoes for everyone. Of course, clothes of any style should be clean and in good repair. Good grooming, too, is a must. Like the store itself, you want the people working in it to make a good impression on your customers.

The Approach

While the steps to retail selling are basic to all selling, there are some major differences in the first step. Instead of prospecting and seeking out the customer at his home or place of business, the customer comes to you. He should be greeted by a neat, well-groomed, enthusiastic salesperson who has the desire and ability to serve people. The salesperson shouldn't be over anxious and rush the customer like a football player. On the other hand, waiting too long gives the customer the impression that no one is interested in making the sale.

The opening greeting should put the customer at ease and get his attention. Two general approaches can be used to greet the customer—the conversational approach and the merchandise approach.

The **conversational approach** should be used to encourage the customer to indicate what he is interested in. It can be used whether or not you recognize the customer. It is especially effective if you recognize the customer's name and use it: "Hi, Jane. It's good to see you! Did everyone at the party like your new silk dress? What can I show you today?"

The **merchandise approach** should be used when you see the customer looking at or touching a specific item. It immediately directs the topic of conversation to the merchandise. To use it effectively without appearing pushy takes a lot of skill. Some salespeople blend it with the conversational approach: "Did you know all the sweaters on this table are 25% off today?" "We just received these knit dresses. Feel how soft the fabric is!"

One approach should never be used; and, unfortunately, it is used most often: "May I help you?" At best, the customer will say, "Just looking." At worst, he'll say, "No." The sale is often lost because there's nothing left for the salesperson to say.

Making the Retail Sale

Determining the needs and wants of the customer begins when he enters the store and continues throughout the sales presentation. Start by observing the customer: Does he march directly to a specific display? Does he take his time walking through the store, looking at various merchandise along the way? Does he immediately put one item down and pick up another? Does he go back to look at an item for the second time?

Asking questions and listening also helps determine needs and wants. How does he intend to use the merchandise? What preferences does he have for color and style? What other conditions must the merchandise meet?

In a retail situation, the way to sell benefits is show and tell. While showing the merchandise, you should tell about its features and benefits. Allowing the customer to handle, try on, or try out the merchandise helps you determine which items are of most interest. It also appeals to several of the customer's senses. You should continue to show different merchandise until the customer's interest is focused on one or two choices. This is the moment to wind down the sales presentation and move toward closing the sale. Showing more merchandise at this point will only distract his attention.

All of the techniques previously discussed for handling objections and closing the sale are effective in retail selling situations.

"Plussing" the Sale

Buying one item usually creates a need for accessories or attachments that would help the customer better use and enjoy the initial purchase. Selling this additional merchandise is "plussing the sale".

"Plussing" the original sale creates a win-win situation. The customer benefits because it often saves him the time necessary to run back to the store for overlooked items. Also, quantity purchases are frequently offered at savings to the customer. You benefit because your sales volume is increased.

Skillful salespeople look for opportunities during the sales presentation to help the customer discover unrealized needs. One technique for plussing the sale is to suggest "go-withs":

Original Item	Go With
shirt	tie
shoes	polish
bed sheets	pillow cases
placemats	napkins
draperies	rods and hooks
lawn mower	grass bag

Other techniques for "plussing" include:

1. Suggesting that buying a larger quantity will save time and money.

2. Telling the customer about specials they might have overlooked.

3. Pointing out new merchandise.

4. Reminding the customer of a special occasion for gift giving.

JANE: THE STORY OF A WELL DONE SALE

Now let's look at the best approach to take to customers who do want our help. Jane, a sales clerk in the Savory Gourmet Cookware Shop, can demonstrate for us. A young woman in her twenties has just walked into the store. After greeting the customer and letting her browse for a few minutes, Jane decides that she looks like she might need some help. The customer is standing in the pots and pans section looking over the displays. Jane goes up to the customer and the following conversation takes place.

> Jane: These enamel pans are very durable. We just got them in last week from Denmark. They're specially treated so they don't chip or discolor.

> Customer: Yes, they are nice. One of my friends is getting married next week and her bridal registry indicated that she needed a frying pan.

> Jane: This particular line of cookware has an excellent model of frying pan. Here, let me show you.

> She picks up a frying pan from the shelf.

> You can see that the sides are much higher than on most other frying pans so food won't spatter as much when it's cooking. Also, this pan is very versatile. Your friend can use it to bake a roast in the oven; then she can make gravy or sauce on the stove. I mentioned that it won't discolor easily, and it comes in just about every color you can think of—even pastels!

> As it happens, we're offering a special introductory price on the cookware. Ordinarily, the frying pan sells for $30.00. You can buy it today for $19.95.

> Customer: Hmmm. That's not a bad price, but I was thinking of spending a little less—maybe around $15.00.

> The customer moves over to another display.

> This pan looks a lot like the one you showed me, but it's only $14.00.

Jane: Yes, you would have to pay a little more for the other pan, but notice the differences. The one you have is smaller and the handle is shorter. The Danish pan I showed you would be a lot safer and easier to manage. Also, the handle is heatproof. You don't have to use a pot holder. With this one, you do.

Customer: Well, maybe it would be worth paying a little extra, then. I'd hate to have Sharon burn herself with an unsafe pan.

Jane: Does Sharon have a preference for one color over another?

Customer: Come to think of it, Sharon did tell me she was planning to do her kitchen in red and black. Does this pan come in red?

Jane: Yes, it does! We also have a spatula with a red handle designed to be used with this cookware. Wouldn't that make a lovely gift for Sharon?

Customer: Yes, they would. You can't really use one without the other, I guess.

Jane: Your friend will get a lot of use out of this pan. She'll appreciate the 5-year warranty, too. May I wrap it for you? There's no charge.

Customer: No, thank you. If you can just get me a box, I can wrap it myself.

Jane: Certainly. I'll get it for you now. As Jane is going back to the stock room, she notices another customer waiting at the counter.

Jane: Good morning! I'll be with you in a minute!

After she has put the pan and spatula in the box, and rung up the transaction, Jane closes the sale with the words every customer deserves to hear.

"Thank you! I hope you'll stop in again."

Jane Continued: A Recipe for Successful Selling

Jane did an excellent job of selling on this transaction. First and most important, she knew her stuff. Customers are interested in three things: features, benefits and price. Jane could describe the **features** of the pan (color, size, the material it was made of). She also gave her customer good reasons to buy the pan, its **benefits.** The pan was specially treated so it wouldn't chip or tarnish; it was designed with higher sides, to keep frying food from spattering on the walls; it was safer to use. Finally, she knew prices, both regular and sale.

Jane didn't just throw a lot of dry facts at her customer. She sparked her interest with some suggestive selling. Customers like to hear about new things. Jane emphasized to her customer that the pans had just come in from Denmark. Sale is a magic word, too. Jane made a point of mentioning that the pans were on special that week only.

Jane demonstrated another valuable sales technique when the customer was considering a less expensive model of pan. She knew that there is a lot more to good value than the price. Sometimes it's worth paying a little more for the better quality product that will last longer and work better. When Jane suggested that the more expensive pan might be a better investment, she was "trading up". Trading up doesn't mean taking advantage of the customer. It doesn't mean tricking him or her into spending more money than he or she wants to. It does mean helping the customer to buy strategically, by choosing either a larger size at a more efficient price or a higher quality product at a higher price.

Jane also remembered to suggest "go-with" items.

The Close: Less Is More

Closing a sale is a delicate art. In this area, too, Jane's performance is a masterpiece. Throughout the sale, she has avoided trying to pressure the customer. She has simply provided the customer with information. The customer then used this information to choose the Danish cookware over the cheaper model. Once she arrived at this decision, Jane **confirmed** it. ("Wouldn't that make a lovely gift **along with the pan**?") In addition, she also **reinforced** the customer's choice by asking **preference** questions. ("Does Sharon prefer one color over another?" "May I wrap it for you?") She reinforced the decision again by complimenting her customer on her choice and pointing out yet another benefit. ("Your friend will get a lot of use out of this pan. She'll really appreciate the 5-year warranty, too.")

Probably the most important thing to notice about Jane's closing technique is that she **knew how to shut up.** Today's customers are, as a rule, sophisticated and knowledgeable. The motormouthed, backslapping, overbearing style of selling turns them off. Once they have made a decision, customers neither want nor need a stream of sales chatter. They aren't convinced by it. On the contrary, they start to wonder if something isn't being put over on them. After confirming and reinforcing her customer's decision, Jane didn't waste any time with needless talking. She got a box, rang up the transaction and let the customer get on with her other business.

What Every Customer Needs to Hear

Note that although Jane didn't say much when closing the sale, she did not forget to thank her customer. This point cannot be emphasized too much. By patronizing your business, the customer has done you a big favor: he or she is helping you to stay in business. A simple thank you is the least your customers deserve.

Keeping the Customers Satisfied: One at a Time

One final point: Throughout the transaction, Jane gave her full attention to her customer. She **acknowledged** the other customer who had come into the store, but she did not make the mistake of trying to wait on two people at once. Neither customer would have received very good service. Most people are willing to wait, so long as they know a salesperson has noticed them and will be getting back to them.

THE TELEPHONE: YOUR CONNECTION TO GOOD CUSTOMER RELATIONS

Not all of your customers will be coming to the store to do business. You and your sales staff will also be responding to phone inquiries. Remember that the telephone magnifies everything you say. You want to be all the more certain that the words you speak are pleasant, courteous, knowledgeable and helpful. Here are some useful pointers to learn and to pass on to your employees.

1. Answer the phone promptly and pleasantly. **Nothing** irritates and discourages a customer more than having to wait on the other end of the line. **No** job is so important that you can't pause for a moment to answer the phone and at least request the customer to hold. Don't lose a customer before you even say the first word.

2. Identify your department and yourself. Don't waste a customer's time. Make sure he knows which department or section of the store he has reached. Transfer the customer promptly if another department could better serve him.

3. Speak clearly. People tend to talk faster when they're in a hurry. Tune in on yourself periodically to make sure you are speaking clearly and understandably. Also, watch the tone of your voice. Remember, the phone amplifies your voice 10 times.

4. The 30 Second Rule. Never leave a customer on hold for more than 30 seconds. If you have other customers waiting or if you can't find what the phone customer wants, check back with him and inform him of the situation. Offer him the choice of either holding longer or of having you call him back. ("I'm sorry, Mr. Cooper. I'm having some trouble finding that particular model. May I take your number and call you back?") If you are really pressed for time, you might also want to ask another employee to take the call.

5. Listen! **Never** interrupt a customer and never assume that you know what he wants better than he does. You need complete information before you can provide good service, and you'll never get this information if you don't let the customer talk. Besides, interrupting another person is the worst kind of rudeness. When you interrupt, you are suggesting that your customer is stupid or unimportant.

6. Write things down. If you have to get back to a phone customer at a later time, **write down** what he wants. Don't trust your memory. As the day goes on, you might forget the customer's request or even the fact that you were supposed to get back to him. Remember, that customer is depending on you. If you don't come through, he won't do business with you.

7. Hang up last. **Never** hang up first! Your customer might not have said everything he wanted to say. Give him enough time to think of everything he needs to ask. Then he won't have to call back or call elsewhere.

Some retail businesses might have a higher volume of phone calls than others. For example, a small engine shop that sells snowblowers will inevitably receive a deluge of calls when the first snow falls. Also, brochures and flyers tend to draw a large number of inquiry calls. If you anticipate attracting a high number of phone customers, then by all means invest in a system that can handle a lot of incoming calls. Don't try to economize by settling for three lines when you need ten. The business you lose from discouraged customers will far outweigh any temporary savings you might get from a smaller phone system.

FIELD SELLING

As stated earlier, field selling differs from retail selling primarily in the manner in which customers are secured. Differences and similarities may be seen in the chart above.

If you plan to go into retailing, don't stop reading here. Many of the same principles apply, and we have expanded on some concepts for application to all selling situations.

How to Find Prospects

The purpose of prospecting is to develop an on-going list of qualified prospects for your product or service. Since you can't expect everyone you call on to buy, the success of your business may depend on how well you play the "numbers game". The more qualified prospects you find, the more you will sell. What are some methods for locating potential customers?

Cold Calls. Go out and knock on doors. This is one of the easiest ways to locate prospects, but often one of the least effective.

Recommendations. Ask family, friends and business contacts for the names of likely prospects.

Referred Leads. Ask satisfied customers to give you the names of people or companies who might be interested in buying your product. This is probably the most valuable prospect source. And, for that reason, it pays to offer an incentive for such leads. Cash or merchandise may be used, but keep it affordable.

Ad or Direct Mail Lead. Media or direct mail advertising can be used to seek inquiries about your products or services.

Newspaper and Trade Magazine Articles. Local newspapers and trade magazines carry many items of interest: birth records, engagements, social events, new jobs, new businesses, promotions, and feature stories on successful businesses and business personalities.

Telephone and City Directories. If your target market is a restricted group, your prospect list may be ready and waiting for you in the yellow pages.

Trade and Professional Associations. If there is an organization for your potential customers, get your hands on the membership roster.

Purchase a Prospect List. You may be able to buy or rent a previously prepared list of names from a list broker or other source.

Fairs, Shows and Conventions. Arrange for booth space at an appropriate event. Have everyone who visits your booth register for a drawing. This is an effective means for getting leads.

Do Your Homework

You have your list of potential customers. Before you contact them, you should find out as much about them as possible. You can start by collecting some basic information through a few discreet phone calls. If you are calling a fairly good sized company, you will need to find out: name and location; basic business; name of the decision maker; and the approximate size of the company.

Then, as you prepare to make your first contact, you should do some in-depth research. You might find out:

1. A more complete description of the company's business.

2. A description of the company's organizational structure.

3. Names and locations of other branches and divisions.

4. Size by dollar volume.

5. Procedures for seeing salespeople.

6. Who your competitors might be.

7. Other information pertinent to your product or service.

How do you find this information? Check the following sources:

1. Corporate reports available from the company or local library.

2. Trade magazines or other industry publications.

3. Direct calls into the company (preferably to a person other than the decision maker).

4. A visit to the company.

5. Conversations with other people who do business with the company.

6. Conversations with your current customers in the same industry.

Preparing in this way will help you tailor your presentation to meet the company's needs. It will also help you uncover what some obstacles might be to making the sale. And, generally, the prospect will be impressed that you took the time to research his company.

What if the prospect is a small business owner, head of household, or some other individual? Collect as much information as you can before making your first contact. Find out:

1. Facts about his present situation.

2. Facts concerning his interests.

3. Facts concerning his needs and goals. What is he dissatisfied with and what would he like to improve?

4. Credit information. Whether he can and will pay.

5. Other information pertinent to selling your product or service.

You can get this information by asking your lead source at the time you are given the prospect's name. You can talk to satisfied customers who know the prospect. Or you can get this information directly from the prospect at the time of the first contact.

Qualify the Prospect

A qualified prospect is one who has a need or use for your product or service. He has the interest and the ability to derive benefits from its use. And he can afford to buy what you are selling.

The information you gathered on the prospect can help you determine:

1. What product or service does he need?

2. How likely is he to buy?

3. What is he likely to buy?

4. What approach would be best to get an appointment?

The First Contact

The first contact with the prospect can be either by cold call, telephone or letter. It is usually best to set an appointment with a larger company instead of cold calling. It saves your time and is standard procedure for most larger companies.

The research you have done so far should help you get an appointment. You know whom to call and enough about the company to create an opening statement that will generate interest.

The first approach you can try is to call the decision maker directly to make an appointment. The second approach is to send a sales letter first and then follow up with a phone call. This method eliminates the initial resistance to your call because it tells the buyer beforehand who you are, what you do, and that you will be calling.

For smaller businesses and individuals, you can cold call to generate interest, collect additional information, and set an appointment for a presentation. Depending on your product or service and your buyer's interest, you can make your sales presentation at the time of the first contact.

Prepare for the Presentation

Once you have the appointment, it's time to plan an effective presentation based on what you know about the prospect so far. Here are some guidelines:

1. Develop an opening statement with a benefit that fits the prospect's needs.

2. Rehearse the flow of your presentation, making sure it is well paced and brief.

3. Prepare any brochures, catalogs or personalized information that you plan to leave with the prospect.

4. Prepare a list of questions you intend to ask the prospect, based on your research.

5. Prepare answers to the objections you think the prospect might present.

6. Prepare examples of how your service has helped others with the same or similar problems or needs.

GETTING OFF
TO A GOOD START

Many salespersons find the first contact with the prospect to be the most difficult part of the presentation. They are afraid of being rejected before they have a chance to tell their story. This fear can be overcome by developing your opening skills.

The Warm-Up

The warm-up is an ice breaker. It is time you set aside to break down the barriers that might get in the way of communicating with the prospect. Here are some methods for prospect warm-up:

1. **Discuss his interests.** This is a logical starting point in warming up the prospect. Examples: "I noticed you're adding on to the building." "You must have quite a green thumb. These plants are beautiful."

2. **Discuss achievements.** All of us like to be complimented. A deserved compliment is likely to get the prospect's quick attention. Examples: "I read in the paper that your daughter just graduated from law school. You must be very proud of her." "I heard you were just promoted to senior vice-president. Congratulations, Mr. Jones."

3. **Refer to a mutual acquaintance.** Someone you both know can often break down communication barriers by providing a mutual point of interest.

You can improve the warm-up several ways:

1. **Make a good first impression.** Be polite and courteous. Speak clearly and business-like. Dress appropriately for the situation and use appropriate language.

2. **Ask questions that show you are interested in the prospect and his needs.** An important objective of the warm-up is to get the prospect talking. Asking a question at the end of a warm-up statement shifts the conversation over to him and encourages him to talk.

3. **Be sincere.** The prospect will quickly spot any phoniness on your part. Be sure your compliments and concerns for his problems are sincere.

4. **Show the prospect you are knowledgeable about his business.** If your customers are farmers, you'd better know something about farming. If your customers are dentists, you'd better know something about dentistry. You will never be able to convince the prospect that your product or service will solve his business problems if you don't understand his business.

The Benefit Offer

The prospect will get excited about what you have to say only if you can give him a personal reason or incentive for listening. The benefit offer is a statement or question that gives him an opportunity to solve a problem or satisfy a need. It gives him a reason, specifically oriented to his self-interest, for talking to you.

The types of benefits that might be used in your benefit offer are almost endless and depend on the nature of your product or service. Some examples are: increase income; reduce expenses, reduce the cost of production; save time; reduce labor costs; increase flexibility; reduce losses; reduce error; simplify procedures; improve quality; add value; and reduce the cost of maintenance.

How do you make the benefit offer?

State it as a question when you want to encourage the prospect to talk and tell you more about his needs: "Would you be interested in having more time to spend on recreation?"

Use multiple benefits to improve your chances of suggesting a benefit the prospect will respond to positively. "Would you be interested in improving the quality of your product, and at the same time, reducing the cost of producing it?"

Make the benefit specific. It will be of more interest to the prospect because he can relate the benefit closely to his needs: "Would you be interested in reducing the cost of heating your home an average of $25 a month?"

Use the words "new" and "free" when appropriate. To the prospect, new means he can take advantage of something the competition doesn't have yet. Or it may mean a new approach to solve an old problem: "Would you be interested in a new way to finance your equipment at below market rates?" Free means he can get something without paying for it: "This free service guide shows how preventive maintenance can save you money."

Don't tell how the benefit can be provided. You are not ready to sell your product yet. Between getting the prospect's attention and explaining your product, you must first develop an understanding of his needs, wants, problems and goals.

ASSESSING THE PROSPECT'S NEEDS

There's no way you can assess the prospect's needs if you're doing all the talking. Remember, a sale isn't in sight until the prospect becomes involved in the selling process. You can involve him by asking the right questions at the right time and knowing when to stop and listen.

Need Identification

What is a need? No business, household or individual can provide, create or produce every product or service it takes to sustain itself. A need is the lack of any saleable product or useful service. Only when the prospect is conscious of a need will he move to satisfy it.

Also, no business, household or individual has the resources or expertise to solve every problem. So a need is any product or service that solves a problem.

The process of assessing the prospect's needs serves two important purposes: it helps the buyer become more conscious of his needs, and it helps you become aware of his needs so you can show how your product can satisfy them.

To understand how your prospect's needs relate to the purchase of your product, think of all the possible reasons he should buy it:

Will it save him money?

Will it be more convenient to use?

Will it out-perform the product he is using now?

Will it cut down on his work?

Will it feed his ego?

Will it give him more control over his situation?

By understanding why customers buy your product or service, you are in a good position to identify the specific reasons important to each prospect.

You can start by asking him about his **present situation:** "Mr. Prospect, how are you presently handling the collection of your delinquent accounts?"

Perhaps, you can ask a question concerning **dissatisfaction** with his present situation. This will give you an understanding of his needs and wants: "Are you satisfied with the accounts receivable balance you are carrying on your books?"

In the same way, you can probe into possible **goals** the prospect has for his business or personal life that may be achieved through the use of your product or service: "What kind of accounts receivable balance would you like to have by the end of the year?"

The information you get will help you determine what features and benefits to present as you progress toward closing the sale.

Questioning Techniques

You can control the prospect's responses by how you ask your questions. Here are some of the questioning techniques you can use to successfully uncover buyer needs.

Ask Closed-Ended Questions only when you need a single, precise answer. The customer gives a very precise answer because there are only a few possible answers. The following are examples of closed-ended questions:

1. Do you guarantee your equipment?

2. How many special functions does your business give each year?

3. How many people attend?

4. What kind of food do you serve?

Ask Open-Ended Questions when you need detailed explanations. There isn't a single answer to an open-ended question. When you ask an open-ended question, you should be prepared to ask more questions which will direct the customer to give you more information. This is called probing. The following are some examples of open-ended questions:

1. On what occasion do you decide to entertain clients?

2. What kind of image do you try to project?

3. How do you feel we can help you make an impression on your client?

Probe to follow up and get more information or a more detailed answer to your question: "What kind of results are you getting?"

Blend Questions with Responses to avoid sounding like a district attorney:

(Observation) "I notice you don't have any quack grass."

(Question) "What type of weed killer are you using?"

(Answer) "Brand X."

(Response) "It seems to be working well for you."

Listening

About half of the time you spend with the buyer will involve listening to what he has to say. Why is listening so important?

1. So you don't misinterpret what the prospect is saying.

2. To encourage the prospect

3. So you know what to say next.

4. So you know how and when to close the sale.

> We were born with
>
> ONE mouth and TWO ears ...
>
> So, we should **speak** only half as much as we **listen.**

Many of us are poor listeners. Often we assume what is being said is uninteresting so we tune out and think about what to say next.

Or we may allow the appearance and speech delivery of the other person to interfere with good listening. Sometimes if we disagree with what is being said, we react emotionally by tuning out or preparing to do verbal battle. Often, we hear only what we want to hear. Physical or audible distractions may also turn our thoughts from the speaker.

Successful selling requires an ability to overcome these roadblocks to effective listening. Here's how:

1. Look for central ideas. Try to identify the main points being made. Main ideas will usually be supported by a number of supporting facts. Don't try so hard to remember the supporting facts.

2. Use extra thought time. You can think much faster than the prospect can talk. Use that time to mentally summarize what is being said to read between the lines. Note the prospect's posture, tone of voice, facial expressions, gestures and other non-verbal cues.

3. Maintain emotional control by reserving judgement until the prospect has finished talking.

4. When possible, minimize high levels of background noise, poor acoustics, uncomfortable seating and temperature, and other barriers to good communication.

SHOW HOW YOUR PRODUCT OR SERVICE WILL MEET THE PROSPECT'S NEEDS

The main purpose of this part of your presentation is to provide facts, features and benefits about your product in a way that will help the prospect evaluate whether or not it will satisfy his needs.

Creating Benefit Statements

Benefit statements are used to incorporate features and benefits into the sales presentation. It is a method to show how the features and benefits of your product will satisfy the specific needs of your prospect.

Following are the steps to making a sales presentation by creating benefit statements:

1. **Support the needs you helped the prospect identify through questions asking and active listening.** Restate his need and get agreement that it does exist: "I understand that you are dissatisfied with your accounts receivable balance and your average collection period."

THE STEPS TO FEATURES AND BENEFITS SELLING

- SUPPORT the prospect's needs
  - state a FEATURE that relates to his needs
    - state a BENEFIT that relates the features to his needs
      - add PROOF to make your claims believable
        - TEST for understanding   acceptance

2. **State a feature of your product or service that relates to the prospect's need:** "We give a 100% guarantee that we can collect any account on your books for an unusually low one-time fixed fee." Then, elaborate on the feature so the prospect can understand how it works and will accept that your claims are possible: "Here's how our service works..."

3. **Now, state a benefit that relates the feature to the prospect's need.** This will describe for the prospect what personally felt needs your product or service will resolve: "Therefore, you can turn those delinquent accounts into cash without spending the usual 33 to 50 percent."

4. If appropriate, **add proof.** This makes your claims more believable: "Many of our clients feel this is an important benefit of our service. In fact, Dr. Smith has found he is saving 30% of the cost of collecting delinquent accounts by using our service."

5. **Test for understanding and acceptance.** This step assures that the prospect understands how he will benefit from the facts you have given him and he agrees the benefits are important. If you forget this step, you may encounter

resistance when you attempt to close the sale and you may not be able to determine why: "Can you see how our service would help you have better control over your accounts receivable?"

Presentation Techniques

Here are some suggestions to help make your presentation more interesting and appealing:

Use Visual Support. It helps the prospect remember key points in your presentation. Some useful visual support consists of sight-sellers, product pamphlets, models, charts, graphs, demonstration aids, or samples of the actual product.

Get the Prospect Involved. Address him by name frequently. Express benefits with the word "you". Let the buyer hold things or fill things out. If appropriate, let him try the product.

Be Enthusiastic. Show that you are sincerely excited about your product and that you believe it to be the best solution he will find anywhere.

Use Words That Sell. Certain words and phrases will tend to impress the prospect: "different", "new", "latest", "just released", "money saver", "lasts longer", "more for your money", "time saver", and "modern styling". Make sure the words you use speak a positive message: "you" and "let's", not "I" and "we"; "our customers tell us", not "I believe"; "investment", not "cost"; and "opportunity", not "problem".

Use Repetition. Be sure to repeat what you want the prospect to remember.

WORK OUT THE PROBLEMS
THAT KEEP THE CUSTOMER FROM BUYING

Handling Objections

What do you do when the prospect says: "Your price is too high"; "I hear people who buy from you have trouble getting service"; "I can get the same results by using Brand X and it's a lot cheaper"; "Your service can't handle all of my collection problems"; or "I don't care for the style"?

Even though the customer says "no" the first time around, he isn't necessarily rejecting your product or service. His objection is an invitation to be sold. No matter how good your sales presentation, the prospect will often resist the first time you ask him to buy. Successful salespersons know that objections are an aid to closing the sale and should be welcomed.

How can you overcome objections to your product or service?

A. **Anticipate the Objection.** You should know your product or service well enough to anticipate the general objections you will get from buyers. You can also put yourself in each prospect's shoes to determine what might cause him to resist. Then, build into your presentation the facts that will answer that potential objection.

B. **Find the Prospect's Real Objection.** Until you understand the true nature of his objection, you have little opportunity to resolve it.

    1. Cushion the objection. This tells the prospect, "I understand you." Example: "I can appreciate your desire to keep down your costs."

    2. Clarify the objection. Example: "How much are you now spending on collecting past due accounts?"

    3. Probe to find out what the prospect is really asking you to do. Example: "If I could show you how other professionals are able to justify the costs of our services, **would you** be interested?"

    4. Answer the objection. Example: "You'll be interested in knowing that one of the benefits of our service is to give you better control of your accounts receivable. Here's what it can mean to you in dollars..."

    5. Provide a testimonial. Does the customer want to know who else is using your service and why they chose it?

    6. Solve a problem. Does the customer have an underlying problem that your service doesn't appear to solve?

C. **Outweigh the Objection with Benefits.** This technique is valuable to show the prospect that the objection he raised should not be so important as the benefits he would enjoy. Example:

(Prospect)   "I can buy Brand X for less money and it will do the same thing for me."

1. Cushion and clarify: "I can understand your concern. Just how much less would Brand X be?"

(Prospect)   "$500."

2. Recognize the objection in smallest terms: Let's spread that $500 savings over the lifo of our product, say 10 years. That's $50 per year. That $50 represents the additional investment you would be making with our product."

3. Build **plus** benefits: "Now, let's see what benefits you would be getting for that $50 per year investment..."

4. Compare: "Now, compare the added $50 per year investment with the added benefits you will enjoy year after year. Is there any question in your mind which is the better value?"

D. **Give the Prospect a Reason to Act Now.** This technique is valuable when the prospect is mentally sold, but wants to procrastinate to be absolutely sure. "I'd like more time to think about it. Why don't you come back next week?" First, cushion and clarify the objection. Then show his losses from delaying his decision and his gains for acting now.

Recognizing and Handling Emotional Resistance

Even though he has made the decision to buy your product, the prospect may resist taking action on that decision. This is especially true if it involves a sizeable investment or a significant departure from his present way of doing things.

Emotional resistance is not a product of rational thought. It will not yield to logic. It does little good to provide the prospect who fears the consequences of his decision with more facts about your product.

How do you recognize emotional resistance? Some indications are:

1. When the prospect repeatedly puts off taking action, even though he agrees your product is the best answer to his problems.

2. When he keeps bringing up the same objections over and over again.

3. When he is worried about what people will think of his purchase.

4. When he is obviously ill at ease when you try to close the sale.

You can resolve emotional resistance by helping the prospect recognize his fears. If possible, introduce the prospect to a satisfied customer who had similar fears before buying your product. Encourage the prospect to express his feelings. As he talks about his feelings, he is more able to deal with them on a rational basis.

The Answer That's Worse Than a "NO"

The worst thing that a customer can say when you make your closing statement is "Oh". In this case, the customer has lost interest in your presentation. The customer doesn't have an objection, a question, a reason to buy or a reason not to buy. The following are the "oh" responses that mean the customer has lost interest:

1. I'll let you know."

2. I don't think so; not today."

3. Perhaps next month."

4. I really don't see a reason to."

At this point, the only thing you can do is create the objection for the customer. You can do this in the following way:

1. Bring up a feature or a benefit that the customer previously disagreed with."

2. Restate it for the customer as an objection.

3. Handle the statement as you would an objection.

4. Ask the customer to buy again.

NOT TODAY... MAYBE NEXT YEAR..!

Another method is to try to grab the customer's attention by stating a new feature and benefit that you didn't bring up before.

However, sometimes you simply lost the customer and it may be wise to move onto the next presentation. You can always call the customer back when you have a new service or special rate to offer.

THE CLOSE

There is one thing you can count on: You won't get the sale unless you ask for it. The "close" is the culmination of your entire sales effort. Throughout the presentation, you have led the prospect up to the buying decision. Now at the end, you close the sale by directly asking him to buy.

Buying Signals

A buying signal is the prospect's way of telling you he has already made the decision to buy. It usually comes in the form of a question or statement about some minor decision that follows the major decision to buy: "When can you make delivery?" or "Which color would look best with my blue chair?" The buying signal tells you to start preparing for the close.

Trial Closes

An important part of setting up the prospect for the close is to periodically test his interest in buying. The trial close is a question you ask to find out where the prospect is in his buying decision. It can be made anytime during the sales presentation: "We want to handle your delinquent accounts." "Would you want the building up by fall?" "Would you need the automatic timing feature?"

How to Close

Many salespeople fail to get the order because: they don't ask; they don't know when to ask; they ask the wrong closing question; or they give up too easily when the answer is "no".

Here's how to ask for the order:

1. **Ask an All-Clear Question.** In response to a buying signal or at the appropriate closing time, ask something like, "Do you have any further questions?" If not, proceed to the close.

HOW TO CLOSE THE SALE

- Ask an "ALL CLEAR" question

- Use the appropriate Closing Technique
- Summary · Assume · Choice · Special Inducement

- Don't talk past the Close

- Don't give up if he says "NO"

- Support his decision to buy

2. **Use the Appropriate Closing Technique.** The **summary close** is an effective way to close sales in most situations:

   - Ask an all-clear question.
   - Review the prospect's needs.
   - Restate the features the customer liked.
   - Summarize the benefits most important to the customer.
   - Ask for the order.
   - Wait for the reply.

   The **assume close** works best for the prospect who has indicated through buying signals an extreme desire to buy. To close the sale, you assume he has agreed to buy: "In order to get delivery by the end of the month, we'll need to fill these papers. First I need to know..."

   The **choice close** is effective in all closing situations. Ask the prospect to order with a choice question that can't be answered "no": "Can we start your service this week or next week?"

   The **special inducement** close gives the prospect a special reason to buy now: "By buying now, you can save 20%."

3. **Don't Talk Past the Close.** Once you have asked the prospect to buy, don't say anything until you get an answer.

4. **Don't Give Up If He Says "No".** It may mean he either has an objection you haven't uncovered yet or he is afraid to make the decision. Handle the objections and attempt to resolve emotional resistance. Then, repeat the appropriate close. Sometimes the special inducement close is effective to overcome a natural reluctance to act. Continue this process until all his objections are exhausted or emotional resistance has been resolved.

5. **Support the Customer's Buying Decision.** When the customer agrees to buy, give him a vote of confidence. Assure him he has made a wise decision. Check all details to avoid unnecessary callbacks. Follow through promptly to make absolutely certain everything happens just the way you told the customer it would.

PERSONAL SELLING		
FIELD SELLING		**RETAIL SELLING**
• Prospecting • Initial Contact • Warm-up and Benefit offer • The Sales Presentation • Overcoming Objections • Closing the Sale		• Greeting the Customer • The Sales Presentation • Overcoming Objections • Closing the Sale • Plussing the Sale

If at First You Don't Succeed...

So you've gone through all the steps and he still says "no"? You haven't necessarily lost the sale forever. If you still feel the prospect is qualified, you should plan to go back and resell him. To make the call back pay off:

1. Assess your strengths and weaknesses in the first sales attempt. Did you "read" the prospect correctly? Did you stress the right features and benefits? Did you try to sell the right person? Did you try to close the sale?

2. Stay in contact with the prospect. Check back personally, by telephone or by letter, when you have new products, services or other information he might find interesting.

3. Try a different route. In large companies you can often get the account by going through a different department or division.

TELEPHONE SELLING

Unless your business is one where customers come to you and you have more business than you want, chances are a certain percentage of your selling could be done over the telephone.

What are the advantages of telephone selling? It can save you money. Personal selling in the field is a lot more expensive today than it was when gasoline sold for 40 cents a gallon and $10 rented a decent motel room.

Telephone selling can also save you time; and time, we all know, is money. Selling is a numbers game. The more presentations you make, the more you sell. Some companies claim if you double the number of presentations made every day, you can more than double your sales volume. The hours you spend clocking "windshield" time and waiting in reception areas to call on the wrong people could be used more productively on the telephone.

Not only can you talk to more prospects in the same amount of time, but you can screen out prospects who are not qualified buyers. You can create enough interest in your product or service to make a solid appointment for a personal sales presentation.

Regardless of what you sell, the telephone offers you the choice of expanding your market. Time and cost constraints may limit your personal selling efforts to a restricted geographical area. Telephone calling can take you beyond those limits.

Some accounts cannot be serviced profitably through personal sales visits. For these marginal accounts, servicing by telephone may be the best solution.

While the phone can be a tremendous boon to a salesperson, there are some disadvantages to watch for. You can't see your customer, for one thing. Visual clues can tell you a lot about your customer and your customer's business. Asking the right questions and listening are particularly important over the phone.

Pre-Call Planning

Whether you are using the phone only to qualify prospects and set up appointments, or you close all your sales over the phone, you must prepare for the call.

The first decision to be made, of course, is **who are you going to call?** If you are calling on new prospects, all of the rules for good prospecting apply. With your list of everyone to be contacted as a base, design a record keeping system to help keep track of: your "completions"—the people you actually speak to regarding your services; your qualified prospects—those interested and willing to hear from you; actual sales presentations made; and new accounts. Prepare index cards for each prospect to record qualifying information and the results of each contact.

Before you make the call, you must determine **why are you calling?** While the telephone can be used for a variety of purposes, you can only accomplish one selling objective per contact. Is the purpose of your call to sell your product? Get an appointment? Gather information to qualify the prospect? Find the decision maker? Follow-up? A good record keeping system can help you keep track of the specific purpose of each call.

What are you going to say? This, of course, will depend on your purpose for calling. The advantage of telephone selling over personal selling is that you can work from notes. Assuming you are speaking to the right person, you should have an opening prepared:

1. Tell who you are.

2. Give the name of your company.

3. Tell what you do.

4. Tell why you are calling.

5. Give a benefit to the prospect for listening.

When should you call? Depending on your product and your market, there are certain times of the day when prospects are likely to be available and more receptive to your call. If you sell your product or service to businesses, call during business hours. Peak phone times are thought to be from 9:00-11:00 a.m. Tuesday, Wednesday and Thursday. On the other hand, if your product or service is sold directly to the consumers, you may consider evening calls. You would definitely want to avoid meal times and early mornings. Experience and common sense will help you determine your prime calling time. Don't waste your prime selling time getting organized. Do your homework in advance.

Getting Through to the Right Person

Making your call is not as easy as dialing the number. Getting through to the right person is essential, whether you sell over the phone or in person. One study estimated that 65% of all sales calls are made on the wrong person! Your time is too valuable to waste on people who can't make the decision to buy what you sell.

Usually when prospecting, you can get the name of the decision maker through the switchboard or receptionist. But what about the "screener"? Usually, a third party stands in the way of you and your prospect. It may be a secretary, an assistant or a spouse. Their job is to screen calls and save the decision maker's time. Here are some techniques for getting through:

1. Be brief and direct.

2. Speak with authority. The screener's job is to screen out **unimportant** calls. Project your importance through your voice.

3. Don't allow yourself to be put on hold. Important people value their time.

4. Never tell the screener more than is asked:

   "I'd like to speak to Mr. Peterson, please."

   "May I tell him who is calling?"

   "Mary Smith. Is he in, please?"

   "Yes, he is. What company are you with?"

   "XYZ Company. Would you please tell Mr. Peterson I'm on the phone?"

   Let the screener ask the questions and ask to speak with the decision maker each time you answer. Persistence pays off.

5. Leave messages with authority and a subtle sense of urgency: "Mention to Mr. Peterson that if I can hear from him today, I'd appreciate it."

6. Establish rapport with the screener when you have to make several calls to get through. Find out his name and use it each time you call back.

The Telephone Presentation

The techniques used in the telephone presentation are basic to all selling. There are some distinct differences between personal and telephone selling:

1. You can control the presentation because the prospect has to concentrate harder on what you have to say.

2. You must compensate for the lack of visual cues.

3. You can work from notes. You can have the prospect's index card and other relevant background information at your fingertips.

The following format can be used in making the call:

1. Opening (basic introduction and benefit statement).

2. Establish rapport (assess needs and interests).

3. State the sales message (present features and benefits, overcome objections, close the sale).

4. Confirm the order or appointment.

5. Arrange for the next step.

6. Thank the customer.

The length of the presentation will depend on the purpose of the call. Most people get impatient after 15–20 minutes on the telephone. If the purpose of the call is to get an order, the majority of the time should be spent overcoming objections and closing the sale.

Follow-Up

Follow-up refers to the events that occur after the call is completed or the sale has been made. It can be summarized in one phrase—tending to details. Here are some suggestions for effective follow-up in telephone selling:

1. When you "sell" an appointment for a personal call, record it in your calendar and note if you should call first to confirm it.

2. When you close a sale, confirm the order by carefully repeating the item, quantity, price, delivery date and other details. Schedule a time and date to call back to make sure the order was delivered or service was rendered as promised. Make detailed notes of the transaction on the prospect's index card.

3. Call back periodically to find out how things are going.

Improving Your Call Success Rate

Suppose you find telephone selling isn't working for you. Before you give up, try to determine some possible reasons for your problems:

If no one is in when you call, you're probably calling at the wrong time. Change your selling times to see if you can get in touch with more prospects.

If they aren't interested in what you're selling, review your prospecting techniques.

If you're not getting enough appointments or closing enough sales, you probably aren't making enough calls.

If your prospects are rude on the phone, are you giving them a reason for listening?

If you are getting complaints about service, how's your record keeping system? Do you follow-up?

DIRECT MAIL

Direct mail is the use of mailed advertising to directly or indirectly develop sales. Selected mailing lists are employed to direct the selling message to the desired audience. Direct mail is used by more advertisers than any other medium and more dollars are spent on it than on any other form of advertising.

Direct mail can be used for anything from pure advertising to direct selling (mail order) to research and market surveys. In this chapter we will look at the following uses for direct mail:

1. To create more effective personal sales contact. Direct mail can be used to get actual inquiries about your product or service from interested prospects. These serve as leads for personal follow-up. It can also pave the way for your personal call by lessening resistance, arousing interest, and educating and informing the prospect.

2. To bring the prospect to you. This applies particularly to retail and service businesses. It generally involves a direct mail offer for reduced prices on products and services or a free product if another is purchased.

3. To take actual orders through the mail. In direct mail selling or mail order selling, every step in the process from the initial contact to the final sale is done exclusively by mail. The

products are generally those not readily available in stores or through other sources. Rarely is a successful mail order business established through the sale of a single product or "one-shot" offer.

How Will Your Prospects Respond?

Direct mail is often misunderstood and assumed to be a waste of money for advertisers, a burden on the post office, and "junk mail" for the consumer. However, research has shown that: 85% of the people have no general dislike for direct mail; at least 75% of them open all direct mail received; for most people, the problem of "cluttered mail boxes" just doesn't exist.

The Basic Elements of Direct Mail

The List. The most important element in any direct mail program is the list of prospects to whom the mailings are sent.

There are a variety of ways to build your mailing list. You can start with your own sales records and then add prospects. Mailing lists covering every conceivable type of market and customer base are available through professional list compilers, brokers and other sources. To rent a list for one-time use usually costs between $25-35 per thousand names. The cost of purchasing a list for continued use may cost as much as $5.00 per name for a highly specialized list, although compilation costs are more likely to run about $50 per thousand names.

HOW TO FIND PROSPECTS

COLD CALLS •RECOMMENDATIONS •REFERRED LEADS

AIR & DIRECT MAIL LEADS •TELEPHONE & CITY DIRECTORIES

•NEWSPAPER & MAGAZINE ARTICLES • PROSPECT LISTS

TRADE AND PROFESSIONAL ASSOCIATIONS

•FAIRS, SHOWS, & CONVENTIONS

A useful directory for locating list sources is the **Direct Mail List Rates and Data**, a comprehensive listing of mailing lists, arranged by subject in consumer, business and farm categories. It is published by the Standard Rate and Data Service and is available at local libraries.

Once you have a list, it is essential to keep it up-to-date. There is at least 25% turnover in the average list each year. Your sales records, sales call reports, new editions of directories, personnel change columns in newspapers and magazines, association rosters, and other sources will help keep your list alive. You can't afford to send direct mail to wrong addresses or to people who are no longer a part of your market.

The Offer. To be effective, you should seek to accomplish specific objective through your direct mail effort. This is referred to as the "offer". It specifies the purpose of your mailing and the action you expect the recipients to take. It may be to send in an order, a request for literature, or a personal sales call.

Once you have your offer clearly in mind, you must develop copy that leads the reader to the offer and makes him want to take the action you request. The oldest and most frequently used outline for effective direct mail copy is AIDA:

- Get **Attention**

- Arouse **Interest**

- Stimulate **Desire**

- Ask for **Action**

Frequently, "the offer" is made in the form of a letter. Here are some tips for writing effective sales letters:

1. Clearly define the purpose of the letter.

2. Make it clear and concise. Use short, crisp sentences.

3. Clearly state the benefit of the product or service early in the letter.

4. Answer as many objections as possible

5. Clearly state a "next step" or the action you want the recipient to take.

The Package. The package is how the material is presented. Whether the mailer is opened and read or tossed in the wastebasket will often depend on the "package".

Careful consideration must be given to such things as the appearance of the sales letter, letterhead, envelopes and postage. The appearance of your sales letter is affected by the datelines, margins, the salutation, underlining, asterisks, color, type and signature. Your product and your market will determine the type of letterhead and paper to use. Color, art and design of the envelope are important in getting your mail opened and read. You must decide whether to use stamps, a postage meter, or printed postage permit, and whether to mail first or third class.

The order form is a very important part of the direct mail package. It can make or break the sale. A well-designed order form will have the following features:

1. The copy is clear and the offer is plainly stated.

2. There is plenty of room for the customer to give his name, address and other information.

3. Your name and address appear on the front or back if the form is not business reply.

4. The form looks important.

If you are making a straight charge offer, your order form could simply be a business reply card. A cash offer will have to include a reply envelope. In either case you need a business reply permit which is available at your post office. The permit number should be printed on your reply cards and/or envelopes.

You should include a circular in the package if:

1. Your product or service is not known.

2. The cost of the product is high.

3. When the product takes a lot of explaining or has to be seen to be appreciated.

4. When a desire for the product has to be created.

5. When you don't expect immediate action but you want the prospect to have information about your product or service before a telephone or personal contact.

If you decide your product or service can be sold better with a circular and a letter, here are some guidelines for a successful circular:

1. It should have an eye-catching headline with reader benefits.

2. It should show the product or service.

3. It should be easy to read with plenty of subheadings.

4. It should include all the information necessary for the prospect to decide to take action.

5. It should include an order form, if applicable, even if a separate order form is included in the package.

Fulfillment. Your objective in direct mail is to get the prospect to act. If he does, your objective is fulfilled. Now your job is to see that he gets what he asked for and gets it promptly.

If your objective was to seek inquiries about your product or service, you should:

1. Answer every request for product literature or a personal sales call.

2. Do it with a personal letter. Tell him when he can expect a call to set up an appointment.

3. Include all the information and literature he requested.

4. Do it **today**.

Handling orders received through the mail is even more important. You have just created a customer and he expects prompt and efficient service. If he is satisfied, he becomes an excellent prospect for future business.

Three Types of Sales Letters

1. **Letter of Introduction.** A letter of introduction is sent to the prospect before you make the first phone call. This letter tells the prospect who you are and what you do. You close this letter with a statement telling the prospect when you are going to call.

   Now, when you call the prospect, it is no longer a cold call. You open the conversation with a statement that refers to your letter. "Did you receive the letter I sent you?" or "As I mentioned in my letter..."

2. **Letter of Confirmation.** A letter of confirmation is sent to the prospect after you have set an appointment by phone. In this letter, you thank the customer for the appointment and state the benefits which will be the highlights of your presentation. If the prospect has asked you to send any specific information before the appointment, it can be included in this letter.

Sales letters can also be used to reinforce the prospect's buying decision:

3. **The Thank-You Letter.** Thank you letters separate the successful salesperson from the average salesperson. Successful salespeople send thank-you letters. This letter thanks the customer for the order an restates your commitment to serving the customer.

The following are the rules for writing sales letters that sell:

- The purpose of the sales letter is clearly defined in the letter.
- There is a clear "next step" stated.
- They are precisely worded with short, crisp statements.
- The main benefits of the product/service are clearly stated.

Customer Service Letters

A lot of a salesperson's follow-up can be done in letter form. Some customers may feel that you are imposing or pushy if you are constantly calling or stopping by. But, everyone likes to get mail that isn't a bill. The following are the two types of customer service letters:

1. **The New Information Letter.** Every time a new service is introduced, you can use a new information letter. The letter explains the new service and the benefits of the service. If you plan to call or stop by to explain the service, you can state a time and date in the letter.

   Any new brochures or catalog sheets can be included with the letter. The new information letter helps you reach all your customers quickly.

2. **The Complaint Service Letter.** The complaint service letter helps you maintain your customer after he has had a problem. It is the personal touch that shows you were concerned about the problem and the problem is now solved. The complaint service letter is sent after the problem has been resolved and the customer has been informed by phone.

The following are the rules for writing customer service letters:

- They are written in a personal and informal manner.
- They are always sent with a benefit message.
- They are brief, no longer than one page.

Proposals

A proposal is used for selling large accounts. The proposal explains in detail the services and prices offered. The following is a brief outline of what should be included in a sales proposal:

1. The purpose of the proposal.
2. The services and prices offered.
3. The benefits of the services.
4. How the customer will be serviced.
5. A description of the next step.

Guidelines for Successful Mail Order

In mail order, it's the repeat sales that yield the profit. Here are some pointers for making your direct mail selling program a success:

1. Address correctly and to the right list. Reaching the right people at the right time is critical to successful direct mail.

2. Make sure the copy shows a benefit.

   a. Promise the reader a benefit in the headline or first paragraph.

b. Immediately expand upon your most important benefit.

c. Tell the reader specifically what he is going to get.

d. Back up your claims with proof.

e. Tell the reader what he'll lose if he doesn't act now.

f. Rephrase your benefit in the closing offer.

g. Ask for immediate action

3. Make the copy "fit" the reader.

4. Make it easy for the reader to take the action you want him to take.

5. Don't forget the customer. Tell your story over and over again through repeat mailings. You would never think of stopping at one sales call in personal   selling if you didn't get results. The same holds true for direct mail.

6. Keep track of your results. Note the packaging and lists that "pull" the most action.

BASIC RULES OF BUSINESS WRITING

The problem most people have in writing a letter or proposal is that they don't know how to get their thoughts out of their head and down on paper. The following step-by-step method is used to solve this problem.

1. **Who is the Reader?**

   Is the reader a new prospect, a new customer or an established customer?

2. **Why Are You Writing?**

   Are you trying to sell a new customer, set an appointment, introduce new services, etc?

3. **How Are You Going To Say It?**

   The information from steps one and two will help you decide what type of letter to write: prospecting letter, thank you letter, proposal, etc. In addition, you will know what the style and tone of the letter should be: formal or informal, handwritten or typewritten, long or short.

4. What Do You Want To Say?

Create an outline of what you want to say. For example, what do you want to say in the first paragraph, the second paragraph, etc. Now, write a first draft of the letter by filling in the outline with the right statements. At this point, don't worry about sentence structure or grammar; just get your thoughts down on paper.

5. Write the Second Draft.

Now, review your first draft. Do you like the style and tone of the letter. Do you like how the letter is organized? Have you stressed benefits throughout the letter? Start with a fresh piece of paper and write a second draft which corrects all the things you didn't like in the first draft.

Many professional writers will write third, fourth and fifth drafts before they get a letter they really like. However, each draft becomes easier because your thoughts were down on paper in the first draft.

6. Edit Your Last Draft.

Finally, correct your letter for any spelling or grammar mistakes that you may have made in the last draft. You can also make any changes in the format or layout of the page before it is finally typed. Any errors in your letter will distract the reader and dilute your selling message.

In this chapter, you learned that your business depends on the art of selling. You learned it takes skill, ability, personality, product knowledge and people knowledge to do it right. You learned the principles basic to all selling and the specific techniques for selling in person, by telephone or by direct mail. The rest is up to you. Your success will depend on your ability to close sales and create satisfied customers. It will depend on your hiring the right people to sell for you...people who enjoy selling and do it well. Remember: "Nothing happens till something is sold."

Chapter 15

Insuring your future

How to keep the sky from falling

A pet shop chimpanzee, usually friendly with strangers, suddenly bites a little girl on the cheek. Her doctor says she'll be scarred for life. The little girl's parents sue the pet shop for damages in the amount of $500,000.

A small TV repair shop is gutted by a fire caused by faulty wiring. The owner's entire inventory, as well as twelve TV's in for repair, are destroyed.

A family is visiting a photography studio for a portrait, when five-year-old Mark uses the men's room. He playfully turns on the water faucet, and leaves it on. Before the flowing water is discovered, it has seeped through an opening in the floor, damaging several very expensive paintings in the art studio directly below.

Without adequate insurance to cover such occurrences, these small business owners would be wiped out.

Accidents are always unpredictable, and they occur by the thousands every day. They inflict every type of injury, from a scratch to sudden death, on their victims. As careful as people try to be, the chance of some kind of injury or disaster remains.

Let's face it, the cost of insurance itself is painful; but what small business can be without it? Even though you may be struggling to stretch your dollars, you should (or in most cases, **must**) make insurance a part of your operating budget.

Think how you would be affected by chance events like:

Fire
Earthquake
Windstorm
Flood
Theft
Vandalism
Automobile accidents
Anyone injured on your business premises
Employees injured on the job
Illness which prevents you or an employee from performing on
    the job for a long time
Death or injury to you or a key employee

Such occurrences are called "pure risks" because the victims are always unwilling. It is for this type of risk that insurance exists.

Insurance first came about by people pooling funds or goods on their own to share risk. A disaster is likely to happen to only a few people in any give year, but nobody knows which few. If a group of people pools funds and sets the money aside, everyone can be protected from fire or other disasters and illness with a modest individual investment.

A small business owner can become overwhelmed by all the insurance needs and options. You could use the help of a good insurance agent to develop a sound insurance package for your business. You'll also want to be armed with a knowledge of insurance principles and an understanding of the many different types of insurance available.

In this chapter you will learn:

1. Basic principles common to many types of insurance.

2. How to choose insurance agents and companies.

3. The basic types of insurance for small businesses, including:

    A. Property and liability insurance.

    B. Employee plans and workers' compensation.

    C. Special life and health insurance concerns for small business owners and partners.

    D. Special insurance concerns for one-person or at-home businesses.

4. How to reduce your chance of loss.

5. Insurance requirements are continually changing, along with changes in your business and in the insurance industry.

BASIC INSURANCE PRINCIPLES

Insurance companies play the odds.

Insurance company rates are based on hundreds of statistics. These statistics allow them to determine the odds of particular disasters common to your business. The odds are influenced by factors such as your location, the age of your building, and the nature of what you do. These factors go into the formula that computes your insurance rates. Your age, sex, and health history are factors which affect the insurance company's calculation of your odds for life and health insurance premiums.

Because an insurance company has many policyholders, it can calculate closely what it will pay out in claims each year based on the law of averages.

When insurance companies play the odds, they build in a "house advantage," just like a gambling casino. They charge enough in premiums to cover their expected claims and produce a profit.

Insurance is for large losses, not trivial ones.

Insurance will not pay for itself by paying for claims equalling what was paid in premiums. This will happen only for a few people who suffer large losses.

You don't want to buy insurance for every possible loss. If you break a $50 piece of equipment, you can handle that loss without insurance. You should think of insurance as protection against only those events which would cause your company serious financial hardship.

One way of reducing insurance costs is to buy policies with deductible claim portions. Higher deductibles reduce your premium. In turn, you pay for small losses - those below the stated deductible - yourself. Automobile insurance, for example, can usually be purchased with deductibles of $100, $250, or $500. Obviously, a policy with the $500 deductible will cost less than the other two.

In general, when you buy a policy with a higher deductible, the money you save in premiums can more than make up for the money you'd spend to take care of small losses yourself.

Buy insurance with high enough policy limits.

If you insure a building that costs $100,000 to rebuild, you should insure it for 80% of its replacement cost or its actual cash value.

Lawsuits against small businesses sometimes run into the millions of dollars. So give serious thought to the possibility of liability insurance for large claims against your business. It pays to have insurance with limits high enough to cover losses which you could reasonably expect to pay. Higher limits usually add a relatively small extra premium.

Don't over-insure or expect to profit from insurance.

People should not think they can profit from some disaster by buying insurance worth more than the true value of the property covered, or by buying several policies with overlapping coverage. Insurance companies and state governments have many rules to prevent the fraudulent use of insurance for personal gain.

Be open with your insurance agents and companies

Only through honest and complete communication can insurance agents and companies meet your needs with appropriate policies. Some people try to save money by concealing facts. However, misleading answers to application questions can be grounds for cancellation of the policy or denial of claims. Be sure your insurance agent knows all the facts about your company. Otherwise, you may wind up with coverage that doesn't meet your needs.

Open, honest, unadulterated, factual, explicit, lily-white, literal truth.

Don't shop by price only.

Price is important when shopping for insurance, but it shouldn't be your only consideration. Different companies charge different rates for identical policies. However, sometimes you get only what you pay for. A cheaper policy may exclude important items from coverage. Read the fine print. The deductibles on a cheaper policy may be too high, or the policy limits may be too low. Some companies are known for providing superior service, and their premiums may be higher as a result. Good service from your insurance agent is very valuable. This will be discussed in the next section.

Make a safe business.

Even with insurance, a loss will cost you time and money. Also, human lives may be at stake. So when you are planning an insurance package, think also about ways to make your business safer. Measures such as high-quality locks, fire alarms and other fire-safety measures, careful driving, and so forth, give you peace of mind. They can also reduce your insurance premiums.

You'll never insure everything.

Insuring your business against every possible chance event that could produce a financial loss would be impossible. To come even close would be very expensive. You need to decide what risks are most important for your business. Develop an insurance plan which goes as far as possible given your finances.

Risks you choose not to insure, you "assume." For example, some people go without collision insurance on automobiles, especially older cars of low value. They have chosen to face the cost of possible damage to their cars personally

Some large corporations go a step further through "self-insurance." They maintain large funds of their own to cover certain risks.

Summary

Insurance companies play the odds. They take in more in total premiums than they expect to pay out. When they don't, they raise the premiums. Think of insurance as protection against large losses that could cause serious hardship - not as protection for all trivial losses. Deductibles save you premium dollars, but you will then pay for small losses yourself. Buy insurance with policy limits high enough to cover potentially large losses. At the same time, don't carry excess insurance thinking you could make a profit. Be open with your agents and companies. Price is important but must be balanced by other concerns. Finally, look for ways to make your business safer.

CHOOSING INSURANCE AGENTS AND COMPANIES

A good agent (or two) is crucial.

Many people buy their individual insurance from a relative or friend. Or they are sold policies by friendly agents who are good at patting people on the back and making small talk about sports. Be careful when choosing insurance agents for your business. You need a true business insurance expert.

Your agent must help you make sense of all your insurance options and considerations. He or she also serves as your contact with the insurance company. Your agent will have to go to bat for you should a claim arise.

You may need several agents for various types of insurance. One agent may specialize in property and liability insurance. Another may specialize in employee benefit plans or life and health insurance.

A good agent will not just sell you insurance. He or she will help you study the important risks involved in your business.

What To Look For in Insurance Agents

In view of the fact that an insurance policy is so often obsolete before it is printed, the agent's role takes on a special significance. You'll know you've found a good one when he demonstrates his ability to tailor and interpret a proper policy for your business

Choose an agent the same way you would choose any other business associate or supplier. Look for someone with a good reputation

in your community. Ask other small business people you know to recommend agents.

Interview several competing agents. This will help you find one who really knows the business. Ask lots of questions. Don't be afraid to plead ignorance or any matters like coverage or vocabulary. After all, you need all the raw information and understanding you can get.

Look for someone who seems willing to spend enough time to carefully evaluate your insurance needs. You'll want an agent with whom you can develop a long-standing relationship of trust. As your company grows and changes, you'll want your agent to help you determine your changing insurance needs.

The insurance industry awards some designations - they're like diplomas - to agents who have demonstrated their knowledge. A CPCU designation (Chartered Property and Casualty Underwriter) means that an agent has passed a series of difficult tests on property and casualty insurance. A CLU designation (Chartered Life Underwriter) shows life and health insurance expertise

Some agents are independent and represent several insurance companies at once. Others represent only one company. A broker is also independent and can place your insurance with many companies. There are pluses and minuses to each kind. For your purposes, these differences are not as important as business insurance expertise.

Once you have chosen an agent, it is a good idea to ask him to function as though he were on your board of directors, interpreting your insurance needs.

Choosing Insurance Companies

Your choice of an insurance agent often comes before your choice of an insurance company. The agent can help you make that choice.

Look for a company with:

1. The specialized types of products you need.

2. A good reputation for service.

3. Financial stability.

4. Competitive prices.

There are more than 3,000 insurance companies in the United States. If a company has a name you've never heard, it doesn't mean it's not a good company for a particular insurance need. Many smaller companies have developed fine reputations for catering to specialized types of businesses or needs.

Your state government protects you against many unethical practices by insurance companies, but it still pays you to ask as many questions as you can about different companies. You can also check at the public library for publications by A.M. Best Company that rate the management and stability of insurance companies.

Summary

Choosing the right agent or agents is your first important insurance decision. Look for one with the expertise to match your insurance needs. Carefully interview several, and get some recommendations from other small business people. With the help of an agent you trust, choose insurance companies with solid reputations, the specialized products you need, and competitive prices.

TYPES OF INSURANCE

Insurance is divided into two main categories. **Property** and **Liability** (or property and casualty) is the first. The second is **Life** and **Health.** Property and Liability coverages are the most important types of insurance for business. Property coverage includes insurance on your buildings and other property. Liability protects you against claims of injury or protects you against claims of injury or property loss resulting from negligence on your part. Automobile insurance falls into this category. Life and Health coverage may be part of your employee benefit package. It may also be for the owners and partners themselves.

We will review these main types of property and liability insurance:

- Property and liability package policies

- Business interruption

- Marine and inland marine

- Product and professional liability

- Motor vehicle

- Other special types

In the "Your Employees" section of this chapter, we will cover group life and health and related employee benefits. We will also discuss workers' compensation, actually a form of liability coverage.

The "Personal Insurance for Business Owners and Partners" section will discuss business-related uses of life, health and long-term disability considerations. Credit life, used in connection with loans, will also be looked at.

PROPERTY AND LIABILITY INSURANCE

As an owner of a small business, your major need will most likely be property and liability insurance. There are many different types of property to be covered and many potential areas of liability. You don't have to buy a separate policy for each item and each risk, however. One package policy can cover many property and liability risks at once. You may need separate policies to cover risks left out of the primary package, however. Motor vehicle insurance, for example, comes separately.

Before we discuss types of policies, let's look at the range of risks involved.

Property Risks

As you work out a program with your agent, list all the property your business owns to help you understand your insurance needs.

Let's take a look at Harry, the owner of a small office supply business, as an example. His business owns a building worth an estimated $200,000. The business furniture and equipment are worth more than $30,000. Inventory varies, but its value at one time can be more than $50,000. The business also owns an automobile ($8,000) and a delivery van ($10,000). Every item of business property that Harry owns is subject to a variety of risks. He has listed their value in terms of replacement cost and would be wise to insure them against loss.

After you've made an inventory of your business property, stop to consider again all the various types of disasters to which it is exposed. Fire comes to mind immediately. Similarly, there are dangers of explosion, windstorm, flood, earthquake and so forth.

Consider crime risks of theft or burglary, or the possibility of vandalism or riot. Which risks are most important for your business depend on their nature and location. For example, a business located near a river has a greater need for flood coverage.

Liability Risks

For what types of damage to others might you be held financially responsible? For what could you possibly be sued? Harry knows that a customer, or even a passer-by, could be injured on his business premises. A fire or explosion could originate at his building and damage the building next door. A defective product could cause an injury.

Many business owners have a hard time imagining a major lawsuit could actually be brought against them for almost any reason. But anyone who reads the newspapers knows we live in a "suit-happy" world. Here's a story, based on an actual occurrence, to illustrate why you should be concerned about liability risks:

An electrician, a small businessman, was called by a large corporation to do some wiring at its headquarters. While completing his work, the electrician unknowingly damaged some other wiring. Several days later, the electrician's slip-up created a chain of events leading to a $250,000 fire.

The corporation's insurance company came after the electrician. He had liability coverage, but with policy limits of only $50,000. The result: One ruined business, and it wasn't the major corporation or the insurance company.

Business Property and Liability Package Policies

A "package" property and liability policy covers many risks at once. Most people are familiar with standard homeowners policies. They cover your home and your personal property, as well as your personal liability needs. Similarly, business "multiple-lines" policies include both property and liability coverages and protect against many perils.

One warning about package plans: Don't assume they cover all your property and liability needs. Be sure you and your agent review your plan carefully to determine exactly what it does and does not cover.

For example, a common type of package policy is called an "all-risk" policy. Because of the multitude of risks it covers, the insurance company prefers to list those risks it **does not** cover. Examples of some exclusions would be ground seepage, earthquake, landslide, normal wear and tear, animal damage, etc.

When you find important property and liability items or risks not covered in your multiple-lines policy, add appropriate separate policies to your insurance package. Or, you may be able to add "endorsements" which will extend your package policy. This is like adding "options" when you buy a new car.

Your basic business liability needs can likewise be covered under such a package policy. Some businesses will purchase separate business and liability package policies. But this is not usually true for small businesses.

As mentioned earlier, policy limits are a very important part of your liability coverage. Because businesses are often prime targets for lawsuits, some agents recommend that small businesses have liability limits of $1,000,000 or more.

Standard liability coverage protects you against many types of judgements for bodily injury or property damage. It also covers expenses for immediate medical care required by third parties at the time of an accident. It covers legal expenses in lawsuits against you, and the settlement of expenses such as court bonds.

Property Insurance: Replacement Cost or Actual Value?

In your property coverage, you can buy either "replacement cost" or "actual value" insurance.

- Replacement cost insurance is more expensive. If you have a loss, you can receive a claim payment to cover the cost of **new** buildings and goods to replace those lost.

- Actual value insurance will pay claims based on the estimated **depreciation** value of the property and goods damaged or destroyed.

How do you decide? If you think you can afford to make up the difference yourself between depreciated value and replacement cost should you suffer a loss, buy actual value insurance. If that difference would cause your business a serious financial hardship, buy replacement cost insurance.

Business Interruption Insurance

In addition to being costly in and of themselves, many disasters can create a business-interruption loss. If a fire hits Harry's business, it might take weeks or months to reopen in the same location or some other location. Meanwhile, Harry could lose

Perhaps its time we looked into a business interruption policy...

thousands of dollars in revenue.

Business interruption insurance makes up for such lost revenue. It comes either as an endorsement to a multiple-line package property and liability policy, or as a separate policy.

Marine and Inland Marine Insurance

Among the many specialized types of insurance are marine and inland marine. Marine insurance covers ships and their cargoes. "Inland marine" insurance may seem to be a contradiction in terms. It covers many types of goods in transit on trucks, trains, and so forth.

Inland marine has also become a sort of "catch-all" for many different types of coverage difficult to get under other policies. Some examples might include salespersons' samples, or data processing equipment used by a worker at home.

Products and Completed Operations

A **product liability** case arises when someone claims that one of your company's products has caused an injury or property loss due to a product defect or design flaw. Such lawsuits have grown both in number and dollar amounts in recent years. You can purchase product liability insurance as protection.

Completed Operations insurance applies to any legal liability on your part arising out of work completed by or for you.

Comprehensive General Liability insurance includes both of the above types, and premiums are based on an annual audit of your sales and receipts.

Professional Liability

Medical malpractice is the best-known form of **professional liability** insurance. This insurance protects people whose business involves services or consulting. People in such fields as law, engineering, accounting, and even insurance sales, are finding a need for professional liability insurance.

Motor Vehicle Insurance

Motor vehicle insurance is separate from other property and liability policies. Commercial motor vehicle coverage is not much different from the automobile insurance most of us carry on our personal cars.

Most policies include property coverage for your vehicle itself, as well as liability coverage for damage caused by the driver of your car to other vehicles and persons. Policies also cover the costs of injuries to the driver and passengers of your vehicle. There are several standard commercial policies available. Some vary in terms of who may drive your vehicle and be covered.

Most states require that you carry at least liability and personal injury coverage on any car you own. This protects all motorists from the danger of uninsured drivers. Otherwise, you must usually show that you have assets up to certain limits on which to draw if you have an accident.

If your company has many vehicles, you can buy "fleet insurance" to cover them all on one policy. You'll need a special type of policy if your business involves vehicles used for transporting people for a fee. If you use your personal vehicle for business, your premiums will be slightly higher than for other personal vehicles because of increased use.

Deductibles are useful in reducing your motor vehicle insurance premium. High policy limits often cost only a small added premium.

Other Special Types of Property and Liability Insurance

Many special types of property and liability insurance have been developed for special risks and unusual categories of property. These often come as separate policies.

One example is **credit insurance,** which can protect a business from unusually high losses on accounts receivable. **Title insurance** covers losses which may occur if a title to real estate proves to be contestable. **Aviation insurance** has been developed especially for airplanes. There are many other special categories, from **cast insurance** for theatrical or film producers, to **crop insurance** for those involved in agriculture. If your business is of a special or unusual nature, or if you have special types of property, your agent can tell you about special coverages available.

Bonds are closely related to insurance. You buy a bond as insurance for a customer or other third party to guarantee that you will perform some specific action. For example, a construction contractor can buy a bond to help ease the mind of a client. If the contractor fails to perform as agreed, the client can get a settlement.

Summary

Every business is different and will need its own combination of property and liability policies and coverages. You should begin with a careful analysis of your property and your possible property and liability risks.

A package property and liability package can serve most small businesses well. But be sure you know what the package leaves out. You may need special endorsements to a package, or some separate policies, to get all the property and liability insurance you need. Coverage for your vehicles comes in separate policies. It is a must, for at least liability and personal injury protection. Other special property and liability coverages include business interruption, product or professional liability, marine or inland marine insurance, and other less common types.

We haven't yet discussed liability involving employees injured on the job. Workers' compensation insurance will be covered in the next section of this chapter, "Your Employees."

YOUR EMPLOYEES

Employee benefits, such as group life and health coverage, are commonly offered as additional compensation in lieu of salaries or wages. Small businesses offer benefits such as these to attract and hold good employees.

Group Life and Heath Insurance

Employers sponsor and help administer group life and health plans. The employer usually pays part or all of the costs for each employee.

Group insurance is usually cheaper, per person involved, than comparable individual insurance because an insurance company can administer group insurance more efficiently than individual insurance.

In most group life and health coverage, a person's health condition does not affect his or her rates or eligibility. However, if your business has fewer than 10 employees, you probably cannot buy that kind of group policy. You will most likely be able to provide only the type of group insurance that uses a health questionnaire for each employee. Employees with health problems may be ineligible for the plan, or they may be charged a higher rate.

Group health insurance includes three main types of coverage:

1. **Basic** medical and hospitalization takes care of most day-to-day expenses of illnesses.

2. **Major medical** covers more severe health problems.

3. **Disability income** provides a regular income for employees who suffer disabilities making them unable to work for long periods of time.

Most employers provide a package of the first two. The major medical portion of the coverage is designed to "kick-in" after the basic coverage has been exhausted for a sick or injured employee.

Deductibles are common in group health basic coverage. The insurance cost will be less with deductibles, and employees will pay for small medical expenses themselves. "Co-insurance" in group health is similar to a deductible. A co-insurance provision might state that each employee will pay 20% of his or her medical expenses up to $2,000 in a given year. If such a co-insurance provision were obtained with a $250 annual deductible, here's how the coverage would work:

Employee's 1-Year Medical Expenses	Group Health Pays	Employee Pays
$ 250	$ 0	$250
$ 500	$ 200	$300
$1,000	$ 600	$400
$2,000	$1,400	$600
$3,000	$2,400	$600

An alternative to a group health insurance plan is a **Health Maintenance Organization**, or HMO. In many areas, HMO's have only recently become an option for small companies. An HMO is a large medical organization, usually including one or more medical clinics affiliated with one or more hospitals.

When you join an HMO, you pre-pay a flat amount, and the HMO will take care of all your medical needs while you are enrolled. Because HMO's don't have deductibles, they are usually more expensive than group health plans. However, those enrolled pay no medical expenses out of their own pockets.

Large employers can often offer employees a choice of an HMO or a basic health/major medical plan. Small employers can usually offer only one of the two options. With small employers, most insurers and HMO's require that all eligible employees must participate in the plan for the company to be eligible.

Employees' spouses and dependent children can be included in the group health plan or HMO at an additional cost.

As an employer, you can pay all of the group insurance costs or a percentage. Small employers usually must pay the entire cost for employees - although, not necessarily the added costs for spouses or dependents.

Many employers neglect long-term **disability insurance**. It can be a valuable employee benefit. Let's go back to Harry. He hadn't even thought about disability insurance, trying to save money by providing only a minimal group health plan for employees.

Jim, one of Harry's employees, suffers a stroke, is hospitalized for months, and may not be able to work for more than a year. Jim uses up all his group health benefits. He has a family to support, more medical bills, and no money coming in. So, naturally, he expects more help from his employer. Harry feels bad, but he can't do any more for Jim. He can't pay Jim's salary while he can't work.

Harry wishes we would have provided a group long-term disability benefit for his employees that would now give Jim a regular income to help him and his family through the disability.

Some employers have a policy of continuing a disabled employee's salary out of business revenues, which can be expensive. If you plan to offer no disability benefits at all, make your policy clear to employees so they won't expect to be covered.

Group life insurance follows many of the same rules for small employers. It's a form of annually renewable term insurance, which means that each employee re-enrolls once a year at a rate based on his or her age.

If you decide to offer group life insurance for your employees, one decision will be how much life insurance to provide for each employee. Coverage of $10,000 per employee is a common starting point. Some companies offer different levels for each employee, frequently equal to each individual's annual salary.

The insurer usually cannot cancel insurance for one person in your group once the insurance is issued. This prevents the insurance company from trying to cancel coverage for people who develop health problems. The insurer can, with due notice, cancel the policy for an entire group, however.

An employee who leaves your firm will often be able to continue group life or health coverage in some form at his or her own expense upon leaving.

Group dental insurance has become a common employee benefit. Insurance companies have experimented with other types of group coverages, such as group automobile insurance, but such plans are not common.

You may wish to purchase **individual life or health** insurance for some employees as an added benefit. A life

Never mind the pay Miss! How's your Group Insurance Program?

APPLY HERE

insurance policy as a benefit for an employee, for example, can be a form of tax-deferred compensation.

"**Key Man**" insurance is a life insurance policy taken out by the company on a key employee. The company itself is named as beneficiary as protection against the severe financial hardship it would suffer.

Workers' Compensation

In a way, workers' compensation is an employee benefit. It protects employees from medical costs and lost income caused by on-the-job injuries. It also protects you, the employer. By providing workers' compensation, you are protected from the threat of lawsuits by employees over on-the-job injuries. So, workers' compensation is considered liability insurance.

Workers' compensation is an expensive worry for many businesses. But if you have employees, you don't want to go without it. This is true for almost all types of businesses. Most states have strict laws requiring workers' compensation.

Workers' compensation laws vary from state to state. Your property and liability agent can help you understand the laws in your state. You can also consult state government agencies or an attorney if you are not familiar with your state's requirements.

While you are looking into workers' compensation, find out if you should - or must - include yourself in the coverage.

Summary

Your employees are very important to your business. Employers provide benefits such as group life and health insurance to help keep and attract good employees. Your employees' health and happiness should be a major concern, and (if you're really gung-ho) this concern should extend even to their diet, exercise and accident prevention practices. Even if your company has only two employees, you can provide some type of insurance benefits. Long-term disability coverage should be considered along with group health. Workers' compensation protects both your company and your employees. You can also benefit from participation in most employee insurance plans.

PERSONAL INSURANCE FOR
BUSINESS OWNERS OR PARTNERS

You've developed a good insurance program to cover your business property and liability needs. Your employees have a good benefit plan and workers' compensation. Have you looked after yourself and your family? As a small business owner or partner, your individual insurance needs may be larger than other people's.

Life Insurance

A small business owner or partner may want a lot of life insurance. Here's why. Most small businesses, even very successful ones, are usually in debt. They borrowed heavily over the years, especially to get started. The business owner may have used his own personal assets as collateral for loans for the business.

This debt is not a big problem as long as the business keeps generating revenue to make the payments and the owner remains alive. An owner often wants to be sure that his family can retire business debts in the event of his death. Life insurance can be a way to take care of this problem. It can also help the family keep the business in operation, or at least pay estate costs.

With partnerships or small corporations, there's another twist. Partners often buy life insurance on each other. If one dies, the other will be able to buy out the deceased partner's share in the business. This use of life insurance works to the benefit of both the surviving partner and the deceased partner's family. In a small corporation, the corporation itself may buy life insurance on each owner involved.

Types of Individual Life Insurance

There are two main kinds of life insurance: term and whole life. Term insurance is cheaper. It provides coverage for a specified number of years. Term insurance pays only a death benefit, thus, there is no cash value to draw upon. Some term insurance is "guaranteed renewable," which means the policyholder can renew the policy every time it expires regardless of changing health. The rate will be higher every time the policyholder renews, however, because of increasing age.

Whole life insurance guarantees you a flat insurance premium, regardless of your changing age and health, for as long as you continue paying premiums. The rate is based on your age and health when you first buy the policy. Whole life also features an accumulating cash value which can be drawn out while you are still alive. You can use the policy as collateral on loans.

Which type of life insurance is better? Whole life policies have been attacked by some financial experts who say that other investments will provide a better interest rate. Term is cheaper, but it has no investment value and no guarantee of life-long, flat-rate coverage. Insurance companies have recently developed new, more competitive types of whole life insurance.

Credit Life Insurance

Credit life is often required by lenders before approving loans, naming themselves as the beneficiaries. If the borrower dies, the insurance pays off the outstanding loan balance. Lenders may either require you to buy and pay for the coverage or it may buy and pay for the insurance itself.

If you buy the credit life, it is individual insurance. If the lender buys it, it is a form of group insurance. Consider the cost of credit life as a factor in choosing among various loans.

Your Health and Disability Needs

If your company has a group life and health policy, as described in the last section of the chapter, you'll almost always want to take advantage of it for yourself. This is because group insurance is cheaper than individual insurance. Remember that disability insurance can also be important.

If you have no group health or disability benefits, see the following section of this chapter which describes some options.

SPECIAL CONCERNS FOR ONE-PERSON OR HOME BUSINESSES

If you run a business out of your home, and/or if you run a one-person business, most of the principles discussed in this chapter still apply.

If you assume that your homeowners or renters policy takes care of your professional equipment stored at your home and also takes care of your business liability needs, you are probably wrong! Most homeowners and renters policies specifically exclude coverage for property used in a business pursuit, and for liability arising out of business pursuits. If your business is new, and your business property is of low value, and liability problems are unlikely, you may decide to "assume" the risks and go without coverage. Or you could add coverage of incidental business items by endorsement to your homeowners policy.

The basic rule is this: If your home-based business involves products, inventory or walk-in customers, you need a business insurance policy. Then your personal property would be insured separately under a "renters policy" as though you were renting space from your business.

You may have to call around (use the yellow pages) to find an agent who knows how to take care of your unusual insurance needs. Many business insurance agents have neither the expertise nor the time to work with you. (Agents earn their livings

ALL THIS FOR A LOUSY $10.29 COMMISSION

through commissions on premiums.) For many business-oriented agents, your premiums would be so small they wouldn't take the time to help you.

However, since "cottage industries" are a trend right now, some insurance companies are developing special insurance policies for at-home businesses. Such packages could be an easy solution to your property and liability needs.

Unless you are also working somewhere else, you probably have no employer-sponsored group plans to take care of your life and health insurance needs. You may have to shop around for individual policies. Individual health insurance can be expensive. You may want to find a policy with high deductibles.

You have a few other options to explore, through which you might be able to get cheaper group life and health coverage. If your spouse works, you may be insurable under his or her employer's plan. You may also be able to take advantage of group insurance through associations or professional organizations to which you belong.

WHEN YOU HAVE A CLAIM

When a disaster strikes, you suddenly realize why you have insurance in the first place. Your first step is to tell your insurance agent. If you chose your agent carefully, he or she will bend over backwards to help you through the claim procedures. Your insurance materials may also include addresses and phone numbers for appropriate insurance company claim offices. While a phone call may be sufficient, it's a good idea to also notify the company of the loss in writing. Claim procedures vary for different companies and policies. In addition to help from your agent, you can find out about claim procedures by reading your policy and related materials.

Here are some additional guidelines for various types of claim situations:

1. Plan for claims before they happen. For property insurance, keep complete and accurate records of your property in a safe place. For life and health insurance, let your loved ones know what policies you have and where to find them.

2. In cases of theft or other crimes, notify the police immediately in addition to your insurance company.

3. With fires, window breakage, or similar property losses, take steps to protect your property from further damage.

4. If an accident occurs which may involve liability, notify your insurer even before the injured party files any type of claim or lawsuit.

5. If any liability situation arises — a customer is injured at your business, for example — do not admit your fault or liability. This admission could later be used against you in a costly lawsuit. You may also be violating a requirement of your insurance policy. Don't offer the injured person a financial settlement before you have contacted your insurance company. This can be taken as an admission of blame. Be courteous and make sure the injured person gets the immediate medical help needed. Let your insurance company know about everything that happens in connection with the event, and, generally, let them handle the situation.

CONCLUSION AND REVIEW

Congratulations! You have completed the chapter on insurance. Insurance is a very complicated subject; one which people can study for a lifetime - and still not know completely. But armed with a knowledge of insurance basics, you will be far better able to make sound decisions about your business insurance needs. Here is a review of some of the main points covered in this chapter:

1. Risk is a fact of life for the small business person. "Speculative" risks are those you take willingly for a chance of gain. Insurance involves "pure" risks, potential accidents and disasters which are balanced by no chance of gain.

2. You can't cover all pure risks through insurance. You want to cover risks too large to bear without coverage.

3. Insurance is based on calculations of "the odds."

4. You can rarely, if ever, arrange insurance so you can profit from a loss.

5. People should be honest and open with insurance companies and agents.

6. Policy limits should be high enough to cover potentially large losses.

7. Your choice of insurance agents may be your most important insurance decision. A good agent will be of great value to you.

8. Price is important in insurance, but other considerations, such as making sure you get the policy provisions you need and finding an insurance company with a reputation for good service, are equally important.

9. Property and liability (or property and casualty) is one broad category of insurance. Life and health is the other.

10. You should make a realistic assessment of the broad range of risks faced by your business.

11. You can often cover many property and liability insurance needs through a package policy. But you'll probably need to add endorsements or separate policies for special coverage.

12. Motor vehicle insurance comes separately.

13. Property risks may also involve business-interruption risks. Consider business-interruption insurance.

14. There are many possibilities of lawsuits which could be brought against you. Product liability and professional liability may require special insurance treatment.

15. Some type of group life and health insurance can be provided as an employee benefit even in very small companies.

16. Disability income insurance is an important, but often neglected, employee benefit.

17. Workers' compensation insurance protects both a business and its employees. It is required for employees in most states.

18. Small business owners and partners may have special needs for life insurance.

19. Term and whole life are the two basic types of life insurance.

20. A homeowner's or renter's policy does not usually cover property used for business in your home, or liability claims which may result from your business pursuits. Separate policies or endorsements may be needed.

21. Notify your insurance agent and/or company immediately following any event which may involve your insurance.

Chapter 16

The Small Business Administration Programs

WHAT ASSISTANCE WILL THEY PROVIDE?

The Small Business Administration offers a wide variety of services for the entrepreneur. Since 1953 the SBA has helped small businesses succeed from start-up through the many stages of growth. In fact, many big businesses whose names are now household words – FedEx, Intel, Nike, Apple, Ben & Jerry's, Compaq, and AOL, just to name a few – received help from the SBA along the way.

SBA History

Officially established in 1953, the SBA philosophy and mission began to take shape years earlier in a number of predecessor agencies, largely as a response to the pressures of the Great Depression and World War II.

The Reconstruction Finance Corporation (RFC), created by President Herbert Hoover in 1932 to alleviate the financial crisis of the Great Depression, was SBA's grandparent. The RFC was basically a federal lending program for all businesses hurt by the Depression, large and small. It was adopted as the personal project of Hoover's successor, President Franklin D. Roosevelt, and was staffed by some of Roosevelt's most capable and dedicated workers.

Concern for small business intensified during World War II, when large industries beefed up production to accommodate wartime defense contracts and smaller businesses were left unable to compete. To help small business participate in war production and give them financial viability, Congress created the Smaller War Plants Corporation (SWPC) in 1942. The SWPC provided direct loans to private entrepreneurs, encouraged large financial institutions to make credit available to small enterprises, and advocated small business interests to federal procurement agencies and big businesses.

The SWPC was dissolved after the war, and its lending and contract powers were handed over to the RFC. At this time, the Office of Small Business (OSB) in the Department of Commerce also assumed some responsibilities that would later become characteristic duties of the SBA. Its services were primarily educational. Believing that a lack of information and expertise was the main cause of small business failure, the OSB produced brochures and conducted management counseling for individual entrepreneurs.

Congress created another wartime organization to handle small business concerns during the Korean War; this time they called it the Small Defense Plants Administration (SDPA). Its functions were

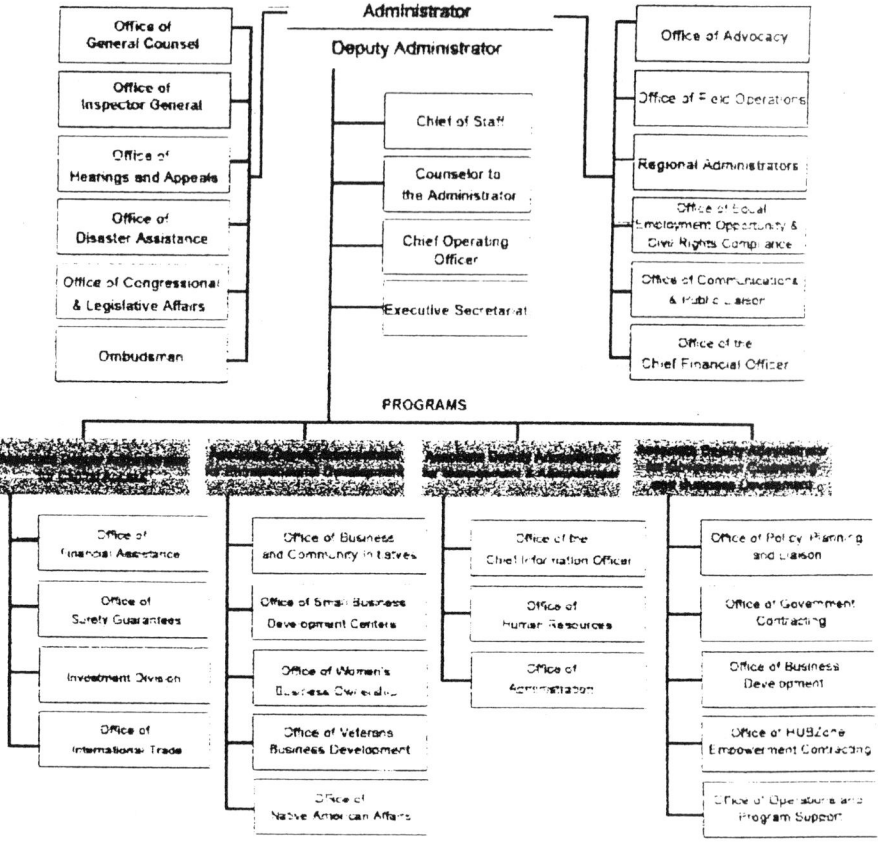

similar to those of the SWPC, except that ultimate lending authority was retained by the RFC. The SDPA certified small businesses to the RFC when it had determined the businesses to be competent to perform the work of government contracts.

By 1952, a move was on to abolish the RFC. To continue the important functions of the earlier agencies, President Dwight Eisenhower proposed creation of a new small business agency -- the Small Business Administration (SBA).

In the Small Business Act of July 30, 1953, Congress created the Small Business Administration, whose function was to "aid, counsel, assist and protect, insofar as is possible, the interests of small business concerns." The charter also stipulated that the SBA would ensure small businesses a "fair proportion" of government contracts and sales of surplus property.

By 1954, SBA already was making direct business loans and guaranteeing bank loans to small businesses, as well as making loans to victims of natural disasters, working to get government procurement contracts for small businesses and helping business owners with management and technical assistance and business training.

Over the past 40 years, SBA has grown in terms of total assistance provided and its array of programs tailored to encourage small enterprises in all areas. SBA's programs now include financial and federal contract procurement assistance, management assistance, and specialized outreach to women, minorities and armed forces veterans. The SBA also provides loans to victims of natural disasters and specialized advice and assistance in international trade.

SBA continues to branch out to increase business participation by women and minorities along new avenues such as the minority small business program, microloans and the publication of Spanish language informational materials.

Small businesses have become a driving force in the U.S. economy. Nearly 21 million strong, they now employ 54 percent of the private work force, produce 50 percent of private sector output and create two out of every three new jobs.

Small business is where the innovations take place. Swifter, more flexible and often more daring than big businesses, small firms produce the items that line the shelves of America's museums, shops and homes. They keep intact the heritage of ingenuity and enterprise and they help keep the "American Dream" within the reach of millions of Americans. Every step of the way, SBA is there to help them.

SBA PROGRAMS

The U.S. Small Business Administration is dedicated to providing customer-oriented, full-service programs and accurate, timely information to the entrepreneurial community. All of the SBA's programs and services are provided to the public on a nondiscriminatory basis.

FINANCING
www.sba.gov/financing

7(a) Loan Guaranty

Its function is to provide short- and long-term loans to eligible, credit-worthy start-up and existing small businesses that cannot obtain financing on reasonable terms through normal lending channels. The SBA provides financial assistance through its participating lenders in the form of loan guaranties, **not direct loans**. The agency **does not provide grants** for business start-up or expansion. The SBA Office of Capital Access administers the 7(a) Loan Guaranty Program. Loans under the program are available for most business purposes, including purchasing real estate, machinery, equipment, and inventory, or for working capital. The loans cannot be used for speculative purposes. The SBA can guarantee a maximum of $750,000 under the 7(a) program. The guaranty rate is 85 percent for loans of $150,000 or less, and 90 percent for loans made under the Export Working Capital Program. Generally the interest rate cannot exceed 2.75 percent over the prime lending rate as published in The Wall Street Journal, except for loans less than $50,000, where the rates may be slightly higher. Maturity is up to 10 years for working capital and up to 25 years for fixed assets.

Those that use this program are start-up and existing small businesses and commercial lending institutions

Funding is established through commercial lending institutions

Certified and Preferred Lenders

Its function is to designate the most active and expert SBA participating lenders as either Certified or Preferred. Certified lenders receive a partial SBA delegation of authority to approve loans. Preferred lenders receive full delegation of lending authority. A listing of participants in the Certified and Preferred Lenders Program is available from SBA district offices.

Those that use this program are Small businesses and commercial lending institutions participating in SBA-guaranteed lending programs

Funding is established through commercial lending institutions

Secondary Market

Its function is to give lenders holding business loans guaranteed by the SBA an opportunity to improve their liquidity by selling the guaranteed and unguaranteed portions of the loans to investors. Frequent secondary market buyers include banks, savings and loan companies, credit unions, pension funds and insurance companies.

Those that use this program are Commercial lending institutions participating in SBA-guaranteed lending programs, securities dealers

Funding is established through lenders, securities dealers, and secondary market for guaranteed government obligations

Low Documentation Loan (SBALowDoc), a 7(a) Loan Program

Its function is to reduce the paperwork involved in loan requests of $150,000 or less. The SBA uses a one-page application for SBALowDoc that relies on the strength of the applicant's character and credit history. Once an applicant satisfies all of the lender's requirements, the lender may request an SBALowDoc guaranty from the SBA.

Those that use this program are start-up and existing small businesses
Funding is established through commercial lending institutions

SBAExpress, a 7(a) Loan Program

Its function is to encourage lenders to make more small loans to small businesses. Participating banks use their own documentation and procedures to approve, service and liquidate loans of up to $150,000. In return, the SBA agrees to guarantee up to 50 percent of each loan. SBAExpress is a new loan program being piloted with selected banks nationwide.

Those that use this program are start-up and existing small businesses
Funding is established through SBA-designated commercial lending institutions

CAPLines, a 7(a) Loan Program

Its function is to finance small businesses' short-term and cyclical working-capital needs. Under CAPLines, there are five distinct short-term working-capital loans: Seasonal, Contract, Builders, Standard Asset-Based, and Small Asset-Based lines. For the most part, the SBA regulations governing the 7(a) Loan Guaranty Program also apply to CAPLines. The SBA generally can guarantee a maximum of $750,000 under the program.

Those that use this program are start-up and existing small businesses
Funding is established through commercial lending institutions

SBA Loan Prequalification, a 7(a) Loan Program

Its function is to enable the SBA to prequalify an applicant for a 7(a) loan guaranty on a loan application of $250,000 or less before the applicant goes to a bank. The program focuses on the applicant's character, credit, experience and reliability rather than assets. SBA-designated intermediaries work with the business owner to review and strengthen the loan application. The review is based on key financial ratios, credit and business history, and the loan-request terms. The program is administered by the Office of Field Operations.

Those that use this program are small businesses owned by women, minorities, veterans, exporters, plus rural small businesses and those in certain designated industries and geographical areas

Funding is established through nonprofit intermediaries such as small business development centers and certified development companies operating in specific geographic areas.

Defense Loan & Technical Assistance (DELTA), a 7(a) Loan Program

Its function is to help defense-dependent small firms that are adversely affected by defense cuts diversify into the commercial market through financial and technical assistance. Loans must be used for the following: to retain jobs of defense workers, create new jobs in impacted communities, or modernize/expand in order to remain in the national technical and industrial base. DELTA uses the following loan programs: 7(a), with a maximum total loan of $1.25 million; and/or 504, with a maximum guaranteed debenture of $1 million. 7(a) loans carry a maximum guaranty of 80 percent. Federal, state and private-sector resources provide a full range of management and technical assistance.

Those that use this program are defense-dependent small firms adversely impacted by defense cuts

Funding is established through SBA district offices, and resource partners

Community Adjustment and Investment Program (CAIP), a 7(a) Loan Program

Its function is to create new sustainable jobs and preserves existing jobs in businesses at risk due to changed trade patterns with Canada and Mexico. Business applicants must be located in a CAIP-eligible community. They also must demonstrate that within 24 months and as a result of the loan they will create or preserve at least one job per $70,000 of federally guaranteed funds they receive. CAIP is a partnership between the federal government (primarily the SBA and U.S. Department of Agriculture) and the North American Development Bank.

Those that use this program are Businesses in communities with significant job losses related to the North American Free Trade Agreement.

Funding is established through NADBank, SBA, and U.S. Department of Agriculture

Export Working Capital Program (EWCP), a 7(a) Loan Program

Its function is to enable the SBA to guarantee up to 90 percent of a secured loan, or $750,000, whichever is less. Loan maturity may be for up to three years with annual renewals. Loans can be for single or multiple export sales and can be extended for pre-shipment working capital, post-shipment exposure coverage or a combination of the two. Proceeds can only be used to finance export transactions. See also Assistance for Exporters.

Those that use this program are export-ready small businesses

Funding is established through commercial lending institutions

International Trade Loan (ITL), a 7(a) Loan Program

Its function is to offer long-term financing to small businesses engaged or preparing to engage in international trade, as well as to small businesses adversely affected by import competition. The SBA can guarantee up to $1.25 million for a combination of fixed-asset financing and working capital. The working-capital portion cannot exceed $750,000. See also Assistance for Exporters.

Those that use this program are export-ready small businesses

Funding is established through commercial lending institutions

Energy & Conservation Loan, a 7(a) Loan Program

Its function is to provide financing for eligible small businesses engaged in engineering, manufacturing, distributing, marketing, and installing or servicing products or services designed to conserve the nation's energy resources. The maximum guaranty for loans up to $100,000 is 80 percent. For higher loans up to $750,000, the maximum guaranty is 75 percent.

Those that use this program are small businesses

Funding is established through commercial lending institutions

Pollution Control Loan, a 7(a) Loan Program

Its function is to assists businesses that are planning, designing or installing a pollution control facility. This includes most real or personal property that will reduce pollution. The program has a maximum SBA exposure of $1 million, less any outstanding balance due the SBA on other loans.

Those that use this program are businesses building, installing, or servicing a pollution control facility

Funding is established through commercial lending institutions

MicroLoan, a 7(m) Loan Program

Its function is to provide short-term loans of up to $25,000 to small businesses for working capital or the purchase of inventory, supplies, furniture, fixtures, machinery and/or equipment. Proceeds cannot be used to pay existing debts or to purchase real estate. Loans are made through SBA-approved nonprofit groups. These lenders also receive SBA grants to provide technical assistance to their borrowers. Additional entities also receive grants to provide technical assistance to other businesses selecting non-SBA-backed financing. The MicroLaon Program is available in selected locations in 46 states.

Those that use this program are small businesses needing small-scale financing and technical assistance for start-up or expansion

Funding is established through intermediary lenders (nonprofit organizations with experience in lending and technical assistance)

The Facts About . . . The MicroLoan Program for Entrepreneurs

The MicroLoan Program combines the resources and experience of the U.S. Small Business Administration with those of locally based nonprofit organizations to provide small loans and technical assistance to small businesses.

Under the MicroLoan Program, the SBA makes funds available to qualified nonprofit organizations, which act as intermediary lenders. The intermediaries use these funds to make loans of up to $25,000 to new and existing small businesses. The intermediaries also provide management and technical assistance to help ensure success.

Eligibility Requirements

Virtually any type of for-profit small business is eligible for the MicroLoan Program. The form of the business, whether a proprietorship, partnership or corporation, is not a determining factor. It must, however, meet the SBA's size standards at the time of application. Generally, businesses applying for this type of loan will fall well within these standards. Not-for-profit child-care centers are also eligible to apply.

Use of Loan Funds

MicroLoan funds may be used for working capital or to purchase inventory, supplies, furniture, fixtures, machinery and equipment. Funds may not be used to purchase real estate or to provide a down payment on real estate.

Loan Terms

The maximum MicroLoan is $25,000. The average-sized loan is around $10,500. The maximum term allowed for a loan is six years. Terms may vary according to the size of the loan, the planned use of funds, the requirements of the intermediary lender, and the needs of the borrower. MicroLoans are direct loans from the intermediary lenders and are not guaranteed by the SBA. Interest rates vary, depending upon the intermediary lender.

Credit Requirements

A MicroLoan applicant must meet the credit requirements of the local intermediary lender. Generally, the applicant will be expected to have good character, a strong commitment to his/her business idea, and a credit history that provides reasonable assurance that the loan will be repaid. In addition, the applicant should have some management expertise or be willing to participate in training designed to strengthen management skills.

Collateral Requirements

As with credit standards, collateral requirements for the MicroLoan Program are set by each local intermediary lender. In most cases, loans are at least partially collateralized by equipment, contracts, inventory or other property. Lenders may also require personal guaranties.

Applying for a MicroLoan

The first step in applying for a MicroLoan is to contact your local intermediary lender. Since the MicroLoan Program is not available everywhere, contact your local SBA district office to find out if there is a MicroLoan intermediary in your area. The intermediary lender will provide information on applying for a loan and receiving technical assistance.

Certified Development Companies (CDCs), a 504 Loan Program

Its function is to provide long-term, fixed-rate financing to small businesses to acquire real estate, machinery or equipment to expand or modernize. Typically at least 10 percent of the loan proceeds are provided by the borrower, at least 50 percent by an unguaranteed bank loan, and the remainder by an SBA-guaranteed debenture. The maximum SBA debenture is $1 million. DELTA funding is also available under this program.

Those that use this program are small businesses requiring "brick and mortar" financing

Funding is established through certified development companies (private, nonprofit corporations set up to contribute to the economic development of their communities or regions)

INVESTMENT
www.sba.gov/inv

Small Business Investment Companies (SBICs)

Its function is to provide equity capital, long-term loans, debt-equity investments and management assistance to small businesses particularly during their growth stages. The SBA's role consists of licensing the SBICs and supplementing their capital with U.S. government-guaranteed debentures or participating securities. SBICs are privately owned and managed, profit-motivated companies, investing with the prospect of sharing in the success of the funded small businesses as they grow and prosper.

Those that use this program are small businesses seeking long-term capital
Funding is established through small business investment companies.

Specialized Small Business Investment Companies (SSBICs)

Its function is to provide businesses owned by socially and economically disadvantaged individuals with equity capital, long-term loans, debt-equity investments and management assistance, particularly during business growth stages. SSBICs are a significant component of the SBIC program, accounting for more than a third of the program's financings. The SSBICs typically make smaller investments than SBICs.

Those that use this program are socially or economically disadvantaged small businesses seeking long-term capital
Funding is established through specialized small business investment companies

Angel Capital Electronic Network (ACE-Net)

Its function is to provide an Internet-based secure listing service for entrepreneurs seeking equity financing of $250,000 to $5 million from accredited "angel" investors. The "angels" using ACE-Net can negotiate directly with listed companies to provide equity capital funding and advice for a stake in the entrepreneur's corporation. ACE-Net is operated as a partnership between the SBA's Office of Advocacy and a number of nonprofit organizations nationwide. It will ultimately be turned over to a private nonprofit organization.

Those that use this program are entrepreneurs and "angel" investors

SURETY BONDS
www.sba.gov/osg

Surety Bond Guarantee

Its function is to guarantee bid, performance and payment bonds for contracts up to $1.25 million for eligible small businesses that cannot obtain surety bonds through regular commercial channels. By law, prime contractors to the federal government must post surety bonds on federal construction projects valued at $100,000 or more. In addition, many states, counties, municipalities, and private-sector projects and subcontracts also require surety bonds. Contractors must apply through a surety bonding agent, since the SBA's guaranty goes to the surety company.

Those that use this program are small construction and service contractors; surety and insurance companies, and their agents; federal and state agencies; state insurance departments -- federal, state and other procurement officials

Funding is established through surety and insurance companies and their agents; four SBA area offices: Atlanta, Denver, Philadelphia, and Seattle.

FEDERAL PROCUREMENT
www.sba.gov/gc and pronet.sba.gov

Breakout Procurement

Its function is to encourage the breakout of subsystems, components or spare parts from historically sole-source contracts into full and open competition in order to effect significant savings to the federal government.

Those that use this program are Other federal agencies, large and small businesses

Funding is established through SBA breakout procurement center representatives (BPCRs)

Prime Contracting

Its function is to increase small business opportunities in the federal acquisition process. This is accomplished through initiating small business set-asides, identifying new small business sources, counseling small businesses on doing business with the federal government, and assessing compliance with the Small Business Act through surveillance reviews.

Those that use this program are small businesses, other federal government agencies

Funding is established through SBA procurement center representatives (PCRs)

Subcontracting

Its function is to ensure that small businesses receive the maximum practical opportunity to participate in federal contracts as subcontractors and suppliers.

Those that use this program are large and small contractors, other federal government agencies

Funding is established through SBA commercial market representatives (CMRs)

Certificate of Competency (CoC)

Its function is to help small businesses secure government contracts by providing an appeal process to low-bidder businesses denied government contracts for a perceived lack of ability to perform satisfactorily.

Those that use this program are small businesses that have been denied government contracts for perceived lack of ability

Funding is established through SBA field office industrial and financial specialists.

Women-Owned Business Procurement

Its function is to use a multifaceted outreach and educational program to teach women business owners to market to the federal government.

This program is for women-owned businesses

Funding is established through SBA Office of Government Contracting

Procurement Marketing & Access Network (PRO-Net&trade)

Its function is to serve as a search engine for contracting officers, a marketing tool for small firms, and a "link" to procurement opportunities and other important information. Pro-Net™ contains business information on thousands of small firms. It also provides links to the online Commerce Business Daily, federal-agency home pages and other sources of procurement opportunities. Administered by the SBA Office of Government Contracting, PRO-Net™ registration is free.

Those that use this program are contracting officers, small firms seeking federal procurement opportunities, federal and large prime contractors

Size Standards

Its function is to determine which businesses are eligible for the SBA's financial- and procurement-assistance programs. The SBA Office of Size Standards develops and prepares regulations on size standards as needed following agency and federal government rule-making procedures.

Those that use this program are small businesses, large and small federal contractors, federal agencies and financial institutions

See SBA Office of Size Standards, www.sba.gov/size

HUBZone Empowerment Contracting

Its function is to encourage economic development in historically underutilized business zones — "HUBZones" — through the establishment of federal contract award preferences for small businesses located in such areas. After determining eligibility, the SBA lists qualified businesses in its PRO-Net™ database.

Those that use this program are Small businesses located in historically underutilized business zones

See the SBA Office of HUBZone Empowerment Contracting Program, www.sba.gov/hubzone

RESEARCH & DEVELOPMENT

Small Business Innovation Research (SBIR)

Its function is to provide a vehicle for small businesses to propose innovative ideas in competition for Phase I and Phase II awards, which represent specific R&D needs of the participating federal agencies. These awards may result in commercialization of the effort at the Phase III level. Administered by the SBA Office of Technology.

Those that use this program are Innovative small businesses interested in competing for federal R&D awards

See the ten participating federal agencies with $100 million in extramural R&D budgets at www.sba.gov/sbir

Small Business Technology Transfer (STTR)

Its function is to require each small firm competing for an R&D project to collaborate with a nonprofit research institution. This program is a joint venture from the initial proposal to the project's completion. Administered by the SBA Office of Technology.

Those that use this program are Small innovative R&D firms

Funding is established through Five federal agencies with extramural research and R&D budgets of $1 billion: NASA, the National Science Foundation, and the departments of Defense, Energy, and Health & Human Services

Small Business Research, R&D Goaling

Its function is to measure and report the amount of federal funding for research and R&D (excluding the amounts for SBIR and STTR) awarded to small businesses each year by the major research and R&D federal agencies. Administered by the SBA Office of Technology.

Those that use this program are Small businesses that compete for federal R&D awards

Funding is established through 18 federal agencies with annual research or R&D budgets in excess of $20 million

BUSINESS COUNSELING & TRAINING

The SBA provides most business counseling and training programs through its resource partners.

Small Business Development Centers (SBDCs)

Its function is to provide management and technical assistance, counseling and training to current and prospective small business owners. Administered by the SBA, the program is a cooperative effort of the private sector, the educational community, and federal, state and local governments. See also Business Information Services.

Those that use this program are pre-business, start-up and existing small businesses

There are more than 1,000 locations, including universities, colleges, state governments, private-sector organizations, www.sba.gov/sbdc

Business Information Centers (BICs)

Its function is to provide the latest in high-tech hardware, software and telecommunications to help small businesses start and grow. BIC counseling and training are provided by the Service Corps of Retired Executives (SCORE), other community organizations and SBA resource partners. See also Business Information Services.

Those that use this program are pre-business, start-up and existing small businesses

There are more than 45 locations throughout the country. www.sba.gov/bi/bics

Service Corps of Retired Executives (SCORE)

Its function is to offers counseling and training for small business owners who are starting, building or growing a business. Sponsored by the SBA, SCORE's services are free of charge. See also Business Information Services.

Those that use this program are small businesses, start-ups, pre-business start-ups

There are more than 12,000 volunteers in 389 chapters with 700 locations, www.score.org

There is also specialized business counseling and training, see Assistance for Armed Forces; Assistance for Exporters; Assistance for Native Americans; Assistance for Small & Disadvantaged Businesses; and Assistance for Women.

BUSINESS INFORMATION SERVICES

Answer Desk

Its function is to help callers with questions and problems about starting and running businesses. The computerized telephone message system is available nationwide 24 hours a day, seven days a week. Counselors are available Monday through Friday, 9:00 a.m. to 5:00 p.m. Eastern Time.

This is open to the general public

Toll-free telephone number: 1-800-U-ASK-SBA

Publications

SBA field offices and the Answer Desk (see above) offer free publications that describe the SBA's programs and services. The SBA also produces and maintains a library of business-management publications, videos and computer programs. These are available by mail for a nominal fee (to defray reproduction and shipping costs). A complete listing of these products can be found in the Resource Directory for Small Business Management (SBA no. CO-0042).

These are available to the general public

Available at SBA field offices, Answer Desk and SBA resource partners, the federal Consumer Information Center, etc., www.sba.gov/library

SBA Online

Its function is to provide fast and easy help to the small business community via a computer-based electronic bulletin board. Operating 23 hours a day, 7 days a week, SBA OnLine offers relevant, current information to the public. SBA OnLine services include: SBA publications, access to SBA programs and services, points of contact, calendars of local events, on-line training, access to other federal agency on-line services and data, electronic and Internet mail, information exchange by special-interest groups, and down-loadable files.

This is open to the general public
Limited access: 1-800-697-4636
Full access: 1-900-463-4636
D.C. metro area: 202-401-9600
SBA home page: www.sba.gov
SBA gopher: gopher://www.sba.gov
Telnet: telnet://sbaonline.sba.gov
U.S. Business Advisor: www.business.gov

U.S. Business Advisor

Its function is to provide a one-stop electronic link to the government's business information and services. With the U.S. Business Advisor, small businesses no longer have to contact dozens of agencies and departments to access applicable laws and regulations, or figure out on their own how to comply. They can download business forms and conduct a myriad of other business transactions through this web site.

Those that use this program are the General Public
Accessible through the Internet at web site www.business.gov

ADVOCACY
www.sba.gov/advo

Office of Interagency Affairs

Its function is to monitor regulatory and other policy proposals of more than 20 federal agencies to assess their impact on small business and suggests alternatives for consideration. The office provides information to Congress on legislative issues and drafts testimony on public policy issues of concern to small business. Monitors regulatory agencies' compliance with the Regulatory Flexibility Act, as amended by the Small Business Regulatory Enforcement Fairness Act, and reports annually to Congress on the agencies' activities.

Those that use this program are small businesses, regulatory agencies, Congress

Office of Economic Research

Its function is to produce the annual report to Congress, "The State of Small Business: A Report of the President"; oversees research on small business issues, banking and the economy; and compiles and interprets statistics on small businesses according to size, industry and geographic distribution.

Those that use this program are Congress, the media, academic institutions, government agencies, foreign governments

Funding is established through the White House, federal agencies, Congress, state and local governments, the media, and independent researchers

Office of Public Information

Its function is to publicize and disseminate information on small business issues, statistics, research and advocacy publications; prepares printed material for Office of Advocacy-sponsored economic research, policy and conferences; and provides outreach to small businesses, trade associations, the legal community and others interested in small business policy.

Those that benefit from this program are small businesses, Congress, state legislatures, the media, government agencies, economic-research organizations

See Office of Advocacy, the SBA home page, under Offices & Services. www.sba.gov/advo

Regional Advocates

Its function is to serve as the SBA chief counsel's direct link to local communities. Regional advocates monitor the impact of federal and state regulations and policies on communities within their regions. They also work with state officials to develop policy and legislation that shape an environment in which small companies can prosper and grow.

Those that use this program are local business owners, state and local government agencies and legislatures

Small Business Regulatory Enforcement Ombudsman

Its function is to receive comments from small businesses about the regulatory enforcement and compliance activities of federal agencies and refers comments to the appropriate agency's Inspector General on a confidential basis. Coordinates the efforts of the 10 small business regulatory fairness boards and reports annually to the SBA Administrator and to the heads of the affected agencies on the boards' activities, findings, and recommendations.

Those that use this program are small businesses, federal agencies

For more information see SBA ombudsman, 10 SBA regional fairness boards, SBA Office of Field Operations, toll-free number: 1-888-REG-FAIR. www.sba.gov/regfair

DISASTER ASSISTANCE
www.sba.gov/disaster

Administered by the Office of Disaster Assistance, the SBA Disaster Assistance Program is the primary federally funded disaster assistance loan program for funding long-range recovery for private-sector, nonagricultural disaster victims. Eligibility is based on financial criteria. Interest rates fluctuate according to statutory formulas. A maximum interest rate of 4 percent is provided to applicants without credit available elsewhere; a higher maximum of 8 percent is for those with credit available elsewhere. In addition to presidential declarations, the program handles disaster loans when a declaration is made by the SBA Administrator. There are three disaster loan programs: loans for homes and personal property, physical disaster loans to businesses of any size, and economic injury loans to small businesses without credit available elsewhere.

Loans for Homes and Personal Property

Real Property Loans

Its function is to provide loans to qualified homeowners for uninsured losses up to $200,000 to repair or restore a primary residence to pre-disaster condition. Homeowners may apply for an additional 20 percent for disaster mitigation. This is the major long-term recovery program for an individual's disaster loss.

Those that use this program are Individuals

Personal Property Loans

Its function is to provide loans to qualified homeowners and renters for uninsured losses up to $40,000 to repair or replace personal property such as clothing, furniture, cars, etc. This loan is not intended to replace extraordinarily expensive or irreplaceable items such as antiques, pleasure crafts, recreational vehicles, fur coats, etc.

Those that use this program are Individuals

Loans for Businesses Physical Disaster Business Loans

Its function is to provide loans for uninsured losses up to $1.5 million to qualified businesses of any size to repair or replace business property to pre-disaster conditions. Loans may be used to replace or repair equipment, fixtures and inventory and to make leasehold improvements.

Those that use this program are sarge and small businesses, and nonprofit organizations

Economic Injury Disaster Loans (EIDLs)

Its function is to provide up to $1.5 million in working-capital loans for businesses that suffer economic injury as a direct result of a disaster, regardless of whether the property was damaged. The loans are made to help small businesses pay ordinary and necessary operating expenses that they would have been able to pay if the disaster had not happened. NOTE: The maximum loan amount is $1.5 million for EIDL and physical disaster business loans combined, unless the business meets the criteria for a major source of employment (see below).

Those that use this program are small businesses without credit available elsewhere

Loans for Major Source of Employment (MSE)

Its function is to waive the $1.5 million loan limit for businesses that are a major source of employment, as defined in the SBA regulations. Generally, businesses that employ 250 or more persons in the disaster area are considered major employers.

Those that use this program are large and small businesses, nonprofit organizations

ASSISTANCE FOR ARMED FORCES VETERANS
www.sba.gov/vets

Veterans' Entrepreneurial Training (VET)

Its function is to provide up to 18 months of in-depth business training. Workshops include accounting, marketing, computer training, business-plan preparation and loan packaging.

Those that use this program are armed forces veterans (primarily disabled veterans)

Funding is established through SBA grant recipients and their subcontractors

Transition Assistance Program (TAP)

Its function is to provide nationwide assistance and information to all military personnel about to be discharged. Offers information on how to start a business and available SBA resources.

Those that use this program are armed forces veterans and active-duty personnel

Funding is established through the Department of Labor, Department of Defense (includes individual armed services), and SBA field offices

Veterans Business Development and Procurement Conferences

Its function is to assist veteran-owned businesses and start-ups, primarily in areas impacted by military downsizing. Start-ups receive information on how to market and finance their businesses; existing businesses seeking to sell products and services can network with federal procurement representatives. The conferences are co-sponsored by the Department of Veterans Affairs.

Those that use this program are veteran-owned contracting businesses

Funding is established through the Department of Veterans Affairs

Technology Transfer Conferences

Its function is to provide assistance to defense-dependent firms adversely affected by reductions in defense spending and non-defense-dependent small firms interested in buying or selling technology.

Those that use this program are high-tech, veteran-owned small businesses and defense-dependent and non-defense-dependent small firms

Funding is established through the SBA Office of Veterans' Affairs and small business development centers

ASSISTANCE FOR EXPORTERS
www.sba.gov/oit

U.S. Export Assistance Centers (USEACs)

Its function is to combine the trade-promotion and export-finance resources of the SBA, the U.S. Department of Commerce, the Export-Import Bank and, in some locations, the Agency for International Development. Designed to improve delivery of services to small- and medium-sized businesses, USEACs work closely with other federal, state and trade partners in local communities.

Those that use this program are export-willing, export-ready and exporting small businesses

Export Legal Assistance Network (ELAN)

Its function is to provide free initial legal consultations to export-willing and exporting small businesses. Under an agreement among the SBA, the U.S. Department of Commerce and the Federal Bar Association, experienced trade attorneys volunteer their time to answer exporters' legal questions.

Those that use this program are export-willing and export-ready small businesses

Funding is established through the SBA, U.S. Department of Commerce, and the Federal Bar Association

Strategic Partnerships

Its function is to foster improved cooperation and business opportunities for small businesses in international markets. The partnership agreements are between the SBA and its counterparts in other countries.

Those that use this program are export-willing, export-ready and exporting small businesses

Funding is established through the SBA, the 19 USEACs

ASSISTANCE FOR NATIVE AMERICANS
www.sba.gov/naa

Native American Affairs

Its function is to develop initiatives that ensure native individuals have access to business-development resources, training and services in their communities. The primary focus of the Office of Native American Affairs is economic development and job creation through small business ownership and education. The office works with the following: individual and tribally owned organizations; other federal, state and local agencies; nonprofit organizations; and national Native American organizations.

Those that use this program are American Indians, Alaskan Natives and Native Hawaiians

Funding is established through the SBA field offices, small business development centers, and reservation-based tribal business information centers (TBICs)

Tribal Business Information Centers (TBICs)

Its function is to provide access to state-of-the-art computer software technology, individualized business counseling services and business management workshops. TBICs serve Native American reservation communities in the states of Montana, North Dakota, South Dakota, California, Minnesota, North Carolina and the Navajo Nation. TBICs are SBA resource partners.

Those that use this program are American Indians

ASSISTANCE FOR SMALL & DISADVANTAGED BUSINESSES

Small Disadvantaged Business (SDB) Certification

Its function is to ensure that small businesses owned and controlled by individuals claiming to be socially and economically disadvantaged meet the eligibility criteria. Once certified, the businesses are eligible to receive price evaluation credits when bidding on federal contracts.

Those that use this program are small socially and economically disadvantaged businesses

8(a) Business Development

Its function is to utilize the SBA's statutory authority to provide business development and federal contract support to small disadvantaged firms.

Those that use this program are small socially and economically disadvantaged businesses

Funding is established through the SBA and other federal contracting officers, small business specialists at federal procurement activities.

7(j) Management & Technical Assistance

Its function is to authorize the SBA to provide grants and enter into cooperative agreements with service providers for specialized assistance in areas such as accounting, marketing and proposal/bid preparation. (The SBA does not provide grants to start or expand a business.) Industry-specific technical assistance and entrepreneurial training also are available.

Those that use this program are small disadvantaged businesses, low-income individuals, firms in either labor-surplus areas or areas with a high proportion of low-income individuals

Funding is established through service providers (including small businesses and educational institutions), and SBA Office of 8(a) Business Development

ASSISTANCE FOR WOMEN
www.sba.gov/womeninbusiness

Women's Business Centers

Its function is to provide long-term training and counseling in all aspects of owning or managing a business, including financial, management, marketing and technical assistance, and procurement.

Those that use this program are women-owned small businesses, start-ups, pre-business start-ups

Online Women's Business Center

Its function is to serve as an interactive, state-of-the art web site that offers the information an entrepreneur needs to start and build a successful business. The center is a public-private partnership between the SBA and several major U.S. corporations. The numerous features of the center include training, mentoring, individual counseling, and topic forums and newsgroups. Information is available in several languages.

Those that use this program are women-owned small businesses, start-ups, pre-business start-ups

Women's Network for Entrepreneurial Training (WNET)

Its function is to provide a vehicle for established women business owners to serve as mentors, passing on knowledge, skills and support to protégées who are ready to expand their businesses. WNET roundtables offer support and guidance in a group setting. Sponsors include small business development centers, local business leaders, government representatives and SCORE.

Those that use this program are women-owned small businesses

Funding is established through the SBA field offices, women's business and professional organizations, SBDCs, women's business centers, SCORE, more than 110 WNET roundtables around the country

EMPOWERMENT ZONES/ENTERPRISE COMMUNITIES
www.sba.gov/onestop

One Stop Capital Shops (OSCSs)

Its function is to provide centralized access to the full range of a community's small business resources, including entrepreneurial development, access to capital and federal procurement. Clients can do the following: access a range of small business information resources (through the Business Information Center located in the OSCS); receive counseling (from SCORE volunteers) and training (from a local SBDC); learn to develop a business plan or mend damaged credit; and apply for financing (typically under the SBA's MicroLoan Program). An OSCS is a partnership between the federal government — primarily the SBA — and a local community designed to offer small business assistance from a single, easy to access, retail location. Created through the federal government's Empowerment Zone (EZ) Initiative, an OSCS is located in a distressed area, and is generally targeted to under served communities.

Those that use this program are potential entrepreneurs and small businesses

Small Business Welfare to Work Initiative

Its function is to help small businesses gain access to a new pool of workers by connecting them to local service providers and job-ready workers. Targets efforts toward small businesses in industries that are experiencing labor shortages. Provides entrepreneurial counseling and training to persons currently or formerly on welfare who are interested in starting a business as a means to self-sufficiency. The Welfare to Work Initiative is a function of the SBA Office of Entrepreneurial Development.

Those that use this program are small businesses and former welfare recipients

Provided through the SBA headquarters, field offices, resource partners, and service providers

HOW CAN THE SBA HELP YOU?

Can the SBA help you get started in business?

The U.S. Small Business Administration provides a wealth of information on starting a business at the SBA home page (www.sba.gov). You can take advantage of SBA's resource partners; the Service Corps of Retired Executives (SCORE) and the Small Business Development Center (SBDC) provide free one-on-one counseling to those interested in starting and expanding a business. This includes, critiquing your business plan, legal requirements, marketing, and licenses needed for your business. To find the location nearest you, please visit www.sba.gov/regions/states.html and click on your state.

Business Information Centers (BICs), supported by local SBA District Offices, can assist you by providing access to state-of-the-art computer hardware and software, and through counseling by Service Corps of Retired Executives (SCORE) volunteers. BICs have resources for addressing a broad variety of business start-up and development issues. You can receive help with writing a comprehensive business plan, evaluating and improving your marketing and sales techniques, diversifying into a new product and/or service areas, pricing your products, or exploring exporting opportunities. The BIC web site is www.sba.gov/bi/bics

How do you get a small business loan from the SBA?

The SBA does not lend money. It guarantees loans to you. The loan is actually provided by your local lender.

You should prepare a business plan, including your loan proposal and submit it to a local lender. If the lender is unable to approve your loan, you may request that your application be submitted, by the lender, to the SBA. The SBA can guaranty up to 85% of a small business loan; however, the lender must agree to lending the money with the SBA guaranty. The lender will then forward your loan application and a credit analysis to the nearest SBA District Office. Upon SBA approval, the lending institution closes the loan and disburses the funds.

How do you get a small business grant from the SBA?

At this time, Congress has not set aside any monies for grants to start and/or expand a small business.

How do I write a business plan?

Chapter 18 will assist you in writing a business plan, also, at the SBA's home page select "Starting," you will find information on starting a business and writing a business plan.

How do you get a business license?

Licensing is generally handled through your state or local government. You will need to consult your local telephone directory in the "Government" section for an office that will assist you with a license or permit. See www.sba.gov/hotlist/license.html

How do you get a tax identification number?

For a Federal Tax ID number, please contact the Internal Revenue Service for Form SS4. This form is available through their web site at www.irs.gov. Or you may call the IRS at 1-800-829-3676 (Publications) and ask for the Small Business Tax Kit #454.

You will need to contact your state Department of Revenue for state taxes (if any). Please consult your local telephone directory in the "State Government" section for the office in your state.

What type of collateral do you need for a loan?

Repayment ability from the cash flow of the business is a primary consideration in the SBA loan decision process but good character, management capability, collateral, and owner's equity contribution are also important considerations. All owners of twenty percent (20%) or more of the business are required to personally guarantee SBA loans.

The SBA does not deny approval for an SBA Guaranty Loan solely due to lack of collateral. However, it can be used as a reason, in addition to, other credit factors.

What SBA business assistance is available in your area?

There are 12,400 Service Corps of Retired Executives (SCORE) chapters and approximately 1,000 Small Business Development Centers (SBDC) nationwide. SCORE provides free, expert advice based on many years of firsthand experience and shared knowledge, on virtually every aspect of business. The SBDC provides a variety of management and technical assistance services to small businesses and potential entrepreneurs.

You may also want to visit one of the Business Information Centers (BICs) that have various books, videotapes, and training workshops on starting and expanding your business. This includes marketing, business planning, legal requirements, bookkeeping, etc.

What classifies a business as "small?"

There is no "official" certification process to be determined as a small business. The U.S. Small Business Administration (SBA) uses Standard Industrial Classification (SIC) codes in determining size standards. To see if your business is considered small by the federal government, or to determine which SIC code(s) is applicable to your business, please go to www.sba.gov/regulations/siccodes/.

It is considered a self-certifying process; therefore, no paperwork needs to be filled out.

How can you get your business certified as a woman or minority owned?

On a Federal level, Congress considers a minority-owned business as generally anyone other than white. The business MUST be owned and at least 51% controlled by one or more minorities. Women are not considered minorities. It is a self-certifying process and no paperwork needs to be filled out.

However, your state and local government may have different rules and regulations regarding their contracts and what their definitions are. Consult your state and local government for rules and requirements.

There is a certification process to be considered a Small Disadvantaged Business (SDB). The SDB certification ensures that small businesses are owned and controlled by socially and economically disadvantaged individuals meeting SDB eligibility criteria. If you are considered an SDB, you may receive a price evaluation credit of up to 10% when you bid on a federal contract. For more information on this program, please go to: www.sba.gov/sdb

The HUBZone Empowerment Contracting Program encourages economic development in historically underutilized business zones, through the establishment of federal contract award preferences for small businesses located in such areas. To learn more about this program, please go to www.sba.gov/hubzone

The SBA offers many services to the entrepreneur for starting or expanding his/her business. Some of them are specifically for minorities, women, and the disabled. This chapter gave you a brief history and overview of the numerous programs of the Small Business Administration. See Appendix D for a list of the US SBA Offices

Chapter 17

Managing people

How to get the most out of anyone you hire

"Have you been to Olson's Variety Store lately? They have a new sales clerk there and she was so nice! She not only knew the difference between all the different toasters, she offered to gift wrap the one I selected at no extra charge!" (Customer A.)

"Oh, I've never met such a rude salesperson in all my life! I practically had to beg her to wait on me and then she acted like she was doing **me** a favor. I can tell you one thing - I wouldn't go back to Albrecht's Hardware Store if they were giving toasters away!" (Customer B.)

You've heard comments and conversations like the ones above all your life. In fact, you've probably even been involved in a few. So, how seriously should you take what your customers are saying?

The answer is **very.**

In a small business, your reputation can mean the difference between success and failure. And reputation is what Customer A and Customer B are talking about. One is telling everyone what a marvelous experience she has had. The other is telling all her friends and relatives how awful it was to shop at Albrecht's. There is no way of telling how many customers would be lost as a result of Customer B's experience.

Often the only contact the public has with your business is the people you hire. Therefore, it's very important that you hire the **right** person for the **right** job.

How employees feel about their jobs will directly influence how they treat your customers. For example, note the following comments of two employees:

"I just love my job. The Johnsons couldn't be better bosses. They treat me with respect and seem to value my opinion. I feel that what I'm doing is really important." (Employee A.)

"I hate this place; I hate everything about the people I work for. As far as I'm concerned, they can all jump off a bridge. I can't wait until a better job comes along." (Employee B.)

Again, it doesn't take an expert to see that you have a problem if Employee B works for you.

In this chapter we will deal with the hiring and supervision of employees for your small business. You will learn:

1. How to hire an employee.

2. Where to look when you want to hire employees.

3. How to conduct an interview.

4. How to discipline and train employees.

5. How to motivate employees.

6. The principles of good management.

7. How to discharge an employee.

HIRING EMPLOYEES

As an owner/manager of your small business, you must decide whether to hire employees to do part of your work for you. While some people think this involves just "going out and hiring someone," it's not that easy.

A manager does not manage work — he manages the people who do the work. The better the job done by the people who do the work, the easier the manager's job. The opposite is just as true.

So, what's needed is a plan — a logical progression of steps to help you hire the best people for the job. The steps are:

1. Identify a need.

2. Write a job description.

3. Recruit applicants.

4. Conduct interviews of possible candidates.

5. Check references.

6. Make the offer.

Let's take a closer look at each.

Identify a Need

This step should be self-explanatory. At some point, you realize you're spending virtually all of your waking hours working at or for your small business. That may be a commitment to its success. But it might also be inefficient.

Sooner or later you realize more and more time is spent handling details and tasks someone else could do for you at a lower cost. (Remember, your time has value, too.) "I feel like I'm buried in paperwork," is a common complaint. Or, "the telephone won't give me a minute's peace to do the work I need to do." Perhaps it might be something like, "I need to be out there selling."

Whatever the words, the complaint is the same: "I'm spending too much time doing one thing, and I need to do something else. I need some help."

Okay, in general terms, ask yourself what you **need** to spend your time doing and what you are **actually** spending your time on. Find some surprises? Most business people would be surprised at how they spent their time if they really knew.

Armed with this information, you can decide what tasks you should do yourself and which someone else should do for you. You may find what you need is a production manager, or a salesperson, or an office clerk — which brings us to step 2.

WRITE A JOB DESCRIPTION

A job description spells out clearly what duties, responsibilities, special requirements and conditions are included in an employee's job. It should also state what percentage of time will normally be spent on each part of the job. For example, a receptionist's description might say that 75% of the time will be spent answering the phone and greeting customers and clients, 15% of the time will be spent filing and 10% of the time will be spent typing.

A job description is important for both you and your employees. It tells everyone what is expected of them and specifies their duties and responsibilities. It also gives you the basis for appraising each employee's performance.

The job description should include authority limits. Responsibility and authority are not the same thing. If you hire a retail salesperson, that employee is "responsible" for selling as much merchandise as possible. However, along with that responsibility, you may or may not delegate "authority" to make certain types of decisions. For example, if a customer comes in and says he will buy 25 team uniforms if he can get a discount, it is important for the salesperson to know if he can authorize such a discount. Perhaps in your business, no discounts are allowed. In that case, make sure the employee understands and follows the policy.

You should also think about the following as you write: How many people do I need to hire? Do I want full-time or part-time help? What should their specialties be? Will the hours be regular or will there be special projects requiring last minute work?

Write a job description for the position you want to fill. A sample form has been included on the following page. Format is not as important as content. Below is a list of the kinds of things you'll want to include in any description you write:

Job title

Effective date of the description

Who the position reports to

Job summary

Detailed list of all duties.

Any special requirements of the person performing the job.

Special qualifications and/or skills necessary, such as education, office machine skills, etc.

THE GREAT GIZMO COMPANY
(SAMPLE) JOB DESCRIPTION

JOB TITLE: Receptionist   DATE:

HOURS: 8 a.m. - 5 p.m.

POSITION REPORTS TO: —————————————————————

JOB SUMMARY: Answer all incoming telephone calls. Greet and direct customers, visitors and vendors. Type all reports and correspondence and maintain files.

JOB DUTIES:

1. Answer all incoming telephone calls, responding or directing to proper staff member. Screen out nuisance calls.
2. Keep accurate message file. When possible, inform caller when to expect an answer.
3. Greet all customers, visitors and vendors, directing them to the person they wish to see.
4. Type reports and correspondence as directed. Neatness and accuracy is required.
5. Maintain all records and files in neat and orderly fashion.
6. Review files quarterly, separating active from inactive files.

JOB REQUIREMENTS: Punctuality; accuracy in typing and record maintenance; friendly and cheerful manner with visitors; even disposition with people who may have complaints; neat appearance; good interpersonal skills.

QUALIFICATIONS:

Education: High School graduate, preferably some business school or office work experience.
Business machine: Electric typewriter, 60 WPM minimum.

RECRUITING APPLICANTS

Once you know exactly what you need from a potential employee, it will be much easier to decide how to go about finding that person. And with the current level of unemployment, you should have no problem finding applicants. In fact, you may find your problem is "weeding" through all the applications. So, before you choose any methods of finding employees, consider the following:

- How many applicants do you want to interview before making the final decision.

- Do you want them to call or send a resume?

- Have you been specific enough about what you need from an applicant? (i.e., number of years of experience, schooling, etc.)

- What is your salary range? Can you vary from that amount?

1. Classified Advertising

An advertisement placed in the "Help Wanted" section of your local newspaper is the most popular method of finding new employees.

"Help Wanted" ads are listed in alphabetical order, with a special section for part-time work and sales. These ads are relatively inexpensive and can be placed over the phone.

SECRETARY
Full time, sharp, efficient, type min. 80 wpm, org. skills, responsible handling customer calls, small office, ideal conditions, $1050 per mo. GIZMOS UNLIMITED. 999-1000 Mr. Gizmo
TYPESETTER

Generally, Sunday is considered the best day for placing such an ad. However, if you live in a community where a local paper or "shopper" (as it is sometimes called) comes out on Wednesday or Thursday, you should consider placing your ad in that paper as well.

2. Employment Agencies

Almost every community has one or more employment agencies. These agencies have a list or file of unemployed people who have come to them to find a job.

The agency has already done preliminary interviewing to learn individual strengths and weaknesses; therefore, your job has become that much easier.

Employment agencies make their money by charging either the company or the individual a certain percentage of the first month or two months salary.

3. Government Agencies

Every state unemployment office (where unemployment checks are issued) also has a job placement bureau.

You can call these offices and tell them what job openings you have available. If your needs match up with someone who is registered for unemployment, the agency will put the two of you in contact with each other.

4. Schools

Schools are a good source for job applicants, especially if you are looking for part-time help. There are two ways you can go about this: either contact the vocational counselor at the high school or college, or place a sign of your own in the student union or individual classroom buildings.

Going through the vocational counselor will save you the trouble of doing preliminary interviewing yourself.

5. Churches and Synagogues

Churches and synagogues are good places to find job applicants. Because of the high unemployment rate during recent years, some places of worship have started running job ads in their church bulletins. Priests, ministers and rabbis can also give you good leads on people in their congregation out of work.

6. Walk-Ins

If your business is already well-established, you will frequently have people walk in and ask you if you're hiring. If you have the time, ask them a few questions about their background and work experience.

It's a good idea to have a supply of employment application forms on hand for these walk-ins. When you are ready to hire, check through these applications. You might find exactly the applicant you are looking for and avoid having to go through the other channels listed here.

7. Current Employees

Your employees can often provide you with good leads for potential employees. When you know you will have a job opening, ask your employees if they know of anyone who might qualify.

Generally speaking, your employees will recommend only someone they feel will do a good job for you. One warning: Good friends may be more interested in socializing on the job than in working.

8. Friends and Relatives

This can be one of your best sources and one of your worst. And, as with reviewing any other group of applicants, you must rely on your own judgement.

For example, if a friend says: "Hey, great! I've been wondering how I can keep John out of trouble for the summer. You know, at his age, all he thinks about is girls," you may have a problem. You have enough to worry about without watching John for the summer.

Another friend might say: "My son, Bill, just graduated from the University and he's always wanted to work in a business like yours. I'm sure he could do a good job for you." In that case, you might be well-advised to consider Bill for the position.

However, you might be misled in both cases. John might turn out to be a very hard working individual and fit right into your company. And Bill might just be looking for a "stepping stone" until another job comes along. The best thing for you to do is say, "I'll be setting up interviews next week. Have him give me a call on Monday."

Never hire anyone to keep peace in the family or maintain a friendship. An employee should be hired only if he or she is the best person for the job and for no other reason. There's no harm in giving your family and friends special consideration, but don't be swayed by your loyalty to them. Refusing to hire them in the beginning is much better than having to dismiss them later on.

9. Temporary Agencies

This might be the ideal solution for your employment needs, particularly if you need someone only at certain times during the year or for an immediate project. Call the agency, tell them what type of help you need, for how long, and they can send you someone that same day. The cost for this service will be slightly higher than what you would pay an employee doing the same work, but the temporary agency takes care of insurance, worker's compensation and any other problems that could develop.

If the employee does not work out, call the agency and have them send out someone else. The temporary is not your problem.

Temporary help is often used for routine, easy-to-train assignments, or highly specialized work such as accounting or computer technologies. Also, some companies find temporary help a good source of full time employees. If you are considering this, be sure of your arrangements with the temporary agency.

10. Posting Neighborhood Signs

Sometimes finding an employee for your small business can be as easy as placing a "Help Wanted" sign in your local supermarket or drug store.

The Employment Application

Before reading this section, please refer to the employment application form at the back of this chapter.

As we review the application form, you will see it's designed to give you a great deal of information about the applicant in a very small amount of space.

The "Personal Information" part of the application deals with simple facts: name, address, social security number, etc.

The "Special Questions" section may include questions not applicable to your situation. If this is the case, simply ask the applicant not to fill out that section.

The "Employment Desired" section will tell you if the applicant is employed currently and what he expects in the way of salary. It also asks if the present employer may be contacted. If the applicant answers "No", don't immediately assume there is something to hide. Often an employee feels uncomfortable telling his boss he is looking for another job.

The sections on "Education", "Former Employers", and "References", will be by far the most important for you to read. They give you a good idea of what the employee's history has been. One thing you will want to look at closely is how long they have stayed on a job and why they left. If the employee has held several jobs in the past few years, you should ask why. It's possible that there is a satisfactory explanation, but it is more likely this is an employee who is not willing to stay in one place long.

Conforming With Government Regulations

The United States Civil Rights Act of 1964 deals with discrimination in hiring on the basis of race, color, religion, sex or national origin.

It is unlawful for any employer of more than 15 persons to refuse to hire, to discharge, or to treat employees differently because of the above factors. In addition, many states have their own anti-discrimination laws dealing with age, sexual preference, and handicaps, which would directly affect small business or any business that has one or more employees.

To make sure your hiring practices are not in violation of any state or federal law, contact your state employment office. Inform them of your business, the number of people employed and the type of work you do. They will be able to tell you the laws governing hiring, training, discharge and any pre-employment tests given to applicants.

CONDUCT INTERVIEWS

The job interview is the most important step in finding an employee. Often this is the only contact you will have with potential employees before you hire them. Therefore, it is extremely important you take time to do a thorough job.

Start preparing for interviews well ahead of time by jotting down a list of questions to guide you. Don't feel you have to follow it to the letter if an interview goes in an unexpected direction. But a list does have its benefits. First, by asking all the applicants the same or similar questions, you can compare their answers easily.

Second, the list serves as a reminder of what you need to know about an applicant. It's easy to forget what needs to be asked when in the middle of an interview.

A third reason is you don't always know when you'll have to conduct an interview, as in the case of someone walking in to apply for work. One business owner has said, "I pick up employees when I find them, not when I need them." As a result, he feels he's avoided the past mistake of having to find the right person under pressure.

It may be helpful to think of the interview itself as having three component parts:

1. The Structure

2. Questions and Answers

3. Observations

The Structure

Have the applicant come in a few minutes early to fill out an application form. (You will find a sample form later in this chapter.) When this is completed, give yourself at least five minutes to review it before beginning the interview. You might give the applicants any literature you have on your company to look through while they're waiting.

Conduct the interview in privacy. Make it understood that you will take no phone calls or visitors during this time. This will give both of you a chance to relax and talk without being bothered.

Put the applicant at ease. Offer a cup of coffee or a soft drink. Most applicants will be nervous about the interview, and you will help them relax if you feel at ease yourself. It's also helpful to "make small talk" for a few minutes rather than jumping right into business. The basic rule to follow is treat an applicant the way you would like to be treated during a job interview.

Be conversational. Many inexperienced interviewers question job candidates as if they were in a police investigation. This really defeats the purpose. Putting an applicant on the defensive makes it much tougher to find out what he's really like.

Make sure you take notes during the interview. After two days of interviews, you won't remember who said what without notes in front of you. You might put a star or some other notation on the applications of the people you're especially interested in.

Be open and honest about the job. If you are hiring a receptionist, you might ask, "Sometimes we get between 40 and 50 phone calls a day from customers. Do you think you could handle that?" Or, "If an order comes in after 5:30 on a Friday, will you be prepared to stay and send it out?"

Be careful about asking personal questions. If, for example, a woman stated during the interview she has three young children, it is reasonable for you to ask if she sees any attendance problem if they are sick. It is definitely **not** all right to ask a young woman if she plans on getting pregnant within the next year.

Legitimate qualifications for the job are acceptable. When asking such questions, state the requirements of the job first. Show the applicant your written job description to let them know exactly what will be expected of them.

At the end of the interview, thank the applicant for coming in and tell them you'll let them know in a few days whether or not they've been selected. Be sure to follow through. Telling an applicant they didn't get the job isn't easy, but it has to be done. If you can, take the time to tell them why you selected another individual. This may help them on other job interviews.

Questions and Answers

Instead of just asking where an employee has worked (which the application tells you, anyway), ask what they liked best about that job, what was the worst problem they faced there, and how they solved it. Do they know anything about your business? Can they work under pressure?

One business owner decided to ask each applicant: "If I asked you to do something you felt was wrong, would you do it?"

He wasn't looking for a specific answer — he wanted to see how each individual would handle such a situation. Many applicants were taken aback and assumed he was either looking for honesty or loyalty. The applicant who finally got the job replied, "I don't really know. I guess I would tell you why I objected to doing it, but if you still insisted, I'd do it."

Check skills and abilities closely, asking specific questions about their current or previous job, such as: What do (did) you do? How do you do it? Why is it done?

Ask questions that cannot be answered in one or two words, like, "Are you working now?" Instead, say, "Tell me about your current job." Encourage the applicant to do most of the talking. Remember, too, that they are trying to learn about you, so give them the opportunity to ask questions.

Observing the Applicant

Observe the person during the interview. You want to hire someone who will fit in well with your business, so it's important to use your own judgement here. How is the applicant dressed? Does he or she appear clean and neat? Do they talk too loudly or too softly? Do they smoke?

Pay attention to personality. You'll be working closely with this person. Look, also, for non-verbal clues. Does the applicant avoid eye contact? Fidget? Chew nails or cuticles or have other annoying mannerisms?

Listen for ideas, not only facts. Particularly, listen for how something is being said. Listen, also, for what is not said. Are the answers to your questions direct?

At the end of the interview, ask the applicant to get back to you if you think you might be interested in him or her. A call from them in a day or two will tell you much about how interested they are in coming to work for you. Don't commit yourself until you've had a chance to interview all applicants.

Check References

If the applicant is someone you are interested in, it is up to you whether or not to contact the references provided. Generally, it is a good idea to get in touch with at least one.

The key question in talking to a former employer is "Would you hire this individual again?"

Many firms and former employers will give a good reference to a former employee even though their work was not always satisfactory. To avoid this, you might ask a number of specific questions, such as: Was the employee punctual? Did they take their training seriously? Were they often corrected on the same types of mistakes? Did they follow instructions well? Did they need constant supervision or could they be left to do their work alone? Were they overly social at work? Was there ever any type of problem with this employee? A 20-minute chat with a former boss should give you all the information you need to know.

Make The Offer

Once you've made up your mind, call the candidate you've selected and offer the job. Be specific about the job, how much the pay will be, and when they will start.

You can follow-up in writing to confirm the offer if you want. This usually isn't necessary for clerical positions.

You should notify all other candidates someone else was selected for the job. A letter is okay here. Don't go into why the applicant was not selected. Don't send out these letters until the applicant you want has accepted. If your offer is rejected, you'll have to extend it to the second-best applicant.

A rejection like the following can be used:

Dear   :

Thank you for applying with (Company Name) for the job of   . We have now filled that position but will keep your application on file.

Again, thank you.

Sincerely,

TRAINING

Employee training is an on-going process. People are always learning something new at their jobs. The training may not always be seen, but it's there. Quite often it can take the form of what an employee learns sitting at a desk, talking with a customer, or working in the plant.

Before you can give training to an employee, you need

to have a clear picture of what you want to accomplish.

Possible goals include:

- Orienting the new employees to their positions.

- Improving the performance of present employees.

- Retraining present employees for new responsibilities.

As a small business person, most of your training will be with new employees. For them, you'll need to devote some time to the company's history and background, products or services, and rules and regulations, along with the details of the job they will be doing.

The best way to do this is to give new employees any pamphlets, brochures, newsletters or articles you may have. These can be read and reviewed several times. If none are available, jot down a few ideas on paper, such as, "Joe's Truck Repair was started in 1979. We service approximately 50 trucks per week and specialize in complete engine overhauls..." to hand out.

If there is nothing in writing, set aside some time to discuss your business with the new employee. Encourage them to take notes and ask questions about anything that isn't clear.

Most training for small businesses will be on-the-job — the employee will learn by doing.

Use the job description you wrote as a teaching outline, working your way down the list. Such things as telephone answering procedures are usually straightforward unless your system is complicated.

Job tasks may require more planning and extensive training. Are there unusual skills they need to develop? Safety hazards to be aware of? Special ways to handle materials or tools? Any production standards the new employee will have to maintain? These should all be spelled out clearly.

For unfamiliar tasks, demonstrate them the first time yourself. Give your new employee a chance to observe it slowly at first, then at the regular pace. Have them do it under your supervision. Later they can do it on their own.

If there are forms to be filled out, such as sales receipts or invoices, have a sample handy they can follow.

Be patient and offer encouragement.

New employees are usually a little nervous but want to do well. Being positive about what they do well will get them productive much faster.

Everyone makes mistakes. It's very important to call them to the attention of the person who did it as soon as possible. This feedback is what keeps things running smoothly. Since we all want to do things well and please the people we work for, constructive suggestions are usually well received. Show the mistake, what probably caused it and how it can be avoided in the future.

Repeated mistakes must be dealt with quickly. But you need to know what the problem really is to correct it properly. Is the employee not suited to the job, or were they inadequately trained?

Your training should also include any standing policies or practices employees are expected to follow. Be sure they are understood. Go over each item individually and answer any questions at that time. The policies below are common; you may think of several others for your particular business.

1. **Product and/or Service Knowledge**

   Your employees, especially those involved with the selling or promotion of your product or service, should know as much as possible about your business.

   Every new employee should be given complete training on all your products and services. Keep in mind there may be a great deal of material to absorb in a very short amount of time. It would be a good idea for you to say, "I realize this is a lot of information. Why don't you take a few days to look it over, then ask me any questions you come up with." If practical, include new employees in any meetings or business calls that might help them become familiar with your company.

2. **Pricing Policy**

   This can also be included in your product and service policies. Instruct your employees on all pricing policies, including discounts, sales, and large orders.

3. **Working with Customers**

Every small business owner has his own ideas and policies on how customers are to be treated. If it's your policy that any customer in your store should be approached within two minutes after arriving, make sure your employees know. If certain customers are allowed to write checks without having credit checked, make sure your new employees know who these customers are. If cash refunds are not given for merchandise, that policy should be clearly understood before an employee starts work.

Many companies have a "breaking-in" period where new employees work with experienced ones. Often, close supervision and observation are the best ways to present your policies and rules.

4. **How to Work with Co-Workers**

Every week, there is at least one letter in Ann Landers' column about problems between co-workers. One employee whistles constantly at his desk, another wears too much perfume, another gossips, another chain smokes, another steals typewriter ribbons, etc. It seems there is an endless list of problems people have when working with each other.

Of course, you **want** your employees to get along, but there isn't any set of rules to guarantee this. What you **can** do is have certain guidelines for employees to follow.

For example, you may want a company rule forbidding any employee from going through another employee's desk. Or a rule dividing your office into smoking/no smoking areas. Maybe you want to state any employee suspecting another employee of wrong-doing is expected to tell you.

You will be the best judge of what rules and policies are necessary for your business. And it's very important to put them in writing, and up-date them regularly to include "sensitive" subjects as they occur. The best rule might be an "open door" policy which allows employees to come to you with any problems or suggestions they have.

Rules and Regulations

Every business has its own set of rules and regulations. Rules may be as simple as making the coffee in the morning and shutting off the lights at night, or as structured as a 3-ring binder filled with them. Generally, it is better to have your business rules and regulations in writing to avoid misunderstandings and to answer questions.

Each new employee should be given a copy to keep and review. Your manual may not include a section on every topic below, but you should give some thought to each to decide which you do want.

Your policy manual could be structured to include the topics we have outlined below:

I.   Employment Policy
     Probationary Period
     Performance Reviews
     Grounds for Termination

II. Attendance
     Absences
     Sick Time/Disability
     Leaves of Absence

III. Wages
     Time Cards
     Work Schedules
     Overtime
     Pay Periods
     Salary Reviews
     Advance Wages
     Travel and Other Work Expenses

IV.   Benefits
      Insurance
      Paid Holidays
      Vacation
      Personal Days

V.   Professional Growth
      Professional Memberships
      Courses/Seminars/Conventions

VI.   Office
      Confidentiality
      Dress Code
      Hygiene
      Smoking
      Parking
      Meals
      Breaks
      Personal Phone Calls
      Housekeeping

DISCIPLINE

No one enjoys disciplining employees, but it is sometimes a necessary part of being a supervisor or manager. Here is how you should handle a disciplinary problem:

• Tell the employee exactly what they are doing wrong.

• Explain how this adversely affects your business.

• Tell them what you want them to do.

• Offer them some constructive suggestions on how to improve.

Agree on a deadline by which the improvement should be made.

Now, before going into detail on the above, it is important to keep in mind that there is also a proper way to discipline. Here are some tips:

1. Never discipline an employee in front of other employees.

2. Try not to lose your temper. Do not raise your voice.

3. Discipline only when the mistake merits it. If you are constantly criticizing, your employees will soon lose their motivation for doing a good job.

When an employee makes a mistake that cannot be overlooked, set aside some time to discuss it. Make arrangements not to be disturbed. Do this in a discreet manner so other employees are not aware the employee is being disciplined.

Detail the mistake. You might start by saying: "Joan, the report you turned in last Tuesday had several errors in it. You had already left for the day and Mary had to retype it so it could go out on time."

Allow Joan to explain why it happened and decide if what she says is a valid explanation. If so, and this is the first time it has happened, simply calling it to her attention should be adequate.

However, if Joan has made a number of mistakes like this in the past, you will have to decide how to handle it. Point out that the mistakes are putting an extra burden on other employees and wasting valuable time.

You might say: "Joan, I'm going to be watching your work very carefully for the next few weeks. We can't afford any more mistakes like this. If there are any, I'm afraid I'll have to reevaluate your position with the company."

If there are any extenuating circumstances (the employee has personal problems or too much work to handle), take that into consideration. Perhaps the employee needs some time off or finds the work too difficult to handle. This is what you want to find out before deciding what type of action you are going to take.

If the employee has been accused of something by another employee, make sure you have all the facts before making a judgement.

Remember, your employees are human, and entitled to make mistakes. Discipline should never be harsh or unfair, and should always be well thought out beforehand.

MOTIVATION AND REWARD

A very important part of your job as a small business owner will be motivating and rewarding your employees. Your employees must **want to** do a good job; they should be rewarded when they do.

This doesn't always come in the form of a bonus or gift, although that is a good way to show appreciation. It can be as simple as saying: "I noticed the good job you did on making that sale to Mrs. Goodwin. I'm really proud of you." Or, "I saw the repair job you did on Joe's motor. It turned out very, very well and I know that you did it quickly. You really seem to have a good understanding of engines." Or, "How did your first day of work go? Let me tell you, I'm very pleased with the way you dress and the pleasant manner you have with all our clients."

This type of comment lets employees know you really have been paying attention and you do appreciate their work. And when you make employees feel good about themselves, they will continue to put their best effort into the job.

If you can afford to, you might include bonuses in the paychecks at 3- or 6-month intervals. It doesn't have to be a lot of money, but rather something to show the employee his hard work has paid off.

It's your goal to establish a good working environment, opportunities for growth and a system of recognition and rewards.

Remuneration

As a small business owner, it is up to you to decide how you want employees to be paid: hourly, weekly, semi-monthly or monthly.

Generally, employees working part-time or odd shifts should be paid by the hour. The advantage is that you pay employees only for the hours they work, which can vary depending on the needs of your business.

Usually, most employees appreciate a weekly or semi-monthly check because it is easier to balance their own finances this way. It can be advantageous for your planning as well. Monthly paychecks take a larger part of your finances at one time.

No matter how you decide to pay your employees, the important thing is that they understand how and when they will be paid. Check with the state employment agency to make sure you are deducting the proper amounts for State and Federal taxes, Social Security, unemployment compensation, worker's compensation, temporary disability insurance, and any other deductions.

COMMUNICATION: THE KEY TO MANAGING PEOPLE

Coordination of activities depends upon the careful selection of people and equipment as well as effective communication. In fact, there is nothing that will foul up coordination faster than poor communication. It is the supervisor's responsibility to develop plans, and to communicate them to the employees. This means, of course, that he assigns tasks. But it also means that he monitors the progress of the employees as they complete those tasks. If the supervisor is unclear with his instructions or about how to implement tasks, problems will occur and progress will be slowed. Communicating well involves:

1. **Speaking distinctly.** Some people slur their words. Think for a moment of the artist who tries very hard to keep his paintings from becoming smeared. The string of sounds which emerges from the speaker shouldn't be piled up in a heap. Perhaps it's just a matter of remembering to slow down.

2. **Writing clearly.** Sometimes the written word carries more weight than the spoken word. This is particularly true over long periods of time since we tend to forget some of the things we've said. It pays to find a few extra moments to select words you know will be understood. Get into the habit of editing all notes which leave your office. Keep a dictionary nearby. Use short sentences. Perhaps a follow-up phone call or visit will underscore the precise meaning of your written message.

3. **Writing neatly.** Often it's much easier to write out a memo by hand than to use a typewriter. If that's the case, take pity on the one who has to read your note. I've often wondered about the poorly written prescriptions that are being filled at the local pharmacy. How many of those prescriptions do you suppose have been filled improperly? In that kind of situation it might be a matter of life and death. Let's hope not. The message here to all of us is that sloppy writing can be very expensive.

4. **Being specific with directions.** Don't beat around the bush. State precisely what your needs are and then help your subordinates to get started with their tasks.

5. **Being timely with communications.** How often have we heard someone say: "Well, nobody told me about it"? In general, people will be fair and cooperative if they know what is expected of them. All they need is some lead time to prepare. Surprise messages, especially important messages, such as those which affect salary and vacation, are apt to rankle people, and rightly so.

6. **Being consistent with information.** Planning your directives carefully so your employees will learn to depend upon you will increase their confidence and keep costs low. Get into the practice of not changing business plans for casual reasons. Changing plans halfway into a major project can be devastating. For a small company it is imperative that big mistakes not occur.

7. **Listening carefully to feedback from employees.** Sometimes employees are too timid to discuss a problem with their supervisor. As a result, it might be necessary for you to initiate a discussion to find out how the employee feels about his work. You can bet that the employee has opinions. You will gain his respect if you regularly ask how things are going. This might prevent a serious problem from developing.

8. **Communicating regularly.** Try very hard to be available to your employees. Find the time to visit with them on a regular basis. They must know that their concerns are being addressed. If you have their confidence, they will inform you when a problem occurs. Very significant, too, is their need to be reassured that they are keeping on task satisfactorily. A word of encouragement, a pat on the back, a simple compliment — these are indicators that you are pleased with their work.

Communicating effectively is a fundamental part of being well organized. Most people probably sense that this is true, but are sometimes confused by the English language. After all, many of the words in our language have more than one meaning. We're all used to hearing junior high and high school students say: "he goes" instead of "he says," aren't we? If you say, "she's neat," you might mean: 1) she's a wonderful person; 2) she's exciting; 3) she's very clean in her work; or 4) she's well-dressed.

Perhaps the easiest way to overcome this difficulty is to give an example after your statement: "She's neat." "See how trim she is in that summer dress."

Another problem stems from the use of "insider" language, particularly in highly technical fields. All too often, people assume that their own special vocabulary is understood by others around them. People must be given a chance to learn special vocabularies.

Of course, the bottom line in effective communications is the need for clarity. If you are delivering a speech or sales pitch and your delivery is too fast, you can't expect your audience to listen faster. They will understand you only if you set a reasonable pace. Temper your voice with pleasant sounds, emphasize key words, and provide illustrations.

What Do You Want Me To Do?

The most effective employees are those who are able to place what they are learning into a context. For example, a manager might say: "Jane, I want you to get on the phone and sell this set of books. Here's the list of phone numbers." How many books do you suppose Jane will sell with such a brief explanation? Not many.

First of all, the problem was not presented well. The manager didn't bother to cover a tried and true sales pitch with Jane. No training time and practice time were provided either. Also, Jane would apparently have to learn the hard way who her customers are.

For the sake of argument, let's suppose that the customers are retired couples who are living on fixed incomes. How eager will they be to buy a book when an amateurish pitch is made over the phone? Probably not too eager. They might even be provoked at Jane for calling. However difficult some sales might appear, they can be enhanced with the proper sales perspective. Give the employee a fighting chance. Make sure he understands how valuable the products are. Give him a chance to "believe" in the product. Then help him study how such a product should be presented to the public. Have him review the sales pitch and procedures of the sale. Top this off with an understanding of who the audience is, and how that audience is apt to respond, and you'll have a good part of the required perspective.

Hearing From Your Employees

Ideally, employees should be informed about the company's plans; about its marketing strategy; its anticipated growth; and its revenues. But the wise manager will want to know how all of this is perceived by the employees, and how

it's being accepted by them. The manager should make it a priority of his business to find out how the employees like what they are doing. He might even ask them to help devise a few plans. Today's managers are finding out that the higher the degree of interaction between management and employees, the greater the likelihood for producing quality products. Commitment to quality tends to pick up when one sees his own credibility is on the line. Even if this kind of scheme is implemented, the manager must be alert to potential problems, especially if a "chain of command" supervision structure is in place. That system should not become so rigid that the efforts of the people in the trenches go unrecognized.

Telling Your Employees

Information about the company should be discussed with the employees on a regular basis. This is the manager's chance to put rumors to rest, to discuss plans, and to announce concerns. The employees want to know how well they are doing individually and how well the company is doing. A discussion of this type will reinforce their sense of security and help to keep the company's financial house tidy. Most employees are not interested in a detailed account of the cash flow, but would certainly welcome any news that suggests financial stability and an improved revenue picture. Just a few words will do. For example, at a general staff meeting the manager might say: "I've got some good news for you. Our sales so far this year are 15% ahead of last year's. And Tom tells me that a lot of the customers he calls on are excited about our new product line." The manager should be prepared to answer a few questions, too.

An attempt should be made, too, to let the employees in on long-range plans. This will give them an overall picture of the company's direction and will serve in some measure to outline their future with the company. Just discussing plans openly with the employees is an exercise that should win their trust. They will see the business is organized well and be less prone to upset when changes are announced. Consider taking the employees into your confidence before implementing a plan, especially a plan of some size. By asking for the opinions of the employees and taking the time to learn their concerns, you will be laying the foundation for participative management.

ANNOUNCING EVENTS

How to Announce Events

Keeping your employees informed is not just a matter of talking to them during a staff meeting, although this is very important, too. Most

WE'RE MOVING! YOUR DESK IS ON THE TRUCK!!

employers are sensitive to this need and will, at least, place notices on a bulletin board. Tacking up newspaper clippings (with the dates!) can reveal important business trends which your employees might not have noticed otherwise. A bulletin board is an excellent place to post special recognition announcements, too. All of us need to be recognized for our special contributions, and we appreciate learning about the special contributions of our co-workers. But additional aids might also prove useful. For example, a manager might consider printing a newsletter. It has to be printed regularly, say once a week or once every two weeks, in order to be current and applicable to the employees' perceived interests. But it provides a wide range of information options. It might list such items as: 1) births, deaths, retirements, and facts about new employees; 2) recreational events; 3) want ads; 4) promotions; and 5) business meetings or conventions. A newsletter can be as long or short as you want, but someone will have to take the time to prepare it.

When to Announce Events

It is essential to announce events in time for employees to adapt to new situations. Many people actually cringe when they are informed so late they have little time to prepare for change. Change in today's fast-paced, technical world is the rule rather than the exception. So a note of caution is advised when dealing with new issues of importance. Allow enough lead time so the employees will be able to adjust. For instance, if an employee recognizes that his job is about to be phased out, he might select another career track to follow, and be able to take the kind of training which would support that career. It isn't change employees always fear, but not knowing about it.

PRINCIPLES OF MANAGERIAL LEADERSHIP

Leadership defined: The ability to direct associates in the completion of an assigned task.

Qualities of Leadership

Leadership appears to come in so many forms that it would be very difficult to list all of the characteristics which leaders have in common. However, Hodgetts, in his Management: Theory, Process, and Practice (p. 289), identifies several qualities which leaders often possess:

1. **Intelligence.** Leaders are bright enough to control managerial tasks.

2. **Maturity.** Leaders are emotionally stable, balanced, and have a broad base of experiences.

3. **Motivation.** Leaders are high-energy people who have the kind of drive it takes to succeed.

4. **Sensitivity in Human Relations.** Leaders do more than just "get along" with their co-workers. They have an appreciative word for work well done, and are able to stimulate cooperation.

THE MANAGER'S ROLE

The Manager Must Use Good Judgement

Finding the balance between the needs employees have and the production schedule is difficult for some managers. Some managers are so oriented toward production that they fail to support their employees adequately. When this happens, the employees do not feel they are part of a team, and they are not given a chance to succeed. If their opinions don't really matter, productivity will fall off. Sometimes this happens because of the manager's reluctance to assign tasks to others. Either he doesn't trust the employees or he feels like he can do the job faster and better himself. Perhaps, too, the manager works well with ideas, but can't work well with feelings and the implementation of ideas. But if the manager spends too much time in production, his business will suffer from a lack of management. He can spread himself too thin.

The best manager can be sincerely concerned about both employees and production. This calls for outstanding interaction skills.

It is not enough to say that the employees should "work together." The manager must be genuinely concerned about the welfare of his employees. If the production goals are clear and rewards adequate, expectations for success should be high.

THERE ARE ALL KINDS OF MANAGERS. . .

The Domineering Manager

This kind of manager is going to dictate what happens in his business. He's more concerned about production than the needs of his employees, and will use threats and coercion to get what he wants. Consider the following case, for example. As soon as Barney Kruger entered the store, his employees knew something was up, and it was probably going to be a bad day. Kruger was frowning and angry about the pilfering of cup cakes and milk at his store, and he was determined to have it stopped immediately. Each employee was called in and told very directly that the situation had to improve immediately. Kruger also assured each employee that the next time he found out that someone had stolen, he'd fire that person on the spot. There are a number of interesting points about Barney Kruger: 1) He shows evidence of an overbearing personality. He's not the type to seek opinions from his employees. 2) He callously disregarded the feelings of his employees. Did **everyone** steal cup cakes and milk? And, 3) He let his anger override a better approach to solving a difficult problem.

The Team Manager

This kind of manager wants the employees to participate fully in the decision-making process. As an example, one can point to the case of Al Jordan, hospital laboratory manager, who was responsible for tests administered to premature infants.

There had been a severe problem with staff turnover. The patient load had been on the increase, and the doctors and nurses were complaining about the lack of support from the lab. Al wasted no time in arranging a staff meeting to find out how to make the lab situation better. He sought the opinions of his technicians, and learned that the blood samples which came to the lab were too often marked with an emergency label: **stat, red tape,** or sometimes a **verbal directive**, such as "Do it now!" Considering the pressure this put his staff under, Al decided to discuss the matter with his boss. This meeting resulted in greater sensitivity on the part of the doctors and nurses and better organization in the lab. Al Jordan had not isolated himself from his staff. He was able to act promptly to correct a critical situation. In the process, he kept the confidence of his technicians. He knew the value of maintaining good interpersonal relationships.

The Survival Manager

This kind of manager is seldom ahead of the game. He seems unable to meet production deadlines. Take the case of Brian Brimspill. He really enjoyed working with Sally and George, but he knew they couldn't possibly complete their drafting project by Friday. He didn't want to risk hurting their feelings about the deadline; so he decided to ask his supervisor for a one-week extension. Brian was very surprised when his supervisor said: "Sorry, Brian, no deal!" Brian seemed unaware that employees expect — even desire — to have a firm boss. Had he been firm with his staff, chances are they would have found him dependable, and confidence among the team players would have been high. Brian is the kind of manager who places so much stress on maintaining good, interpersonal relationships that he risks losing a project and, perhaps, his job.

The above examples of managerial styles suggest that good managers are highly motivated and interested in the welfare of their employees. On the one hand, this means that the work place should be stable and as free of uncertainties as possible. On the other hand, the manager should expect his employees to perform well. Work well done will bring rewards for all.

HOW TO HANDLE THE PROBLEM EMPLOYEE

Maintaining high standards of productivity in the workplace is sometimes complicated by an interpersonal problem. If you detect that an argument is beginning to interfere with an employee's performance, you must make every effort to discover the reasons for the argument, and find a solution.

Identify Causes of Concern

1. Redefine the job

2. Ask the employee's opinion about the problem

3. Be constructive with criticism

Keep the discussion focused on productive issues.

1. Decide how the situation will be improved

2. Coach and counsel the employee

3. Monitor his progress

HOW TO FIRE AN EMPLOYEE

There can be many reasons for firing an employee. Some are out of the control of both you and the employee. Business may be declining and you may be forced for financial reasons to decrease your work force. Or, you may decide that you've got extra help on your hands. Maybe your business is expanding in more directions than you had envisioned and you need a person with different kinds of skills. Other times, ongoing attitude or performance problems may create a situation that forces you to terminate an employee.

If the situation is out of your control, it will probably be easier for you to fire the person. If he has been a regular employee, he may be eligible to receive unemployment compensation, which will ease the burden of transition. Perhaps you have arranged for some kind of severance pay. Emotionally difficult as these situations may be, they are not as tricky as when you have someone who is not working out because of inadequate behavior or performance. These situations require proof on your part of why you are firing the person. And this means you must document your reasons carefully and fairly. Before you go the route of termination, think about whether the employee might be shifted to another position or department. Maybe there is another job in your organization to which he is more suited.

Difficult as it is to fire someone, with the right approach, it can be turned into an experience that helps both parties grow and learn about themselves.

The Importance of Documentation

It's not easy to fire a person, but it's sometimes necessary. Normally such drastic action occurs only after all other avenues have been tried. To go this route, you will need proof, and the time to start gathering it is now. The proof you need must be documented on a regular basis.

Documentation is simply a record of all communications with the employee about his or her performance. You should document your regular performance evaluation meetings with all your employees as a matter of course, but doing this takes on an urgency when you have an employee you may have to terminate.

In many states, it's the law that an employee must be given written warnings before termination can take place. These written warnings will require **facts, facts, facts,** to back them up. This is to protect you as much as to protect the employee, as it can help prevent a possible suit for discrimination or injury.

The technique to use when you document is to give as many facts as possible. This means recording numbers, measurable data, quotations, or other non-emotional, **objective** facts about the employee. Here are some examples.

WRONG: "Susan acted surly and yelled at a customer. I talked to her about it."

RIGHT: "Date: x/x/8x

"Susan was talking on the phone to a customer. The customer was angry because an important order had been delayed. Susan talked to him for 10 minutes explaining the slowness but the customer remained angry. Susan hung up on the customer and told him to take his business elsewhere. I discussed the incident afterwards with her and said that even when the customer is being unreasonable, he must be treated with respect."

WRONG: "I noticed that we have been coming up short on the daily cash count since Jim started working. I warned him about it."

RIGHT: "Date: x/x/8x

"In the month period before Jim started working here, we averaged a minus $5.55 on the cash box at the end of the day. Since he started working here, the daily count is minus $39.00. Jim is consistently late and disappears during working hours. I told him that we have been noticing shortages since he began working and that he must improve his daily counts, come to work on time, and remain at his register."

You should reread what you have written to make sure it makes sense, and then ask yourself if someone reading the report six months from now will understand it. In summary, after a negative incident with an employee, you should record:

- the date

- who was involved

- what happened

- what you did/said

- what employee did/said

This information will provide you with a record of any incidents that occur. If a series of such incidents occur, you may be forced to terminate the employee. It can be too late three months down the road to realize that what you thought were isolated incidents have become a pattern. If you document regularly, you will have the proof if you need it. However, it is impossible to reconstruct these scenes separately after the fact.

If incidents start occurring with regularity, it is time to have a formal counseling or performance appraisal session. You will be taking on a more **active role,** instead of reacting to behavior by the employee. During counseling sessions, concentrate your discussion on these points:

1. Describe how the employee's problems are perceived. Be specific about the details of his decline in productivity.

2. Describe what the employee's decline in productivity means to the company. Help the employee understand his situation by supplying as much perspective as possible. Young employees, in particular, may not appreciate the importance of doing a good job. You may be the person to mold them into mature productive adults.

3. Remind the employee of his responsibility by asking a challenging question like this: "What do you think you can do to improve this situation?"

4. Ask what the employee thinks you can do to help him. There may be a situation in the employee's personal life that is a

factor in his behavior. If this is so, you may be able to work out a temporary arrangement if the situation is on the way to solution.

5. Discuss the consequences which will result from unimproved performance.

6. Arrange a monitoring schedule. For example, "I expect to see you in my office every Tuesday at 3:00 pm for a counseling session. Remember, too, I plan to look over your shoulder while you're working."

After a counseling session or performance appraisal, document the following points:

- the date

- items discussed

- employee's remarks

- goals agreed upon

- steps for attaining goals

- timetable for goals

- employee's full name

Remember that the information you document is usually available for the employee's inspection (by law). So make extra sure to document clearly, concisely, and fairly.

This is a good time to note the importance of regular performance reviews. These are especially critical for new (and young) employees. For such employees, reviews every three months for the first year can be critical in shaping and guiding their growth. You provide a structured forum for communication and may catch minor problems before they develop into something major.

The Dismissal

When you have tried reason, encouragement, and a formal warning with no success, you may have no recourse but to fire an employee. The meeting where you dismiss the employee should be conducted as fairly as possible and should be focused on the causes of dissatisfaction. Call the person in, probably toward the end of the day at the end of the week, outline his performance history and your expectations. There is room in this session, too, for positive points you've noticed about the person. However, be prepared and be firm. Typically, managers might say: "I'm sorry, it's not working out," or "We've decided to release you," or, perhaps, "We feel your skills might be put to better use elsewhere." However, the employee is owed a reasonable explanation about why the dismissal action has been taken.

Performance Appraisals

Periodically, you should review the performance of all your employees and the work they are doing. Generally, it is a good idea to do this after the first month for a new employee, and every six months after that.

In a performance appraisal, you should set aside about an hour to spend with the employee. Go over their job description and let them know how you think they are doing in each category. This is also a time for you to ask the employee if they are having any problems with the job, or if they have any suggestions.

Show the employee what you have written and ask if they agree. It is a good idea to have all employees sign their performance appraisal for your records. Signature does not imply agreement, only that they've read it.

It is a good idea to keep individual files on all employees to refer to. The file should contain all personnel-related information, including performance appraisals, written notices of discipline, promotions, and salary histories.

Maintaining these employee files will help protect you if an employee must be discharged for any reason. If the discharged employee files for unemployment compensation, you will have to document the reason. They will also help support you if you're accused of breaking anti-discrimination rules and regulations.

There have been an increasing number of suits in recent years alleging discrimination in the treatment of employees. Many cases had merit, some didn't.

When disciplining your employees, be sure to document the events leading up to the discipline. Include meeting times, dates, places, interview notes with the employee in question, as well as others. Note action taken. Keep all of this on file, in case you are ever called into court to defend your actions. Being right and being able to explain it can be worlds apart.

The best protection you can take is a written letter to the employee detailing the events leading up to it, and giving them notice further occurrences will be cause for dismissal. The letter should also indicate specifically how the employee can be reinstated. Give a copy to them. Have them sign and date a copy for your file.

SUMMARY

One of the most important aspects of running a small business is having good employees. Only with good employees can your business grow and prosper. And good employees make for a pleasant working situation.

In this chapter, we have learned:

1. Employees are the life blood of any business; they make it grow.

2. Employees with a good attitude about their jobs and company can help make customers happy and expand your business.

3. An unhappy employee with a bad attitude will hurt your business.

4. There are a number of places to locate potential employees.

5. The job interview is probably the most important part of hiring an employee.

6. Federal and state regulations may affect your hiring, training and termination policies.

7. There are a number of different factors to consider when training a new employee.

8. A job description is important to have when hiring and training new employees.

9. The manner in which you discipline an employee will determine how effective the discipline is.

10. Employees are motivated by praise and rewards for a good job.

11. It is a good idea to give your employees periodic performance appraisals.

12. You should keep a file containing personnel related information for each employee.

APPLICATION FOR EMPLOYMENT
(PRE-EMPLOYMENT QUESTIONNAIRE) (AN EQUAL OPPORTUNITY EMPLOYER)

PERSONAL INFORMATION

DATE _____

NAME _____

          LAST   FIRST   MIDDLE

SOCIAL SECURITY NUMBER _____

PRESENT ADDRESS _____

         STREET   CITY   STATE   ZIP

PERMANENT ADDRESS _____

         STREET   CITY   STATE   ZIP

PHONE NO _____ ARE YOU 18 YEARS OR OLDER? Yes ☐ No ☐

ARE YOU EITHER A U.S. CITIZEN OR AN ALIEN AUTHORIZED TO WORK IN THE UNITED STATES? Yes ☐ No ☐

EMPLOYMENT DESIRED

POSITION _____ DATE YOU CAN START _____ SALARY DESIRED _____

ARE YOU EMPLOYED NOW? _____ IF SO MAY WE INQUIRE OF YOUR PRESENT EMPLOYER? _____

EVER APPLIED TO THIS COMPANY BEFORE? _____ WHERE? _____ WHEN? _____

REFERRED BY _____

EDUCATION	NAME AND LOCATION OF SCHOOL	*NO OF YEARS ATTENDED	*DID YOU GRADUATE?	SUBJECTS STUDIED
GRAMMAR SCHOOL				
HIGH SCHOOL				
COLLEGE				
TRADE, BUSINESS OR CORRESPONDENCE SCHOOL				

GENERAL
SUBJECTS OF SPECIAL STUDY OR RESEARCH WORK _____

_____

SPECIAL SKILLS _____

ACTIVITIES. (CIVIC, ATHLETIC, ETC.) _____

EXCLUDE ORGANIZATIONS. THE NAME OF WHICH INDICATES THE RACE. CREED. SEX. AGE. MARITAL STATUS. COLOR OR NATION OF ORIGIN OF ITS MEMBERS

U.S. MILITARY OR NAVAL SERVICE _____ RANK _____ PRESENT MEMBERSHIP IN NATIONAL GUARD OR RESERVES _____

The Age Discrimination in Employment Act of 1987 prohibits discrimination on the basis of age with respect to individuals who are at least 40 years of age

(CONTINUED ON OTHER SIDE)

17-37

(Right margin vertical labels: LAST, FIRST, MIDDLE)

FORMER EMPLOYERS (LIST BELOW LAST THREE EMPLOYERS, STARTING WITH LAST ONE FIRST).

DATE MONTH AND YEAR	NAME AND ADDRESS OF EMPLOYER	SALARY	POSITION	REASON FOR LEAVING
FROM				
TO				
FROM				
TO				
FROM				
TO				
FROM				
TO				

WHICH OF THESE JOBS DID YOU LIKE BEST?

WHAT DID YOU LIKE MOST ABOUT THIS JOB?

REFERENCES: GIVE THE NAMES OF THREE PERSONS NOT RELATED TO YOU, WHOM YOU HAVE KNOWN AT LEAST ONE YEAR

	NAME	ADDRESS	BUSINESS	YEARS ACQUAINTED
1				
2				
3				

THE FOLLOWING STATEMENT APPLIES IN: MARYLAND & MASSACHUSETTS. (Fill in name of state)
IT IS UNLAWFUL IN THE STATE OF _____ TO REQUIRE OR ADMINISTER A LIE DETECTOR TEST AS A CONDITION OF EMPLOYMENT OR CONTINUED EMPLOYMENT. AN EMPLOYER WHO VIOLATES THIS LAW SHALL BE SUBJECT TO CRIMINAL PENALTIES AND CIVIL LIABILITY.

_____
Signature of Applicant

IN CASE OF
EMERGENCY NOTIFY

NAME	ADDRESS	PHONE NO.

"I CERTIFY THAT THE FACTS CONTAINED IN THIS APPLICATION ARE TRUE AND COMPLETE TO THE BEST OF MY KNOWLEDGE AND UNDERSTAND THAT, IF EMPLOYED, FALSIFIED STATEMENTS ON THIS APPLICATION SHALL BE GROUNDS FOR DISMISSAL.

I AUTHORIZE INVESTIGATION OF ALL STATEMENTS CONTAINED HEREIN AND THE REFERENCES LISTED ABOVE TO GIVE YOU ANY AND ALL INFORMATION CONCERNING MY PREVIOUS EMPLOYMENT AND ANY PERTINENT INFORMATION THEY MAY HAVE, AND RELEASE ALL PARTIES FROM ALL LIABILITY FOR ANY DAMAGE THAT MAY RESULT FROM FURNISHING SAME TO YOU.

I UNDERSTAND AND AGREE THAT, IF HIRED, MY EMPLOYMENT IS FOR NO DEFINITE PERIOD AND MAY, REGARDLESS OF THE DATE OF PAYMENT OF MY WAGES AND SALARY, BE TERMINATED AT ANY TIME WITHOUT PRIOR NOTICE AND WITHOUT CAUSE."

DATE _____   SIGNATURE _____

DO NOT WRITE BELOW THIS LINE

INTERVIEWED BY _____   DATE _____

REMARKS _____

_____

NEATNESS _____   ABILITY _____

HIRED ☐ Yes ☐ No   POSITION _____   DEPT _____

SALARY/WAGE _____   DATE REPORTING TO WORK _____

APPROVED 1 _____   2 _____   3 _____
          EMPLOYMENT MANAGER   DEPT. HEAD   GENERAL MANAGER

Chapter 18

Your business plan

Perhaps the most important document of your business career

As a blossoming entrepreneur, you are part of a gigantic wave that's growing in size and sweeping across America. We are slowly reverting back to pioneer times when cottage industry and small businesses were the backbone of our nation. Indeed, many business experts predict that in the future 95% of all new innovations and changes will come from people like you and me in the small business arena.

While the corporate giants continue to grow, merging and swallowing each other, thousands of energetic, talented people are spun off. Thousands more, who have never been part of the anonymous, faceless existence within a big corporation stand on the sidelines with heads full of ideas, wondering if NOW is the time to start up their own businesses.

Is this you? Well, take heart! You have plenty of company. Last year there were more than 600,000 new incorporations in the United States. And there were at least that many new sole proprietorships and partnerships.

But sadly, about 80% of those start-ups will unnecessarily fall by the wayside within a few years.

YOU DO NOT HAVE TO BE ONE OF THEM!

What can you do to keep your bubble from bursting? Perhaps the best preventive medicine is expressed in a single word...PLANNING.

This chapter deals with two vital areas of planning:

The Business Plan

Operational Planning

THE BUSINESS PLAN

Chapter 5 guided you through the procedure for a loan proposal. While this procedure may be all you need to get a loan from a bank, it may not be adequate when trying to raise **venture capital** from other sources. On the other hand, a complete business plan which **includes** a loan proposal is a document which will not only be a powerful money-raising tool, but it will serve as a road map during the first vital years of your new venture.

A properly developed business plan provides more than mere numbers on paper. It serves three main functions:

1. A communications tool which conveys your ideas, research and plans to others.

2. A basis on which to manage your business.

3. A yardstick by which you may measure progress and evaluate changes.

If these functions don't convince you that you need a business plan, we have a suggestion: Ask any business person who has failed whether or not they had prepared a business plan ahead of time.

Sure, it takes time, effort and maybe even money to prepare a document like this. But if it can make the difference between success and failure, it's worth it. So, let's get started.

How to Prepare Your Business Plan

First, decide right now that your business plan will be neatly typed and well-written. Its final appearance will have a significant effect on others who read it. Therefore, if you are weak in the areas of writing and typewriting, hire someone to help with the final preparation.

Your plan is a reflection of you and your ability to organize, to think, to manage and to communicate. In the eyes of a venture capitalist — one who may invest his money in your new enterprise — it demonstrates on paper your potential ability to compete in the business arena.

Because no two business plans are alike, we prefer not to give you a model plan. Instead, we will suggest the essential elements of a properly prepared business plan.

1. **Your Business Concept.** This is your first - and most important page. It sets the tone for what follows. It can be the "make-or-break" page in the eyes of your banker or a venture capitalist. This page presents a summary of your business idea. It tells why you think it will work, how it fits into the marketplace, what the future should hold. All based on your best research, of course.

2. **Your Product or Service.** You will need to provide a complete description of what you plan to sell or rent. If possible, include an 8 x 10 photograph. Emphasize the basic product or service that will provide the bulk of your income. Explain advantages and benefits and anything about your products or services that will help "sell" your business concept to a complete stranger. If your product is still on the drawing board, explain when it will be available, including any test data you have.

3. **Your Market.** Explain the big picture first. What is the total universe of your market? Is the industry growing or declining? Is anything happening now or expected to happen in the future that will impact your business? Who are your competitors? How successful are they, and why? Do they have any weaknesses? If so, will your business fill a need created by their weakness? Who will your customers be? Why will they buy your product or service?

4. **Your Marketing Strategy.** Describe how your product or service will be sold. Include pricing strategy, estimated sales and market share for each of the first three years. Add your advertising and public relations plans, plus your service and warranty policies.

5. **Your Production Plans.** Cover all the specifics, such as how, where and by whom your product will be produced. What is the raw material? Is it readily available? What is the manufacturing process? What is your anticipated rate of production? Will you use union or non-union labor?

6. **Your Personnel.** Will yours be a sole proprietorship? A partnership? Corporation? If so, include an organizational chart. How many people are involved, and what are their skills? How well are they qualified? At what points in time will you add personnel? If you're running a one-man show, explain convincingly how you have the necessary skills and talent to achieve your goals.

7. **Your Financial Plans.** If yours is a new business, you won't have the benefit of past history. As a bare minimum, you will need a personal financial statement. If your business is already established, include a financial statement for the business. Demonstrate how you plan to elevate existing figures from point A to point B. Ideally, you will be totally familiar with all of the financial details of your business, and will be able to answer — line-by-line — how you arrived at each figure.

If raising venture capital is the primary purpose of your plan, you can readily understand its importance to you. Treat it accordingly. It **must** be well organized, easy to read, sound, logical and factual. Investors must see the direct relationship between **future growth** and past **knowledge** and **experience.** The "blossoms" of tomorrow will be the natural fulfillment of the "seeds" you plant today.

Your business plan should not be treated as a sacred cow. You will probably discover its need for fine-tuning at brief intervals at first. And, certainly, if your initial requests for capital are rejected, you should take another look at it. The idea is to make this document serve **your** needs.

If you have done your homework and the result is an idea that has merit beyond the "better mousetrap" stage, there is a good chance that someone or some group will want to support you financially. Once you sell your idea, it will be up to you to plan well for growth.

OPERATIONAL PLANNING

As you consider the time and energy that must go into the process of planning, remember the old adage: "businesses don't plan to fail, they just fail to plan."

Bob Mallory is like a lot of us: he intuitively knows what he wants to accomplish in his county fair concession business. If you ask him, he can tell to the fraction of a cent how much his materials cost and where he is scheduled to sell throughout the summer months. He's an interesting guy to watch because he knows where he is going.

Bob Mallory is different from many of us, though, because he knows how to **plan.** He has been able to translate his intuition into action and results because of good planning.

You already know that the small business owner must do several types of planning; you also know how important it is. There is probably no need to insult your intelligence with more horror stories of lost opportunities, wrecked home lives, and businesses gone bad. You already intuitively know the consequences of poor planning, incomplete planning, and no planning.

How many of us honestly know more than a small handful of people who really know how to plan well? An even smaller number actually are able to follow their plan.

Good intentions are only a part of the formula; the rest is knowing **what** to plan, **when** to plan, and **how** to plan. In this section, you will learn the basics of good planning. If you have the personal discipline, and this chapter adds the information, you will be prepared to PLAN FOR SUCCESS!

What Is Planning, Anyway?

Our definition of planning is simple: **setting objectives** with the specific **time** and **resources neeeded** to hit the objectives. No matter what type of planning you are trying to do, you will need to know this information.

OBJECTIVE = TIME + RESOURCES

(or)

OBJECTIVE = WHEN + HOW + WHO

This 3-part formula is useful because it organizes your thinking. You may know one or two parts, but don't go charging off until you can fill out all the parts.

An **objective** is nothing more than what you want to do. It is different from a goal, which is much more comprehensive; usually, a series of objectives is needed to accomplish a goal. An objective is quite specific, and probably is the "how" of a larger plan. Here's how objectives and goals fit into plans.

Anatomy of a Plan

OBJECTIVE #1 ⎫
OBJECTIVE #2 ⎬ = GOAL
OBJECTIVE #3 ⎭

The **time** element sets a limit on how long you are giving yourself to do the job.

The **resources** you will need to do the job should be spelled out, too. Who is going to do it? Who will follow up? How will you know when the job is completed?

The complete plan, then, includes the following components:

- The **priority** ranking of each action you plan. This is your estimate of how important each action will be toward accomplishing an objective.

- The **action** that you are going to take, usually in verb form. The action structures what you are actually going to "do". Several separate tasks may be required to meet an objective, and each task in your plan should relate specifically to an objective.

- **When** you are going to do it. The closer you can get to a specific, believable date on the calendar, the better.

- **Who** is going to check to see that it is being done and done right? Who is the person responsible for the action?

- The **results** you achieved; your accomplishment in terms of what the action was intended to do. Of course, these entries on your planning worksheet are made at a later date as results are achieved.

- A **comments** section can include other pertinent details such as reasons for delays, how actions or results will affect other people, how results will be measured, etc.

All of these elements have been combined on the following **PLANNING WORKSHEET.** You should make a lot of copies of this worksheet, and use it whenever you want to plan.

PLANNING WORKSHEET

GOAL:

OBJECTIVES: 1.
2.
3.
4.

Priority	Action (Tasks)	Due Date	Responsible Person	Results

Comments

This is what planning is all about; it is NOT a wish list of vague statements like, "My goal is to be rich." The proper way to say it would be: "I want to make a million dollars by my 45th birthday by selling $17,000 worth of merchandise every month. My monthly sales figures will indicate (measure) my progress." Obviously, you don't pull statements like these out of the air or make them up casually. You have to back them up with some good thinking.

What Kinds of Planning Do You Need?

Now that you know what planning is and is not, you can decide how much you're going to have to do in order to be successful. Try to think of your business as a series of different plans that work together; only the very simplest businesses can do everything with one plan.

Let's think about the purposes for these plans. You will probably need a plan to:

- finance your business
- sell your product or service
- achieve your personal financial objectives
- run the day-to-day operations
- get specific customer orders filled
- setting goals for the organization
- establishing work methods
- budgeting
- establishing vacation schedule
- forecasting production
- etc.

You probably notice that these plans cover different amounts of time. Plans are referred to as **long-term, mid-term** and **short-term** plans.

LONG TERMS PLANS include your financing plan and your strategic plan, which is simply the outline of how you want your business to develop and grow. When the financing plan and the strategic plan are combined, they may also be called a business plan. These plans cover three to five years. One or all of these will usually be required by a banker or other source of money. The reason they want it is simple — they want to make a long-term commitment to you, and they won't feel comfortable doing that unless they can see into your crystal ball and see your best estimate as to what is going to happen down the road. You'll probably do only one or two of these, and you should check to see how you're progressing every six months or so.

MID-TERM PLANS are made up of your "big" objectives. Entrepreneurs are usually very good at this level, i.e. launching new products, opening up new sales territories, building a strong team of employees. Mid-term plans run from one to three years, and are reviewed every month or so.

SHORT-TERM PLANS are the operational, day-to-day plans. These are the plans that get the work out, the orders filled, and the deliveries made on time. Entrepreneurs are usually exceptionally good at this level because we are so resourceful; however, it is easy to get caught up or distracted by these short-term concerns, and we have to work hard to occasionally look up from the grindstone long enough to take a directional bearing on the horizon. In other words, it's fine to stick to the knitting, but don't forget that you have to buy yarn in advance and plan your product line to match the selling seasons. Short-term plans should be reviewed daily or weekly, depending upon your production schedule.

As a bare minimum, you should probably have a version of the following plans that achieve the following purposes:

Financing Plan: How much money will you need? Where are you going to get it? When will you need it?

Marketing Plan: How will you sell your product or service? Who will do it?

Distribution Plan: How will you get your product or service to your customers? What limitations do you have to take into consideration?

Production Plan: How will you do or make what you sell? Who will be responsible for keeping it on track?

Beyond these plans you may need various operational plans that keep your place running smoothly. Planning will help you work things out on paper first, and enable you to set up procedures or systems to handle those things that are routine for your business. Those really smart guys who do a lot of planning say that about 85% of your business can be predicted and anticipated; therefore, you can have a plan in place to deal with it. The remaining 15% are the crises, the things you just have to address personally. Because most of your business is running itself instead of running you, you have the time you need to give the proper amount of attention to the things that matter.

Preparing a Plan Step-By-Step

Now that you know the basics, let's apply them in a hypothetical situation. You are the president of a recently formed corporation. You are one of three principal officers and you have two other employees. Your company sells an exciting, mysterious product called a "unit." But, alas, sales during the first four months of your existence are lagging behind the projections of your business plan. Something must be done to correct this situation!

You call a meeting of your officers for a brainstorming session. "Friends," you begin, "we have a problem. Sales are not what they should be. And unless we show a big improvement soon, we're going to start digging our grave. I figure we need to sell 400 units by the end of the fiscal year..."

"Simple," someone interrupts. "All we have to do is drop our price and they'll sell like hotcakes."

"It's really not that simple," you reply. "Dropping our price would undoubtedly increase our sales, but that's only half the picture. Sales won't do us much good unless they generate profit. And since our price is below our competition, I figure we can raise our profit margin one way or the other without hurting ourselves in the marketplace. Now, are there any other suggestions?"

You write them down as they are voiced. "Buy more advertising"..."Hire a salesman"..."Pay an incentive bonus on each sale"..."Renegotiate our unit cost with our supplier"... "Each of us could spend more time selling and less time in administration"..."Concentrate on more telephone selling"... "Take on another product line". All good ideas, and worthy of consideration.

"One thing we're all forgetting," you say. "What if we have that increase in sales volume? Could our storage room handle it? It would be absolutely necessary to expand our storage capability."

After a lengthy discussion, you cross off some of the less desirable ideas. Then you note that some of the remaining ideas represent **what** you want to accomplish, while others represent **how** they could be accomplished.

Before you resolve that issue, you say, "Let's all agree that we have one major goal, and that is to sell 400 units at, say, a 35% profit margin by the end of our first year." All agree.

"Now," you add, "let's sift through our thinking until we develop a list of **what** we must do to reach our goal. We'll call those our **objectives**."

You take out a Planning Worksheet and fill out the top part as follows:

<u>**PLANNING WORKSHEET**</u>

GOAL: *Sell 400 units at 35% profit margin by end of year*

OBJECTIVES:
1. *Hire and Train one additional salesperson*
2. *Increase profit margin by 5%*
3. *Expand storage capacity 50%*
4. *Secure 500 additional sales leads by Jan 3*

You note that your first objective is to hire and train one additional salesperson. But three separate actions are required to accomplish that objective:

1. "Help Wanted" ads must be placed.

2. A screening process must take place in order to arrive at the most desirable new employee.

3. The new salesperson must be trained.

You continue with your list of each action necessary until your list looks like this:

Priority	Action (Tasks)	Due Date	Responsible Person	Results
	Place "Help Wanted" ads Screen and hire salesperson Conduct training program Study feasibility of price increase Renegotiate unit cost with Supplier Add shelving to store room Revise and increase ad budget Order advertising space			

"Now, I want to schedule all of these tasks as realistically as possible and to coordinate our activity logically," you say. "We should be aware of how much time is required for each task, especially for things like training and advertising lead time. So I'll write in a number in front of each task to show the sequence in which they should begin. Naturally, some actions can run concurrently with others. Then I'll be able to fill out the date by which each task should be accomplished."

You show the group how your Worksheet looks at this point:

Priority	Action (Tasks)	Due Date	Responsible Person	Results
	1. Place "Help Wanted" ads	9-24		
	2. Screen and hire salesperson	10-15		
	3. Conduct training program	11-30		
	2. Study feasibility of price increase	10-3		
	3. Renegotiate unit cost with supplier	11-1		
	4. Add shelving to store room	12-1		
	1. Revise and increase ad budget	9-24		
	2. Order advertising space	10-15		

You still have the floor. "I'm going to place someone in charge of each task, according to your usual responsibilities. If we all pull together as a team, I'm sure we can reach or surpass our common goal. And don't kid yourselves; each task is vitally important. We can't afford to find any piece of the pie missing in December.

"My final step in developing this total plan is to put a priority number on each task. The figure "1" is a top priority, and "3" is lowest. I realize these numbers are a judgement call on my part, but I have an idea up my sleeve that will make these little numbers very important to you.

"If a number one priority is accomplished on time and to my complete satisfaction, the person in charge of that task will receive a $300 bonus. Number two priorities will receive $200. And number three will receive $100. Agreed?"

You dash to the copy machine and pass a copy of your worksheet around. It looks like this:

GOAL: Sell 400 units at 35% profit margin by end of year

OBJECTIVES:
1. Hire and train one additional salesperson
2. Increase profit margin 5%
3. Expand storage capacity 50%
4. Secure 500 additional sales leads by Jan. 3

Priority	Action (Tasks)	Due Date	Responsible Person	Results
2	1. Place "Help Wanted" ads	9-24	Bill H.	
1	2. Screen and hire salesperson	10-15	George M.	
1	3. Conduct Training program	11-30	George M.	
2	2. Study feasibility of price increase.	10-3	Mary J.	
1	3. Renegotiate unit cost with Supplier	11-1	George M.	
3	4. Add shelving to store room	12-1	Hank P.	
1	1. Revise and increase ad budget	9-24	Bill H.	
2	2. Order advertising space	10-15	Bill H.	

The Planning Worksheet proved to be an ideal working document for this small company. Everyone knew exactly what was expected of him; everyone had a sense of teamwork; and the goal was beautifully accomplished. But not without the usual roadblocks and unplanned occurrences. Adjustments had to be made, but they were made with wisdom and fairness to all.

By the end of the fiscal year, March 31, the final version of the Planning Worksheet looked like this:

GOAL: Sell 400 units at 35% profit margin by end of year

OBJECTIVES: 1. Hire and train one additional salesperson
2. Increase profit margin 5%
3. Expand storage capacity 50%
4. Secure 500 additional sales leads by Jan 3

Priority	Action (Tasks)	Due Date	Responsible Person	Results
2	1. Place "Help Wanted" ads	9-24	Bill H.	Two ads placed; 27 applicants
1	2. Screen and hire salesperson	10-15	George M.	Gail B. hired 10-10
1	3. Conduct training program	11-30	George M.	Training completed on time
2	2. Study feasibility of price increase	10-3	Mary J.	Feas. study positive. Report delayed 2 wks. See comments.
1	3. Renegotiate unit cost with supplier	11-1	George M.	Completed 11-1. Need 200 more units for 5% price break
3	4. Add shelving to store room	12-1	Hank P.	Completed 11-24. Capacity up 60%
1	1. Revise and increase ad budget	9-24	Bill H.	Revisions approved 9-22
2	2. Order advertising space	10-15	Bill H.	Delayed until 10-22 due to art lost in mail.

Comments	Mary J. hospitalized 9-24. Function assumed by Bill H. Three suppliers interviewed re price. No deal. Ads produced 623 leads. Turned over to Gail. Sold 421 units!

Before closing the book on our foregoing example, there were several other important planning considerations:

1. **Consider the Constraints.** What limitations do you have to take into account? What resources do you have, including money, people, time, equipment, etc.? What potential problems are you likely to encounter?

2. **Develop a Back-Up Plan.** If the worst happens and your plan falls apart, what will you do? In a particularly important scheduling situation, you may want to actually have two back-up plans.

3. **Establish Control Points.** You must be able to tell how your plan is progressing, and you need to be sensitive to changes in direction. Your control points can be people, written reports, sales ledger, bank account or charts.

4. **Chart Your Plan.** Although the Planning Worksheet is an ideal planning guide, it does not serve the function of a work flow chart. Good planning deserves good follow-up, made possible by a chart like this:

	First Week	Second Week	Third Week	Fourth Week	Fifth Week
ACTIVITY					

SUMMARY

You know planning is important; now you know how to do it and when to do it. If you keep the following guidelines in mind, you will be able to PLAN FOR SUCCESS.

GUIDELINES FOR SUCCESSFUL PLANNING

1. PLANNING IS A PROBLEM-SOLVING PROCESS.

2. PLAN MUST BE FLEXIBLE, AS SITUATIONS CHANGE.

3. PLANS MUST REFLECT REALITY.

4. PLANS SHOULD REFLECT THE SKILLS AND KNOWLEDGE OF THE IMPLEMENTORS.

5. PLANS SHOULD STATE SPECIFIC WAYS TO ACHIEVE THEM.

6. PLANS MUST BE COMMUNICATED TO PERSONS AFFECTED.

Chapter 19

Pitfalls and helpful hints

Every cloud has a silver lining

We considered calling this chapter "Challenges and Opportunities" — for fear "Pitfalls" might be too foreboding. But, let's face it. There **are** some pitfalls out there. But don't think they're going to sneak up on you like Murphy's Law.

Pitfalls are only something to worry about **if you don't know where they are**. Once you know where they are, you just step around them. By itself, a pitfall is harmless.

This chapter is our way of saying, "Be careful out there." We think you're ready to face the challenge of entrepreneurship. If you have studied the previous chapters, you have the knowledge you need to work toward your goals.

"Pitfalls are problems and traps to watch for. Recognize them when you see them. Once identified, they become challenges, or opportunities, or just passing nuisances.

This chapter is about keeping both a mental and physical checklist of potential pitfalls, how to recognize them, and how to avoid them — or make the most of them. Most of the pitfalls are clearly marked. Just look for the signs.

Because most newcomers in the business world fail (NOT YOU, though), we want you to read this chapter several times. Then, read it again six months from now. Then, again one year from now. The idea behind this, of course, is to know those danger signs so well that you will be able to see them miles ahead.

PITFALL NO. 1: GIVING UP TOO SOON

Many would-be entrepreneurs become casualties during the first year of business, leaving a legacy of "No Forwarding Address" and "Has Been Disconnected". Quite often, they self-destruct prematurely. They gave up too soon.

Some of the reasons for throwing in the towel include:

1. It's harder work than they expected.

2. The sacrifices are too great.

3. They're not making enough money.

4. They can't take the "ups and downs" of cash flow.

5. Fear of failure.

6. Impatience.

These can all seem like very real and understandable reasons for becoming discouraged. But ask yourself: "How real is this situation?" Too often the entrepreneur will panic without reason. He or she imagines the situation to be worse than it really is or fails to realize that it may be just a temporary condition.

If you analyze your concerns and decide the situation is probably only temporary, all you need to do is adjust your mental attitude, relax, stick to you plan, and hang in there.

However, if you find these are legitimate concerns requiring attention, you'll need to analyze "what's wrong, and why?"

For example, let's analyze the six reasons we identified above:

1. **It's harder work than you expected.** If you start to experience fatigue and/or "burnout" during the first few months of operation, the first thing to do is give your feeling a reference point. Ask yourself, "Harder than what?" Think back to when you were working for someone else. Did you sometimes feel the same way then? Is this

really worse? How about the satisfaction of working for yourself instead of someone else?

Also, examine your original expectations. What did you expect? Were you too optimistic in your expectations?

Project your situation down the road, one year, two years, three years. Do you still see yourself working this hard? Or do you see yourself leveling off, getting over the start-up efforts, and delegating work to others.

Finally, ask yourself how you might improve the situation with better planning, better organization and better time management. You might be surprised how just a better use of your time can result in shorter hours and/or less work for you.

2. **The sacrifices are too great.** This is a lot like Number 1. You want to start with a reference point and compare your situation now with what it was before. If you feel you've given up something, what might you have also gained in the process? What about over the long-haul? Won't there eventually be more advantages, more to show for your efforts than in an alternative situation? (When you read the next chapter, you will get a better idea of those rewards.) And what of the sacrifices you make in working for someone else? Sometimes when we cross over the fence, the grass looks greener back on the other side in an amazingly short time. A popular song asked the question, "Was it all so simple then?...Or has time rewritten every line?"

3. **You're in business to make a profit.** Unless you're already independently wealthy, no profit...no business. Not making enough money can be the most "real" concern of all.

Of course, you must consider your start-up costs and the initial slow period of establishing customers, of getting your business "up to speed". Still, if your year-end cost projections have you checking the "Help Wanted" ads, the situation is serious.

A business that is not making enough money is usually in one of two general situations: 1) Business is good but profits are too low. 2) Profits are potentially good but business is too slow.

When business is good but profits are too low, it's usually due to one or more of these causes:

a. You've priced your product or service too low.

b. Your overhead or cost of doing business is too high.

Review Chapter 3, "Forecasting Sales & Budget Planning", and other chapters in this manual to be sure you're set up properly to insure maximum profits.

If profits look good but business is slow, there is always a remedy. Don't make the mistake of looking for excuses. ("The economy is down." "Our major industry is on strike." Etc.) Only losers hang their hats on excuses.

Instead, look for ways to get a bigger share of the market. Spend some money on a better advertising program. Try something different! How about publicity? There must be a million new ideas waiting to hatch. Put in some new inventory. A new sign. New decorations. A special sale. A contest. Do the opposite of what your competitors do. Fortunes are made when everyone's singing the blues.

If after convincing yourself that you're doing everything "according to the book", after consulting your accountant or financial advisor, you feel you're tapping your potential to produce income, you may have to examine your lifestyle goals. It may well be that you'll need to make a choice between making a more modest income, selecting a more profitable business, or going to work for someone else. But it is rare that the creative, aggressive entrepreneur cannot figure out a way to "make more money". The typical entrepreneur simply looks at the situation as one more challenge, an opportunity to apply his ingenuity.

4. You can't take the ups and downs of cash flow. This is probably the most common reason of all for small businessmen to "chuck it all" and head for a salaried job with regular pay days. Knowing where your next dollar is coming from can be a welcome relief when you're struggling through a cash-less slump.

A cash flow problem isn't really a lack of income. It's just a lack of regularity, coupled with insecurity. The ups and downs of cash flow in some businesses is especially uncomfortable to the entrepreneur who is used to planning his spending and living expenses around regular pay days. Adjusting to a different system of money management requires proper planning, budgeting and discipline.

If you experience cash flow problems, chances are you can correct the situation by applying the principles outlined in Chapter 3, "Forecasting Sales & Budget Planning".

5. **Fear of failure.** During the crucial first year, the scene often looks like this: marginal financing, sales trickle, tough to pay the bills, a supplier is late with a crucial order, Suzie needs braces, a customer threatens to sue, not much sleep, worry, woe, trouble. They forget to look at the bright spot just over the hill. Instead, they look only at today's bleakness and fear sets in. Fear paralyzes. They lose sight of day-to-day operations. They think they're failing, so they do.

6. **Impatience.** This is an emotional reaction which afflicts many first-year entrepreneurs. It has nothing to do with financial strengths, the readiness for expansion, or any of the rational decisions an owner makes. He simply wants (or needs) to succeed. Fast. Today. But he looks at the realities of where he is now in comparison with where he wants to be, and he becomes discouraged, restless, and too soon...defeated. Like a deflated balloon, he drops out.

The important message here is that many of the reasons for "giving up" can be imagined "ghosts in the closet" — not real at all — or simply temporary problems you can work out. Small business ownership isn't for everyone. But if you think it's what you want, give yourself a good chance to succeed — even when the going gets tough.

When you're getting close to Pitfall No. 1, "Giving Up Before You Get Started", there are some signs to look for. They're all related to your feelings and mental attitude. Look for: Anxiety, Fatigue, Frustration, Impatience...and sometimes Fear bordering on Panic. And sometimes it's just a general feeling of not being happy with the way things are going.

Listen to your feelings, admit there is a problem, see it for what it is, and look for ways to solve it. Step around Pitfall No. 1...and keep going.

HELPFUL HINTS:

1. **Talk to successful entrepreneurs.** Share your feelings, They've been through it all...they can probably help you over the hump.

2. **Share your concerns with family and trusted friends.** Just talking about your fears sometimes helps put them in perspective.

3. **See the big picture.** Don't get so bogged down in details that you neglect the important business functions. Recognize that too much attention to busy-work details is often an escape mechanism.

4. **Stay healthy.** Avoid traps such as heavy drinking, overeating, or having an affair. Escape mechanisms just take time and energy away from digging out the root of the problem. Schedule time for play and exercise, preferably **non-competitive** sports.

5. **Relax and refresh yourself.** A long walk, a hot bath, a good book...can do wonders toward reducing stress, helping you unwind and refreshing your mental outlook.

PITFALL NO. 2: THE WRONG BUSINESS

In Chapter 1, we told you how important it is to select the right business. Important because if you're good at your chosen business and enjoy it, you're more likely to succeed.

Probably nothing is more devastating than to suddenly fear you've chosen the wrong business. And there are some definite signs.

You may have chosen the wrong business when:

1. You're not happy doing what you're doing.

2. You're struggling to be proficient. (You're in over your head.)

3. You discover hidden problems and liabilities that may threaten the success of your business (you've been "taken").

Choosing the wrong business is probably the worst pitfall of all, because it's the most difficult trap from which to escape. Most other problems can be solved and corrected while you stay in business and move on. But discovering you're in the wrong business usually means going back to Square One and starting over again.. Hopefully, with careful study of Chapter 1 and this chapter, you will

recognize the signs before you choose a business. Nevertheless, the sooner you recognize you've made a mistake, the easier it is for you to correct.

Let's look at the signs:

1. **You're not happy doing what you're doing.** Don't confuse this with having **problems,** like the ones we talked about in the first part of this chapter. Problems can be corrected. But if you don't enjoy what you're doing at the start, chances are you never will.

The first sign is right there by your bed when you wake up in the morning. The happy entrepreneur is usually up early, eager to get to his work. The unhappy entrepreneur struggles to push himself out of bed, reluctant to face another day.

Another sign is on the job. The happy entrepreneur, even on his worst days, still says, "I like what I'm doing." The unhappy one, even on his best days, says to himself, "This is pure drudgery."

The happy entrepreneur wants to spend every waking moment at his work—and is usually successful because of it. The unhappy one is forever finding excuses and diversions to avoid work.

YOU CAN AVOID THIS PITFALL by following the guidelines of Chapter 1. Be sure you select a business that suits your interests and goals, both personal and professional goals.

2. **You're struggling to be proficient.** In other words, you feel like you're in over your head. You have the feeling your product or service is substandard, or maybe that your productivity isn't what it should be. Both conditions might be correctable. But if you're doing things about as well as you know how and you still have problems, you may be in the wrong business. To put it bluntly, you may be incompetent at your chosen business.

Quite often, the cause of business failure is described as "lack of capital". Very few enterprises that might be made successful actually fail for lack of capital, however. There is usually a bank or friend willing to lend reasonable funds to a potentially successful business.

The overwhelming cause of failure is incompetency which results in a shortage of capital through waste. As capital is wasted, lender confidence is shaken. The incompetent finds it difficult to borrow more.

YOU CAN AVOID THIS PITFALL by following the guidelines of Chapter 1. Be careful to select a business you know something about. It's hard enough just being on your own. If, on top of everything else, you don't know much about the business you're operating, you are courting disaster.

3. **You discover hidden problems and liabilities.** In other words, you've been "taken". This can happen to even the smartest and shrewdest of entrepreneurs. Unfortunately, the world is full of swindlers and dishonest businessmen. Even reputable franchises or chain operations often, supposedly, "color the truth" by hiding some important information or painting a rosy picture to a trusting buyer.

Problems like financial liabilities, personal injury or liability suits, faulty equipment, incompetent employees, a "dying" neighborhood or a declining market are just some of the "hidden" conditions that can cripple or even kill an otherwise promising business.

YOU CAN AVOID THIS PITFALL by following the guidelines of Chapter 1. Above all, enlist the help of professionals before you go into or buy a business. A lawyer, CPA, marketing consultant, successful entrepreneurs, your banker...all can help you avoid this deadly pitfall.

HELPFUL HINTS:

1. **Study the business you're considering.** Spend some time around it. Get involved, perhaps on a part-time basis. Be sure you're going to like it.

2. If you insist on buying or starting a business you know little about, **hire competent people who know the business —** and use them; learn from them.

3. **Have the former owner sign an agreement not to compete.** That way he can't change his mind next year and go back into business again as your competitor.

4. **Above all, take your time.** Beat the bushes and shake the trees, but don't be in a hurry to pick up the first deal that falls to the ground. Buying a business will be one of the most important capital commitments of your life. Take the time to investigate everything thoroughly. Don't be pressured into making a quick decision for fear of missing an opportunity. There will always be another one.

PITFALL NO. 3: THE WRONG PEOPLE

As you progressed through the chapters of this manual, one message should have come across loud and clear: You can't do it all alone. Even if you are a one-man superstar of your chosen career, you need the help of others to succeed. Even entertainers and athletes need a good agent, a good coach, and back-up help.

In the first chapter we stressed the need for good professionals, such as attorneys, CPAs and bankers, in getting off to the right start. In later chapters you saw the important roles these people and others — advertising people, consultants, and your own employees — will have in helping you succeed. Because people play such a vital role in your success, choosing the wrong ones is a pitfall to beware.

How do you choose the right people? Generally, the same way in which you choose a business...carefully, and with certain criteria in mind.

Choosing Business Professionals

Just as you'll stand a better chance of succeeding in a business you know something about, the professionals who help you will do a better job if they know something about your business. Many a business has gone wrong because a CPA advised the wrong structure, or an attorney approved the wrong deal, or an advertising agency launched the wrong marketing campaign.

These professionals, as well as other consultants, have their specialized areas. Either by choice, or by the clients they deal with, they are familiar with certain types of businesses and unfamiliar with others.

So don't select an attorney, an accountant or an advertising agent just because he or she is a friend, a neighbor, or comes highly recommended by someone in a totally different kind of business. Check their present and past clientele. Ask for references, and check them out. And if you think you've made a wrong choice, be quick to correct the situation.

Choosing Employees

From your key "right-hand-man" manager down to an entry level clerk-typist, the right employees can affect productivity, efficiency, image, and sometimes the success or failure of the business.

When people are behind the scenes, that is, not in contact with your customers, your main concern is their ability to do the job. On the other hand, when it comes to people who will be meeting your customers, your concern is not only what they do, but also how they do it. Appearance, personality, temperament, and so on all come into play; and these people must be chosen with special care.

In addition to our Chapter 17, "Personnel Management", there are many books written about the hiring/firing and management of employees. It would be worth your time to study techniques of writing an effective ad, screening applications and resumes, and conducting meaningful interviews. This chapter will not cover the subject again, but let's review some key guidelines:

1. **Write a job description.** Spell out exactly what the primary function of the job is, plus all the duties and responsibilities expected of the person filling the position.

2. **Be prepared with a list of questions** that will probe the qualifications of the applicant. The more you can find out about your applicants, the easier it will be to compare candidates against one another.

3. **Verify information.** Anyone can fake a resume or lie during an interview. Check to see that the applicant really has done and can do what he or she says. Verify places of employment, reasons for leaving prior jobs, and education.

4. **Check personal references.** Not just the ones the applicant supplies. Ask former employers and peers of the applicant about personality traits. One of the most common mistakes in hiring people is to hire just on functional skills alone, then finding out later that the person is dishonest, can't get along with others, or has peculiar habits that "turn off" fellow employees and/or customers.

5. **Solicit the opinions of others.** If possible, have present employees visit with the applicant. They can often learn or observe things you miss and can sense how well the applicant would fit in with the group.

Don't take the attitude that you can find the right employees by trial and error, hiring and firing until you get the right ones. Besides not being fair to the hired-and-fired, it's a waste of both time and money. (Besides the expense of attracting applicants, you'll also have unemployment contributions to pay.) In addition, the "revolving door" policy can have a disturbing and disruptive effect on both employees and customers.

Choosing Business Partners

Partnerships have about the same mortality rate as marriages, and for many of the same reasons. At first, everything is love and kisses. Partners boost one another's morale and reinforce each other's excitement. They have their first argument, discover traits or hostilities previously hidden, and the honeymoon is over. From then on, it's all downhill.

There isn't a "sure-fire" way to choose a business partner any more than there is to choose a marriage partner. Both decisions should be approached with the same care.

In fact, when it comes to **two-man** partnerships, our best advice is: don't. No matter how compatible you are, eventually there will be a difference of opinion. When you're 50-50, there's no way to reach a consensus. Better to have three or more, preferably an odd number.

In any partnership, be sure to have a written buy-sell agreement. It will eliminate future bickering and lawsuits. Without a prior agreement, should a partner withdraw or die, how do you determine the value of the partner's interest and the terms by which his or her interest is to be paid?

Tips for Choosing Partners

1. Choose a partner who supplies a needed strength you are lacking. Don't just duplicate strengths you already have.

2. Be sure you share similar ideas about business goals and methods of running the business.

3. Stay away from partners who want to run the whole show, or who lack respect for your abilities. What you're after is teamwork and compatibility.

4. Watch out for partners who have personal debts or life style expenses that might put an excessive drain on company funds. Company "draws" and high-roller expense accounts can deplete needed cash.

5. Watch out for partners whose life style, morality and attitudes are markedly different from yours.

PITFALL NO. 4: THE ACTIVITY TRAP

If you find yourself saying, "I'm always busy — but I can't seem to get anything done"...you've probably fallen into The Activity Trap. In other words, you're spending too much time doing "busy work" and not getting the essential work done. The result can be lost business, lost profits — in a nutshell, operating in a manner that's not efficient or cost-effective. People who go into business for the first time often fall into the Activity Trap by getting "too organized" — that is, they create complex and cumbersome record keeping systems, files of things they don't need, and get all caught up in extraneous things like choosing wallpaper for the office, or clerical work that could be delegated to someone else.

If the important things don't seem to be getting done, if you find yourself drowning in a sea of paperwork, if you find yourself working long hours with not enough accomplished to show for it — you may be in the clutches of the Activity Trap. To stay out of it, list priorities on your "To Do" list and then ask yourself:

Why am I doing this?

Is it necessary?

Is there a better way?

Why am I doing this? This is really a double-edged question depending on where you put the accent. If you ask "why am I doing this", the question suggests that perhaps someone else should be doing it. If the question is "why am I **doing** this", it suggests that perhaps what you're doing either isn't necessary or it could be done later.

Be aware of when **you** should be doing a task and when you should be delegating it to someone else. Remember that your job is to manage the business, and anything that isn't contributing toward your business goals is an inappropriate use of your time.

Is it necessary? Watch out for the time wasters — those activities that gobble up your days and leave you with little or nothing to show for them. A meeting that could have been handled with a phone call. A trip across town that could have been handled by mail. A lengthy memo that everyone could do without. These are all examples of time wasters to watch out for. A good "To Do" list, with carefully assigned priorities, can do much toward keeping away the time wasters and keeping you off the treadmill.

Is there a better way? There usually is. "Finding a better way" has made inventors famous, entrepreneurs rich, and companies leaders in their industry. Chances are, when you hear yourself saying "there must be a better way", there probably is, if you think about it. Perhaps a better system, a short cut, or the use of a machine or computer can handle the task in less time. Apply your ingenuity to find better ways of doing things at every opportunity.

HELPFUL HINT: Keep a diary of your time for a week or more, including both business and non-business time. Itemize anything that takes 15 minutes or more. At the end of your sample period, analyze your diary. You may be surprised to see how much time you spend on trivial matters, and how little time is actually spent productively.

If you want to eliminate wasted time, set a reasonable goal of **productive time** daily, then check yourself via the diary routine. Leave adequate time for meals, travel, breaks or other regular non-productive necessities. And remember, your objective is to eliminate waste, not drive yourself into a heart attack.

PITFALL NO. 5: THE MONEY DRAIN

In Chapter 3 you learned the wisdom of realistic sales forecasting and budget planning. Proper forecasting and budgeting will go a long way toward conserving and using your money in a sensible way.

But money can easily "disappear" in seemingly strange and mysterious ways. And pretty soon you're asking, "Where has all the money gone?"

There are three major ways your money can disappear:

1. People can steal it from you.

2. You can "steal" it from yourself.

3. You can overextend your resources.

People can steal your money. Embezzlers and "under-the-table" kickbacks are a fact of life in business. A clever, dishonest employee can rob you of many thousands of dollars without your even suspecting, especially if that person has total responsibility and control of the books **and** the money. For this reason, it's a good idea to split the responsibility for this area between two or more people. Second, regularly check the books yourself. If something "doesn't smell right"...check it out.

You might be stealing from yourself. One of the great temptations for new business owners is to spend money like crazy on anything that can be "written off" - new cars, expensive equipment, entertainment, travel, new furniture. Pretty soon they've just about written off their bank account and find they have a serious cash flow problem: not enough money to pay their bills. Remember that your first year or two are the toughest from a financial standpoint. You need all the cash reserve you can hang on to. So wait awhile before you start living in the manner to which you would like to become accustomed.

Over-extending your resources is another way to drain your available money and cause cash flow problems. The most common way businesses over-extend resources is by expanding too soon, i.e., moving to a bigger office, adding on, remodeling, etc. Too often this kind of expansion is premature. The business owners think, "Hey, things are going great." Business is booming. We can afford a bigger building, more employees, new equipment." And before long, our optimistic business owners have doubled or tripled their overhead. Later, when business falls off or doesn't meet the forecast, the overhead becomes too heavy a financial burden.

Resist the temptation to expand to meet only anticipated sales or growth. You may be riding a peak, but you'll need cash reserves for the valley. Seek advice from your banker and your accountant before committing yourself to a substantially higher overhead.

Tips for avoiding the Money Drain:

1. Keep an eye on your cash, your books, and the people who handle both.

2. Use moderation when it comes to credit cards, charge accounts, and "write-off" expenses.

3. Keep your salary (and those of partners) to a minimum, especially during the first year or two.

4. Put off expansion and additional overhead until you've established a good track record and a strong financial base.

5. Plan for "the-worst-has-happened" contingencies.

6. When your urge to expand is overwhelming and your business is in full bloom, look at all the external factors which

affect your business: market trends, general economy, population shifts, demographics, competitors, new products, etc.

PITFALL NO. 6: EMPLOYEE PROBLEMS

Employees will always play a role in the success or failure of your business. Good ones can help you. Bad ones can hurt you. As an employer, you need to recognize which is which, hopefully before you hire them, but certainly when they're on the job.

Earlier in this chapter, we talked about proper hiring techniques. But once the hiring is done, how do you hang on to the good employees? And how do you weed out the bad ones?

In Chapter 17 you learned the important techniques of motivating and managing people. By putting those principles into practice, you can avoid most people problems. Still, you need to watch for the signs when people problems might be hurting your business.

The following are some of the danger signs to look for in the employee ranks:

1. **Disgruntled employees.** An unhappy, sour employee can turn away customers and upset the morale of other employees. Either way, you're the loser. When someone looks disgruntled, find out why. If you can't satisfy the employee, suggest that he or she find employment elsewhere.

2. **Shrinkage.** Otherwise known as "someone is robbing you blind". This is a two-fold problem. Besides the monetary loss, you have an employee who is disloyal — not on your team. You need to weed out this employee for both reasons.

3. **Bottlenecks.** Someone's holding up progress. There can be many reasons for a bottleneck including just plain overload of work. But it may be a case of the Peter Principle: the employee has been promoted beyond his or her competency. Or it may be personal problems at home. Whatever the cause, a bottleneck is your problem and it must be addressed right away.

4. **Turnover.** If your office or company seems to be a revolving door for employees, you've got real problems. Whether it's your idea or theirs, frequent exiting of employees is expensive, non-productive and, usually, a sign of poor management. Why are they leaving? Are you an unreasonable boss? Is the pay too low? Are conditions intolerable? Is there a lack of purpose, incentive or direction? Get to the heart of the problem and correct it.

Whether it's you and one assistant or a staff of hundreds, employees **are** a valuable resource. Learn to be a good boss and a good manager. Cultivate effective leadership techniques in those that have charge of others. Build a team of loyal and productive people who will help build your business and keep it successful.

Tips for building a loyal team of employees:

1. **Recognize the sour apples** before they spoil the rest of the barrel.

2. **Use leadership instead of a whip.** People will work harder for you and do a better job if they want to than if driven or threatened.

3. **Communicate with them.** You won't know about many problems unless you ask. And listen to what they tell you. You may uncover problems concerning morale, motivation, incentives, working conditions and so on. Then, you can try to correct them.

PITFALL NO. 7: NICE GUYS USUALLY LOSE

There are times when it will pay for you to be unreasonable. The reason is simple: You will often be in the position of adversary.

You will have to engage in hassles and negotiations with employees, suppliers, customers, banks, governmental agencies and competitors. Most such negotiations involve a certain amount of give

and take. That is, each side usually grants a few concessions in order to arrive at a settlement.

You, the small businessman, will be seeking lower wages, less taxes, lower purchase prices, higher sales prices, more advantageous delivery schedules, better bank terms, fewer government restrictions, etc. Your business adversaries will likely be seeking just the opposite.

Most of these conflicts will result in some sort of compromise for both sides. Thus, your aim is to end up as close as possible to what you really want. The key to coming out with the "long end of the stick" is to start from a position of being unreasonable. Ask for a lot more than you're willing to settle for. You'll end up closer to what you want.

Remember, nice guys usually lose. You work hard for your money. Don't let other people con you out of it or jeopardize your ability to stay in business. In money dealings, be aggressive, firm, money-smart. And when you need to be, be unreasonable.

PITFALL NO. 8: BOOKKEEPING & ACCOUNTING FIASCOS

Don't forget that "bookkeeping" and "accounting" are not synonyms.

Bookkeeping is the process of recording details, making entries into journals and ledgers, and making order out of all the invoices, vouchers, checks, receipts, etc.

Accounting is the process of putting it all together. Accounting is a higher level process. It requires more training and background than bookkeeping.

The mistake many businessmen make is confusing bookkeeping with accounting. They will give accounting responsibility to a bookkeeper and end up with a meaningless mess. Or, they'll hire an expensive, highly qualified accountant and expect him to spend his time preparing checks and running the bookkeeping machine. Actually, you need both. If your business is small, you can usually get by with a full-time bookkeeper on the premises and an outside professional accountant coming in periodically for the general ledger work and preparation of financial statements.

Small businessmen also make the mistake of systems overkill. They'll say, "What we need around here is a better system" — and rush to install a complicated barrage of textbook systems: vouchers, journals, subledgers, cost accounting, budgets, etc. — the works. Later, they will find out that: (a) the systems are too complicated for the staff people to implement; or (b) the system is too complicated, period. All they might really need is a simple, basic (and inexpensive) system.

Bookkeeping Hints:

1. **Keep it simple when starting out.** Add systems, people, computers in stages as your business grows.

2. **Use checks instead of cash.** Cancelled checks are your records.

3. **Use credit cards for travel and entertainment.** It's good proof of the amount, time and place for IRS purposes.

4. **Get professional help from an outside accountant.** And do it **before** you set up your bookkeeping and accounting system. Don't take a mixed-up box of receipts and papers to an accountant at the end of the year and expect him to make any sense out of it.

PITFALL NO. 9: INVENTORY OVERKILL

Ever hear of Pareto's Law? Pareto's Law says that within any given group, a few items are important, but most are unimportant.

For example: a small part of the total population owns most of the country's wealth; a small percentage of salesmen create a majority of a company's total sales; and so on.

While the tracking of inventory is necessary, it is, potentially, an area where time can be squandered unnecessarily.

You will find Pareto's Law can be usefully applied to taking inventory. If you analyze your inventory, chances are you will find something like the following:

A. 10% of the items = 60% of the inventory's total value.

B. 30% of the items = 30% of the inventory's total value.

C. 60% of the items = 10% of the inventory's total value.

Now, instead of trying to keep track of every single inventory item, do this:

"A items" - keep track of each individual item.

"B items" - keep track of in total only and count periodically.

"C items" - estimate and count infrequently.

In other words, you keep track of the big ticket items and don't waste your time on the nuts and bolts.

PITFALL NO. 10: QUALITY (NON-) CONTROL

Most companies have a Quality Control department. It might be as sophisticated as a computer-based testing device that measures precision or tolerances to one-millionth of an inch. Or, it may be a little old lady at the end of the production line who gives it her trained eye once-over.

Whatever the degree of sophistication, quality control is an important part of doing business for the following reasons:

1. To avoid returned goods and lost sales.

2. To protect the image and reputation of both the product and the company.

3. To avoid lawsuits and customer liability.

These are all valid reasons for paying attention to the "Q.C." department in your business. In some businesses, restaurants for example, word of an inferior product can spread like wildfire and threaten the very existence of the establishment. Even if you're in a service, if the quality of that service falls off, you may lose overnight the customers it took years to acquire.

Of course, the most serious calamity is a defective product resulting in injury or death. Even with adequate insurance, few companies can survive the financial and mental turmoil that can follow such a tragedy.

You may be tempted to "water down" or compromise your product to cut costs and/or make more profit. But the ultimate cost of such a step may be too high a price to pay.

PITFALL NO. 11: YOUR CHANGING MARKET

Not **all** businesses that fail do so in the first few years. Some become casualties after ten, twenty, thirty years of thriving success. News of these "deaths" usually have people wondering "how did it happen".

More often than not, the reasons can be summed up in one word: **complacency.**

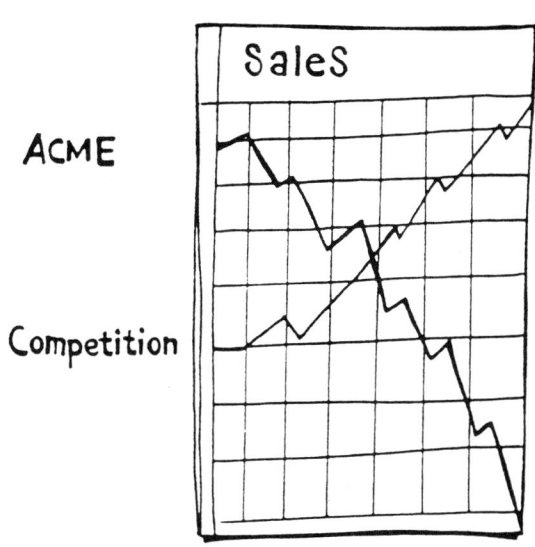

Complacency is a fancy word for becoming too **smug** about success...and assuming it will continue automatically forever. Complacency is what the hare felt when he thought he could afford to take a nap and still finish ahead of the tortoise.

If there is one thing you can count on besides death and taxes, it's change. Customers need change. Buying habits change. The economy, the birth rate, the competition, the mood of the country — all change. Your ability to continue your success, once you've "made it", will depend upon your ability to plan for change, **recognize** it when it's happening, and react to it in positive terms.

Helpful hints for "keeping up" with change:

1. **Have a marketing plan.** You and your marketing professionals should have, at a minimum, a 3-year plan.

2. **Keeping in touch with your customers.** Whether an informal chat or a sophisticated "focus group" study — you need to know your customer wants and needs as they change.

3. **Watch your competition.** Are they taking a bigger market share? Are the "little guys" moving up? Are the big ones pulling away? Find out why and get back in the race. Competition, after all, is what makes life interesting, exciting, and FUN.

4. **Strive for new and better products and services.** If you're standing still, you're probably falling behind. A strong offense is your best defense.

PITFALL NO. 12: NO HELP (SBA TO THE RESCUE)

One of the biggest mistakes you can make is trying to "do it all alone"...especially when the going gets tough. There are times when the best of us must say "HELP" and call for the cavalry...otherwise known as the Small Business Administration.

Your local SBA office is there to help people like you succeed. Toward that end, they can provide you with dozens of pamphlets (most free) filled with sound advice. Everything from "Checklist for Going into Business" to "Handbook of Small Business Finance".

They can also provide you with a list of pamphlets available from the Superintendent of

Documents, Government Printing Office, Washington, D.C. Most of these pamphlets are free.

If you need financial aid, the SBA can help you get a loan and even guarantee up to 90% of it under a special loan program, as we discussed in Chapter 5.

Other SBA programs include:

1. Equal Opportunity Loans and a long list of other special category loans direct from SBA funds.

2. Guaranteed Surety Bonds.

3. Management and technical assistance.

4. Government contract opportunities (they'll get your name on the bidders list).

5. Contacts with consultants and professionals.

6. A variety of courses, conferences, workshops and clinics on the various subjects relating to the successful operation of a small business.

SUMMARY

In this chapter we have pointed out some of the pitfalls that can trip you up along your road to success, and some to watch for after you've "made it".

We're all human; we all make mistakes. No mater how well we learn the principles and guidelines of successful entrepreneurship and good business management, we still end up learning some lessons the hard way.

It is our hope that by pointing out the dangers and the signs to look for you can recognize and avoid the pitfalls. But we have also shown you ways to minimize the damage and solve the problem if, and when, a pitfall "gets you".

Certainly, we don't want you to be frightened or paranoid, imagining monsters around every corner. On the other hand, being a "blind optimist" is inviting trouble. Somewhere in between is the confident yet cautious successful entrepreneur.

Chapter 20

Franchising

How to be in business for yourself, not by yourself.

The business pages of newspapers are full of success stories. All about people who got an idea, got financial backing and started their own enterprises. It's an old story, yet always new and fascinating, especially to people who have decided it's time to stop working for a boss and start working for themselves, taking a chance for independence.

Take caution not to overlook the other stories farther down the page announcing business failures, ie bankruptcies. These people devoted money and effort to create businesses but, for one reason or another, couldn't make a go of it. The news articles hardly ever tell you the real reasons businesses flop–inexperience, lack of knowledge of the market they put themselves in, and lack of understanding basic merchandising principles. It's a sad story, but one you don't have to repeat. There is a way to get the training and continuing guidance that can remove many of the uncertainties of starting and operating a business.

Take the example of John and Mary Samples, a two-income family in their 40s. John was a draftsman, had a pretty good job and had been with his company for fifteen years. Mary was a librarian, worked for the city and had excellent job security. They had two children and an average income. About ten years ago they got the itch, they wanted to start an enterprise of their own.

Neither of these people had the kind of background giving them any specialized know-how for a venture that would provide them a better income or a better life than they already had.

John and Mary had a dream; they talked for years about owning a restaurant. They went to the library and took out a stack of books on small business in general, and restaurants in particular. They discovered a lot of things they never expected pertaining to the pitfalls of running a restaurant. They became aware that restaurant operation was risky–too complicated to give people with their background a good chance at success. It appeared John and Mary were going to

have to look for something that would be more in keeping with their experience.

However, Mary had responded to a magazine ad for a restaurant franchise opportunity. The information they received described a complete franchise program for opening and operating a McDonald's restaurant. It promised continuous direction and support from people who were experts in the field. With that kind of help, it looked more like the opportunity the Samples had been searching for. It answered their questions pertaining to running a business they had never been in and how to make a go of it. Best of all, they discovered the company had a franchise available in their hometown.

They did some research, checked with franchisees and a banker and a lawyer. After a great deal of soul searching they decided to take the plunge. So they invested in their McDonald's franchise, and with the help of some very capable food industry specialists and a lot of hard work, they now have a highly successful restaurant. John and Mary found a business of their own and they had a partner who had as much interest in their success as they did. It turned out to be a winning combination.

Or take the case of Mark Silverstone, a man in his mid-fifties, whose job had been terminated when his employer of 25 years sold the company. Mark and his wife, Emily, decided that it was time they considered a business of their own. They looked into a number of opportunities, but didn't find anything right away that fit in with their experience, money situation or interests.

Then one day they heard about an instant printing franchise that was available. Mark had always been an amateur photographer and Emily had an interest in the graphic arts. It sounded like a possibility. They contacted the Mr. Print company and discovered that the franchise agreement being offered included help in finding a location, outfitting the store, advertising, getting supplies and helping the franchisee establish and operate a print shop.

Without any experience in the printing trade, the Silverstones would have had a hard time making a success of the business. Through the franchise agreement they had all the help they needed to launch and maintain a successful instant print operation. After two years, they're now considering opening a second franchise location.

These are only two examples of the way some people, who have wanted to establish small businesses, have taken advantage of the franchising idea. Franchises enabled the Samples and the Silverstones to set up ventures that wouldn't have made sense for them any other way. It's the course many people have used to get valuable professional help in avoiding the countless traps that are always present in starting and running a business.

This chapter is devoted to explaining the concept of franchising, how it works, what it can do for you, what you should look for in establishing a franchising relationship, how to get financing and where you can find and check out good franchising opportunities.

FRANCHISING-A BIG BUSINESS

There are franchise opportunities in almost every industry: fast foods, motels, automobiles and parts, maid service, business services, dry cleaning, home repair, health clubs, industrial supplies, building products, schools, vending operations - the list is growing every year. Franchising is a business method used by companies that are active in more than 60 different types of business enterprises.

The idea of franchising businesses is not new but its growth in recent years has been outstanding. Government statistics show a tremendous increase in activity in every segment of the franchise economy.

According to a report of the House Government Operations Committee, "The concept of modern franchising, particularly in its evolution since the late 1960s, has opened a remarkable door of opportunity for many of our country's small businessmen and women."

The Commerce Department calls franchising a, "significant part of the U. S. economy ", and reports that franchising, "continues to prove its validity as a marketing method adaptable to an ever-widening array of industries and professions while providing immediate identity and recognition for prospective entrepreneurs joining the system."

FRANCHISING TODAY

In 1988 sales of goods and services through franchises were $640 billion.

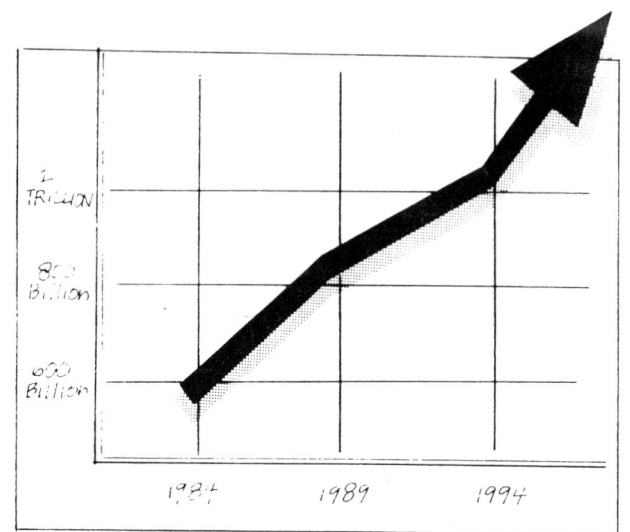

The franchise world has grown more than 35 percent in the past ten years. Sales revenues generated by all franchisors is expected to top $900 billion by the early 1990s. At the current rate of growth, projected sales by 1994 will exceed $1 trillion. That's big business and it's mostly earned by small business people.

The leading association in the field, the International Franchise Association, has more than 700 franchisor members. And they're only part of the growing franchising universe.

In 1988 there were 509,000 franchise outlets in the United States employing 7.3 million people. And, the rate of growth is over 300,000 new employees in franchises every year.

Retail sales generated by franchise establishments already account for more than one-third of all retail sales in the U. S. This proportion may rise to 50 percent near the turn of the century. According to a report by the U. S. Department of Commerce, indications are that, "franchising will be the leading method of doing business in the 1990s."

On an average, a new franchise outlet opens once every 17 minutes around the clock.

WHAT IS FRANCHISING?

A franchise or a franchising operation is a legal agreement between a franchisor - the company offering the franchise, and a franchisee - the party who will own the business.

As a franchisee you use a franchisor's name, special supplies and method of running the business. You pay for the opportunity and operate the way the franchisor tells you. It's your business, but the franchisor controls what you do. The basis of the franchise is an agreement which spells out both the rights and the obligations of you and your franchisor.

The franchisor owns all the trademarks, business methods and supplies that it allows others to use under their contract. The difference between a franchisor and a corporation operating a chain of stores is that the chainstore has store managers who are company employees, whereas the franchise operation is owned and managed by self -employed business people.

The franchisor offers the use of a trade name, a store design, standardized operating methods and a protected territory. In addition the franchisor generally accepts the responsibility of keeping a continuing interest in the business of the franchisee.

The franchisor will usually help in such areas as site location, management training, financing, marketing, promotion, and record keeping. The franchisee, in return, agrees to operate under the conditions specified by the franchisor.

For the help and services provided, the franchisee is usually expected to make a capital investment in the business and to pay fees and royalties to the franchisor. In some cases the franchisee agrees to buy all of his products from the franchisor.

A Practical Partnership

The appeal of franchising for the independent business man or woman is that it is a practical and economic means of fulfilling the franchisee's desire for independence with a minimum of risk and investment and maximum opportunities for success through the use of a proven product or service and a proven marketing method. Franchising is a way to be in business for yourself, not by yourself.

A franchising company depends upon the successful operation of franchise outlets to stay in business and build its profits. It needs individuals who are determined to succeed, are willing to learn the business, and have the energy for hard work. A good franchisor can supply the other basics for successful operation of the business.

KINDS OF FRANCHISES

There are two types of franchise systems:

1. *Product or trade name franchising* is the sales relationship between a supplier and dealer in which the dealer has been given some of the identity of the supplier. Automobile dealerships, gasoline service stations and soft drink bottlers are some examples. As you would guess, they require large amounts of financial investment, frequently in the millions of dollars.

2. The field we're most interested in is called *business format franchising* because it deals with opportunities which are within the reach of millions of Americans. Some business format franchise opportunities require investments as small as a few thousand dollars, and there are many proven franchise businesses that can be started with an initial capital outlay of less than $100,000. Business format franchising accounts for more than 90 percent of the franchise operations in business today.

Business format franchising involves a continuing relationship between the franchisor and its franchisees. That relationship generally involves:

A product or service

A trademark

A marketing system

Location search and assistance in selecting a business site

Lease negotiation

Store design, store development aid and equipment purchasing

Signage

Financial assistance in the establishment of the business

Operating manuals and procedures for standardized procedures and operations

Initial employee and management training, and continuing management counseling training programs

Centralized purchasing with the benefit of cost savings

Advertising and merchandising support .

Advertising counsel and assistance.

Ongoing assistance and guidance from the franchisor.

The greatest attraction of franchising is that it is one opportunity no one has to miss. Even with its impressive growth over the past decade, franchising is a young system of marketing. Thousands of great opportunities still exist for new franchisees.

HOW A FRANCHISE WORKS

In addition to the original idea for the business, the franchisor provides the identity and in many cases, the product which may have taken years and a good deal of money to establish. The franchisor offers a refined and tested operating system developed through years of experience of headquarters specialists and earlier franchisees.

The franchisee is an independent business owner who pays the franchisor for the right to put this recipe for success to use. As a franchisee you provide all or nearly all the working capital to establish and develop the outlet. There is a continuous financial relationship, usually including a fee paid in advance, plus a continuing royalty based on an established percentage of gross revenues.

Ideally, when you purchase a franchise, you are also purchasing a pre-packaged business. Although you own every part of it, you have a partner, your franchisor, who can insist or sometimes merely suggest how you run your business.

As you start searching for the exact franchise business that would meet your requirements, you will notice the large differences among them; the differences in quality of image, polish and approach. Some franchisors will seem aggressive, organized and professional. Others will seem thorough, plodding and simple. Still others may come across as slick, rigid and too anxious to close the deal.

It's important to keep in mind that your franchise decision has three sides: rational, emotional and financial. The following list can help you organize your thoughts, keep the franchise search logical and help you keep from making a costly mistake.

A Respected Identity

The most important thing a franchisor has to offer is a good name in the industry. The worth of a franchise identity is also the result of the recognition, reputation and goodwill of the franchise organization. People who invest in franchises are looking for a successful image. When you take on a franchise, your franchisor's character, in effect, becomes your identity.

The day you open up for business you cease being just an individual and become someone with something special to offer the public; you'll suddenly become Mr. Burger King...Ms. Nutri/ System...or Mr. and Mrs. Dollar Rental.

A Successful Operating System

When you buy a franchise, you are purchasing more than just a trade name; you are also counting on a proven formula for success. So, one of the most important elements of franchising is the simplicity with which the organization's systems and procedures can be transferred to a franchisee.

Some franchisors will offer you a complete "turn-key" outlet; when you are finished with franchise school, you receive the keys to a business in which everything has been set up for a ready-to-run operation. More commonly, a franchisor will provide you with blueprints, manuals, specifications, and training; then it's your responsibility to use your own drive to get the business established.

The franchisor's "how-to" bible is the franchise operating manual. The manual covers everything from accounting procedures to employee supervision. It also spells out standards and policies that all franchisees are expected to follow.

The manual is lent to you for the term of the franchise agreement. When the agreement is ended, you must return the complete manual to the franchisor. This requirement is intended to maintain the condition of secrecy about the franchise system and the know-how it takes to run it. After all, if the formula wasn't a valuable and special secret, why would you pay good money to purchase it?

At the same time, there will be questions that come up as you learn the business and even at times when new situations arise. That's when you'll need continuing help from the franchisee.

Here's what one franchisee has to say:

For Kay Lange, a former data processing consultant, McMaid

proved to be the right decision, bringing her more than $750,000 in annual sales. McMaid appealed to Lange because of its training and franchise services. "Ongoing service support is as important as training. The home office has helped me with everything from bulk purchases of equipment and supplies, to a marketing program. Help is just a phone call away." *

THE FINANCIAL RELATIONSHIP

How does the franchisor receive payment for the franchisee's use of its identity and operating system? It collects a fee from the franchisee. The most usual franchise fee arrangement consists of three parts:

- The initial payment due on signing of the franchise agreement.

- A continuous royalty, usually charged on the gross revenues of the outlet.

- A royalty or contribution to a co-operative advertising fund.

Usually, a new or small franchise will charge a comparatively small fee. On the other hand, the larger the franchise organization, the more you can expect to pay for the privilege of joining.

WHY DO COMPANIES FRANCHISE?

Franchising provides many benefits to commercial organizations. It allows a company to hold on to its own capital and to establish a distribution system in the shortest possible time. It takes a large amount of money and a long while to develop a major distribution system. Using franchises will save time and money for the franchisor. The franchisee finances part of the system through his or her initial franchise fee. At the same time it is easier and faster to sign up independent men and women who will have a financial interest in the success of the business. Also, franchising cuts marketing costs and reduces fixed overhead expenses like personnel administration for the franchisor.

WHY DO PEOPLE FRANCHISE?

For the new entrepreneur, a franchise often makes it easier to go into business because it cuts down on the amount of capital required and provides a sense of security through the experience and help offered by the franchisor. Franchising is one good way for small business operators to avoid problems that can ruin a business.

Everyone who goes into business for him or herself is going after financial independence and security. Those people who are attracted by the franchise idea expect more from life than the day-in day-out grind of wage-earning. They have a high level of ambition and a firm belief that the rewards outweigh the risks.

Another important reason for buying a franchise is the desire to be a winner. We all have the ambition for a positive self-image and a good reputation. Franchisees enjoy the identity of success and, through their national tie-in, the industry importance that goes with the business. Many people buy franchises in the hope that some of their franchisor's successful image will rub off on their small business.

The franchisee is like a middle range executive; not a chief operating officer, but more like a top manager who is qualified to issue orders of his own and relies on the broad objectives and general guidance of a superior.

Even if money may not be the number one consideration in the minds of all franchise owners, it's still high on the list. The franchisee is in the game for financial growth and finally, riches.

WHAT YOU GET

The most powerful reason to buy a franchise is to obtain training and guidance from an experienced insider. Franchisees are more likely than other entrepreneurs to recognize their own limitations. They know it takes a broad range of understanding and skills to develop a successful business. After all, who can lay claim to being an effective chief executive and industry expert, as well as a master advertising director, skilled financial officer and experienced personnel director?

Franchise buyers seek know-how and support in the broader aspects of running a business, especially advertising, accounting and industry practices. Franchising provides a head start in the serious business of starting and running a business.

Lastly, people decide to buy franchises because they perceive the business to be an asset of lasting value. They believe the franchise has more permanence than other businesses, perhaps because a franchise agreement has a defined long term. Most independent businesses are lucky to survive five years. In contrast, the average franchise agreement has a term of ten years, and is almost always renewable.

Tom Fulner "just wanted to make a living" when he bought a PIP printing franchise in 1972. Today, he owns 15 PIP stores in Indianapolis and Nashville with annual sales of more than $4 million.

"My advice to someone starting out in franchising is to go with good franchise company. Check their financial strength. Talk with at least 10 franchisees to see if they are satisfied. That way you can balance the highs and the lows. And once you sign on, utilize the information and system that the company provides to minimize your mistakes. There's no sense reinventing the wheel.

As a franchisee you get certain services for your franchise fee and royalties - equipment, supplies, research and development, legal advice, operations help, and training. You'd be crazy not to take advantage of it.

When I first started out I used to come in an hour or an hour and a half before everyone else in the morning. It was hard to stay away. I was doing what I liked to do. I wouldn't have been there, if I didn't want to do it.

Being a franchisee is a hedge against failure, but it's the individual that makes it go. Take care of the customer. Don't be afraid to work, and don't milk your company. Reinvest in the business. Constantly upgrade equipment and personnel."*

WHAT KIND OF FRANCHISES ARE THERE?

Food

By far the most popular franchise category is restaurants, especially fast food operations. The number of restaurant franchises in the U. S. has grown more than 16 percent since 1986, with a 21 percent increase in total sales. The number of fast food commercials shown on television will give you an idea of the way competition is expanding.   In response fast food outlets and restaurants have been changing the way they do business. A greater emphasis is being placed on customer satisfaction. New or increased services, such as expanded menus, delivery or take-out offerings are becoming more popular.

Convenience Stores

By combining features of grocery stores, restaurants and gas stations, convenience stores answer customer demands for convenience. From 1986 to 1988 the number of convenience stores increased 11percent and sales jumped over 20 percent. As two income families continue to increase the workforce, one-stop shopping convenience and the longer business hours of such stores answer the needs of a growing portion of the population.

General Merchandise

The franchised sale of non-food items such as auto parts, draperies, picture frames and a host of others are also affected by the changing life styles of a growing population. The number of non-food retail outlets increased 16 percent since 1986, and the total sales from this area increased over 23 percent.

Diet Services

Everybody knows about Weight Watchers, but there are numerous other franchisors who offer affordable, popular opportunities in this active market. In diet services alone, the U.S. Department of Commerce reports, franchise sales have grown from $719 million in 1986 to $780 million in 1987 and $868 million in 1988. Industry projections call for sales of more that $975 million, an increase of more than 12% over 1988. Diet franchises are looking at a potential diet base of almost 40 million people according to the National Center for Health Statistics.

The three most popular diet services are Diet Center, Nutri/System and Physicians Weight Loss Centers - one of the fastest growing franchise companies in the United States.

Business Services

A variety of business franchises including accounting services and tax preparation services have experienced growing success in recent years. Since 1986, sales in this area of franchising have increased 27 percent, and the number of business service franchises has increased 20 percent.

Real Estate Services

The number of franchised real estate outlets has increased by 20.7 percent since 1986, and gross commissions from real estate sales have risen 25 percent at the same time.

FRANCHISE OPPORTUNITIES

Employment Services

Since 1986, the number of employment placement service franchises has grown by 23 percent with an increase in revenues of 31.5 percent. At the same time there has been an upswing in demand for temporary employees and for middle-and-upper-management personnel.

Printing/Copying Services

This has been a high-growth area in franchising for several years, and the growth trend is expected to continue. There has been a 30 percent increase since 1986 in the number of printing and copying establishments in this country, with a 32 percent growth in sales.

Automobile/Truck Rental Services

Growth in the automobile/truck rental service area has not been as pronounced in the past two years as it has in the other types of service franchises, with only an 11 percent increase in the number of franchises and a 13 percent increase in sales since 1986.

Construction/Home Improvement Services

Franchised services that include carpet cleaning, sewer and drain cleaning and lawn care are becoming more popular. Within this franchising area, maid service franchises have shown exceptional potential for growth, actually more than a 100 percent increase in revenues during the past two years.

Laundry/Dry Cleaning Services

Although the new textiles and improved home laundry equipment have lowered the demand for laundry and dry cleaning services these establishments continue to thrive. Much of this growth can be traced to expanded service offerings, such as drapery cleaning and alteration services.

Educational Services

This sector includes many different types of specialized franchises. A leader is daycare/early education centers that answer the need of an increasing number of working mothers. The growth trend also includes pre-school and school age educational services that reflect the need felt by many parents for teaching children earlier in life.

Hair Care Services

Both the revenues and the number of hair care franchises have increased by approximately 28 percent. The success of hair care franchises can be traced to the lower prices and quick service they offer.

Leisure and Travel

The amount of money spent in this area increased over 40 percent since 1986. As with other franchises, rising disposable income, greater leisure time especially for retired individuals, and an increase in the number of single member households is responsible for this growth. A weaker U. S. dollar in foreign markets has led to increased domestic travel and greater opportunities for travel agencies in the United States.

Automotive

The auto product/services field has grown 13 percent in the number of establishments and 22 percent in sales since 1986. The expansion of this sector is related to a reduction in the number of gas/ service stations. Services including car washes, muffler and transmission shops, general car care centers and retail tire outlets are becoming increasingly popular. The area that shows the most potential for continued growth is the quick lube and oil change centers, which have increased by almost 90 percent in recent years.

THE VALUE OF EXPERIENCE

Investment in a franchise gains for the new business owner access to important specialized information, which has been developed and organized by people who have already been successful in the business. The franchisor is a source of detailed working information that a new franchisee would find difficult to acquire without spending thousands of dollars and years of effort to acquire.

Franchising sets up a common economic interest between the franchisor and the franchisee, who share risk as well as profit. The franchisor has a built-in interest in helping its franchisee partner.

FUTURE TRENDS

The outlook for franchising depends in large part on the way economic conditions develop as well as continuing acceptance by manufacturers, retailers, service firms and the public.

In recent years, business format franchising has profited by rising incomes and the major entry of women into the labor force. These trends are expected to continue for the immediate future, and the growth in franchising can be expected to remain strong.

Restaurants are expected to remain a leader in the franchise movement. Continued growth also is expected especially for security systems services, automotive maintenance and repair, video equipment and rental stores, travel agencies, home furnishings stores, maid services and home repair services.

In general, franchising has established itself as a marketing idea that offers advantages to both franchisor and franchisee. Prospects seem favorable because an increasing number of firms are finding franchising to be an easy and relatively inexpensive way to expand, and franchisees benefit from their access to the financial and managerial resources of a larger firm. Another consideration is that as a franchisee it's often easier to get loans that are needed to get a business started and keep it running.

Is Franchising Right For You?

Now that you know what a franchise is all about, the big questions are; is franchising right for you, are you right for franchising? Despite all the tempting true success stories about franchising's performance in creating successful small business owners; a franchise is not the ideal method of entrepreneurship for everybody.

Before you spend your money to make the big move, it's especially important to spend some serious thought and time on self-analysis.

Think about it, do the reasons for considering franchising outweigh the advantages of simply making a go of it on your own? You might well come to the conclusion that your personality, abilities and skills place you among the twenty percent of independent business owners who succeed on their own without becoming a franchise owner.

Consider that in a number of ways, the franchisee is not his or her own boss. The franchisor's main interest is to maintain the special conditions and the uniformity of the franchised service he is selling, and to insure that the operations of each outlet will reflect successfully on the organization as a whole.

The franchisor wants to protect and build its good will. So the franchisor generally insists on a large degree of continuing control over the operations of franchisees and requires them to meet the franchisor's special standards. In some cases, franchisees are required to conduct every part of their operation strictly by the book, following every instruction in the franchisor's manual. Desirable or not, to your way of thinking, most franchisees are prepared to follow the franchisor's directions all the way.

What all this means is that the owner of a franchised business must give up some options and freedom of action in business decisions that would be open to the owner of a non-franchised business. When you buy a franchise, you will have to sacrifice some part of your business freedom. The big question is, can you live with the requirements and restrictions of a franchise agreement?

With all of this, as a franchisee, you are still an independent business owner, with the final responsibility for your business' success or failure. Are you willing to accept all the limits to your independence in return for all the benefits you'll receive from a successful franchisor?

Factors to Consider

As you think about whether or not to become a franchisee, you are faced with the necessity of taking on not one, but three types of responsibilities:

1. Financial

The first, of course, is the financial obligation required for the initial fee. Then proceeding with the cost of building and running the business, and giving up a share of the gross revenues. (your royalty cost)

2. Logical

You must be prepared to accept the responsibilities of starting, developing and managing a business with your franchisor. You must be prepared to accept the long hours, the extra effort, the operational headaches, and the burdens of a heavy paper work load.

You must be willing to accept the standards, restrictions, requirements and operating guidelines of your franchisor. You must be prepared to sacrifice some measure of freedom in exchange for the franchisor's ready-to-go business format.

3. Emotional

The emotional commitment is just as important as the financial. Entrepreneurs often have a genuine love/hate relationship with their businesses. It always starts with love. They are enthusiastic about the industry they're in; the product, the image and identity the business provides for them. Eventually, that love may turn to hate when the franchisee realizes the relationship is not working out exactly as planned, and may even turn sour.

As a prospective franchisee, you need to analyze your emotional investment in the business. Think of yourself in the franchise environment. How do you feel about spending a great many of your waking hours there? Will you be proud to call yourself the owner of the business? Does it stimulate pride, enthusiasm, self-esteem? How do you feel about the franchisor and his staff? Do they inspire loyalty, motivation, and confidence? Will you feel comfortable working with your franchisor for the entire term of the agreement?

ARE YOU READY TO MAKE THE COMMITMENTS?

Here are some questions you should be asking yourself before you make any serious moves into franchising.

Financial Questions

With everything you've learned about franchising and the particular franchisor, does the business seem worth the investment?

Considering that most franchisors devote the entire initial fee they collect from a franchisee to setting up the business, do you think the amount they're charging is fair?

How do you *really* feel about paying the franchise royalty every month from your gross revenues?

After deducting your royalty payments, will you still be able to earn a decent profit?

Can you handle the investment?

Logical Questions

What does the franchisor offer that you can't do or accomplish by yourself?

Will the value of the business increase over the years?

Does the franchisor have a solid track record?

Are the franchisor's other franchisees satisfied with their investments?

Emotional Questions

If you had your choice of any business to enter, would this particular franchise be your number one choice?

If you buy the franchise, will you be proud to be its owner?

Do you have a special interest or hobby related to the business?

Are you excited about belonging to this field?

HOW TO RATE A FRANCHISE BEFORE YOU BUY

Once you've decided that a franchise is the best way for you to go, it's time to answer the question that will determine your success or failure in business and may likely have a critical influence on your life for years to come. How can you can tell whether a franchise is worth buying. Since there are thousands of franchises available, there is certainly no quick or easy way to make a decision.

The first thing to decide is the category of business you'll be most interested in, and then to get the necessary information for five to ten franchises in that category.

Most franchisors will send you a package of brochures that contain the information you will need to make an initial decision on which franchises you want to seriously consider. Much of the business data you need for this first step is available from a representative of the franchise through the Uniform Franchise Offering Circular, or UFOC.

Here are some of the factors you' ll definitely want to keep in mind:

Background

Consider the history of the franchise; how it was started, who are the people who started it, who has operated it and what kind of results have they experienced in the past. Obtain additional facts and statistics about the particular industry that include the franchise you're interested in. Your local library can probably supply a great deal of the materials for the information you'll need.

People in your area, who are acquainted with a particular business, can provide another good source. Professional organizations, universities and the local chapter of the American Association of Retired Persons are also good likely sources of background information.

Business Background

Length of experience is one good indicator of the kind of success that can be expected. Consider how many years a company has been in business. How many years has the company been offering franchises? For example, McDonald's has been in business and offering franchises since 1955. No commercial enterprise can stay in business unless it is profitable, so if it has passed the test of time, it's a pretty good bet that it knows how to weather the ups and downs of business conditions.

Look carefully at the franchisor's financial condition. Examine financial documents especially for indications of the company's solidity and credit worthiness.

Number of Franchises

Obviously the more outlets a franchisor has the more acceptance its business program has gained with entrepreneurs and the public. The total size of the business is another indication of how likely it is to be an ongoing operation with the greatest expectation of success.

Minimum Franchise Fee

As always, financial considerations are critical. If you can afford the "price of admission", a more expensive franchise fee is less likely to be a consideration. If your funds are limited, for all practical purposes, you will have to limit your choices to those franchises that will accept a lower entry fee.

Minimum Capital Required

The franchise fee is one thing, the next most important financial consideration is the minimum capital required. This item includes your estimated or the franchisor's required minimum amount of cash and financing needed to begin the franchise operation. For the small investor the less expensive an operation is the more realistic prospect it becomes.

Company-Owned Franchises

Many franchisors also have company-owned franchises. Certainly the fewer of these there are, the better from the franchisee's point of view. If a franchisor's profits are coming mostly from actual franchise operations, it will tend to pay more attention to its franchisees.

Growth Patterns

Consider how many franchises the company has opened in past years. Notice if the trend is up, or if the franchisor has reduced the number of franchises it has. Naturally, older firms may show a pattern of fewer new franchises as they mature, while newer companies may show greater activity shortly after they enter the market.

Total Royalty Fees

This item includes all monthly royalties and payments, advertising royalties and any other payment required from the franchisee by the franchising firm. To get a true picture of the value offered, it will be necessary to compare total royalties to the kind and quantity of services offered.

Financing Provided

Some franchisors will supply financial assistance to the franchisee to pay the initial and ongoing costs of conducting the business. Although an attractive extra, financial assistance should not be considered as a major decision factor; or a substitute for very careful, thorough investigation into all the facts in your choice of any franchise. It is simply another element that can be put into the mix.

How To Get Information

Contact both the national and local Better Business Bureaus. They may be able to give you an informed outsider's look at the company's financial and consumer relations experience.

Call or visit local current and past owners of the kind of franchises that you're interested in. Ask them what they think of the franchise company, its operations and the kind of help the franchisor has given them. Another good idea is to call or write some franchisees in other parts of the country. They may be experiencing better or worse economic situations in their areas and could give you an idea of how the particular business reacts to changed economic conditions.

Talk with your banker. He or she should have access to solid facts that will give you another view of the franchise's economic situation. Your banker may have inside details on the franchises you are considering and a good idea of the problems or opportunities you will have in gaining financing for your franchise venture.

Talk with an accountant. Have him or her check over the pro forma figures provided by the franchisor. These can include projected profit and loss statements, balance sheets, cash flow statements and projections for your location based on a similar demographic location. Have your accountant determine if they make financial sense.

Finally, talk with your lawyer and get a professional analysis of the franchise and the terms you are being offered. It is very important that your lawyer go over the franchise contract with extreme care. Remember, an agreement is just that; a bargain between two or more parties, and it can be changed or modified.

A contract that satisfies the needs of both parties at the beginning of the relationship can spare you grief and financial problems in the future, when it could be too late to change the arrangement.

Most important, avoid financial commitments before the agreement is completely worked out. Some franchisors may push for decisions before you have all the facts by offering special considerations. Avoid these situations at all costs, the final cost may be too high.

WHAT TO EXPECT FROM YOUR FRANCHISOR

Co-op Advertising

Your franchise must be promoted before, during, and after opening. You must sell yourself and your business however and wherever you can. It is rare for even the best product or service to succeed within a reasonable length of time without an active and intelli-gent advertising and promotion program.

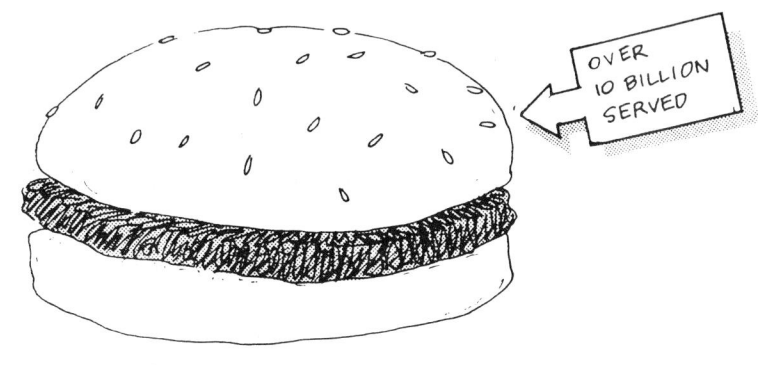

OVER
10 BILLION
SERVED

Besides the initial fee and monthly royalty, most franchisors also require franchisees to pay a monthly ad royalty, usually a small percentage of their gross income, into a co-op fund. Monies gathered in an advertising fund are pooled to finance national and regional advertising campaigns for the benefit of all franchisees.

The franchisor benefits from increased promotion of the trade name and business, which in turn increases the value of your franchise and the amount of royalty dollars you will contribute.

Not all franchisors have a co-op advertising fund. Many franchise systems have no central advertising program but require franchisees to manage and pay for their own advertising. The problem with this arrangement is that it can lead to a loss of control over the franchise image you paid for. Helter skelter promotions by various franchisees can lead to lowering the value of the franchise for all franchisees.

Site Selection

The best franchise companies have established systems that can help you find a good location and acquire it on the best available terms. Actually, working with a franchisee in site selection, helping in the construction of a store or fixing up a storefront, are such important activities in the business mix that franchisors have become more active in these areas over the years.

A favorable site for one type of business will not necessarily be good for another. Each different business requires certain qualities that you will be seeking in a good location: a quality site for a Jiffy Lube shop will definitely be wrong for a Karmelkorn Shoppe or a Mr. Donut. Each business appeals to particular kinds of individuals with different tastes, needs and habits, therefore it may require its own special site.

Many franchise companies have developed exact and scientifically selected requirements for locations in which experience shows their particular franchise operations will do best. Some companies have staffs that include marketing specialists who study census, population distribution and trend information about the best potential areas for franchises. This is valuable information for any entrepreneur who wants to have every possible advantage on his or her side.

The franchisor may have real-estate specialists who constantly seek out and update lists of available sites - vacant land, shopping centers under construction, empty storefronts, and so on within the targeted areas. In some cases, a franchisor may already have made arrangements for ready-to-rent or purchase locations within your territory.

Some franchisors help negotiate the purchase or lease of your land or building. They may help arrange for a contractor to build the facility, or with an owner/ developer to lease it to you. If you are locating in an existing center or mall, the franchise company may lease a storefront and sublet it to you on as good or better terms than you could obtain for yourself.

If you have to build a structure, the franchisor may even provide plans that are already approved by local government agencies. In the case of most fast-food and some other franchises you will be required to build a store according to their set plans; put up required signage, and install the required equipment in a certain way.

Then again, there are franchisors who don't do any of these things. In that case you will have the whole burden of doing market research, finding a suitable location, leasing or buying the space, laying out the interior, fixing up the exterior, even buying a new structure. So it's important to determine what the franchisor will do to help you find the best location and then make sure these steps are put into the agreement in writing.

Getting the Benefits from Training

Most men and women who buy franchises have no experience in the business they're entering. That's natural because a majority of the people who buy franchises are changing careers. But in order to succeed, a new franchisee must learn a great deal about what's involved in their new career before opening for business.

The best way to do this is to make the most out of the franchisor's training program.

The franchisor may offer training at a headquarters "college". These are usually well planned to provide the background you need to get the business off to a good start and to use all the know-how the franchisor has to offer. Formal training sessions are one of the most helpful supports a franchisor can provide to a franchisee and you should take advantage of as much as you can get.

But you should take one step more - to get training at an actual store or franchise location. As part of your franchise arrangement or if necessary, on your own, seek out the opportunity to work for a week or two in a functioning store. Make hamburgers, clean carpets, sell mufflers, sweep floors - learn whatever you can that a seasoned operator knows is needed to make that franchise work. Added to your classroom training, in-the-field practical experience will give you a first hand understanding of what you have to do to make your new business work.

Some franchisors will send a field representative to help train you and your new employees before the grand opening. If your franchisor doesn't offer this service you're on your own, so it's important to find out early how much on-site training is included in the franchise package and where you can locate the help you'll need.

Most franchisors offer some type of on-going training, even if it's only newsletters or regularly scheduled seminars. You'll want to find out about where your franchisor stands on such valuable services as advanced training on accounting and computer systems, new products and supplying a steady stream of marketing ideas.

It's a good idea to check with existing franchisees to find out just how effective the franchisor's training program is. If It looks like you won't be getting all the training support you'll need, the best source of help again is other franchisees who have faced the problem before you. They're usually very willing to help new people in the business and have often set up franchisee committees to provide mutual support.

Operating Practices

The operations manual and the franchise contract will require you to meet the company's standards of quality and uniformity of appearance in these areas among others:

- Product, equipment, fixtures and furniture
- Number, quality, quantity, type, size and shape of products
- Product availability
- Advertising and marketing controls
- Internal security
- Auditing procedures
- Employee conduct

Several court decisions have held that a franchisor cannot require you to buy products or services only from them. Most, however, can and do enforce quality standards and specifications. Violations of these can lead to the termination of your contract. There have been cases in which franchisees have been found in breach of contract for such seemingly minor violations as having smudges on a men's room mirror. Franchisors can get very picky when they think you might be tampering with their image and business. That's why franchisors maintain staffs of company inspectors.

The contract may also dictate the days and business hours you must be open; set any sales quota and penalties for not meeting them and explain any wholesale or discount purchasing plans available through the franchisor

Ongoing Management Assistance

Continuing help for franchisees can range anywhere from advice over the phone to having a company representative visit you whenever you feel the need for guidance and advice. In dealing with some franchisors you may have to pay an hourly rate or flat fee every time you ask the company to help you solve a problem.

One franchisee may be so unsure of himself that he demands a helping hand every time something doesn't go according to the manual. Others may be so confident of their own abilities that they feel no need to ever see the field rep and want no help or interference at all.

Here's how one outstanding franchisor, Midas Muffler supports its franchisees:

A field force of division and district representatives meet on a regular basis with franchisees.

Midas' real-estate, marketing, advertising and sales promotion executives work directly with all franchisees.

There is an open-door policy by which franchisees can go right to the top and get in direct touch with the president of the company.

The company goes to the dealers and asks their advice *before* any new programs are put into effect. Midas understands that the franchisees must believe in and support new programs to make them work.

The franchisor encourages its franchisees to expand. To support such a move Midas provides high quality market research.

Midas has a policy of giving current franchisees first crack at expanding and opening new outlets in their area.

That's how one first-class franchisor deals with its franchisees, builds a happy family of franchisors and a highly successful business.

Ingredients of a Winning Franchise

Now that we've covered some of the main points of how you should go about choosing a franchise it's time to close in on more specific considerations. By this point in the process you should have a pretty firm idea of just what kind of business you want to get into and some initial information on several franchise operations.

Here is a checklist that can help you establish the finalists in your search:

Identity

How well known is the trade name? If it's already a household name like Kentucky Fried Chicken, Baskin-Robbins or 7-Eleven you know their identity is well established. If you're considering a newer company, is the trade name memorable or unique enough to catch the interest of the buying public?

Some new franchisors might purposely choose a trade name that sounds like an already successful business. That may cause legal problems in the future. Another question might be, is the name so similar to another business name or trade mark that it might cause confusion to potential customers?

Will you be comfortable with the identity that's built into the business? Does the image fit in with your feelings of suitability for a venture that will represent you to the community?

Operating System

This is especially important if you're going into a field of business with which you have no previous experience. Does the franchisor offer a training program? If so how long is it? What topics does it cover?

Will the franchisor help you select a site for the business?

Does the franchisor provide an operating manual? If so, does it cover these important subjects:

Opening for business

Training - for yourself and employees

Setting up books and records

Accounting and reports

Advertising and publicity

Purchasing and inventory

Marketing and sales

Daily operating procedures

Technical information

Does the franchisor provide ready-to-use signs, menus, fixtures, decorations, forms etc. If not, will he help you get them?

Can the franchisor help you purchase equipment, supplies or inventory at a discount? Are the prices really better than you can get for yourself?

Financial Relationship

Is there an initial franchise fee?

Does the fee vary from one location to another? If so, what is the amount for the location or territory you have in mind?

Does the franchisor charge an ongoing franchise royalty? If so what is the percentage?

Is the royalty set for the entire term of the franchise, or can it be raised or lowered in the future?

If the royalty is not set, what factors will the franchisor use to determine it?

Does the franchisor charge a co-op advertising royalty in addition to the basic franchise royalty?

Is the co-op advertising royalty set for the entire term of the franchise, or can it be raised or lowered in the future?

Things to Look Out For

We've spent most of this chapter discussing the benefits of operating a franchise operation - and there are plenty of them. There have been success stories enough to fill a raft of magazines and books. But, be warned; as in most things that look too good to be true there are serious downside considerations as well.

As we've mentioned before, and it bears repeating, as a franchisee you are locked into a single company, and are required by contract to accept the company's rules, regulations and methods of doing business. There's always small print in the contract that defines your relationship to the franchise company for better or worse. In some ways a franchise relationship is like a marriage in which each side counts on the other party to provide help and support.

Sometimes this means that you as an entrepreneur are stuck in a situation where you cannot move quickly to meet your business' particular local needs - to take quick action against a competitor or meet changing financial or market conditions. As a franchisee you may have to wait for word from headquarters before you take steps to solve the problem..

Franchise fees are forever, or at least for the duration of the contract. When you sign that contract you are tied to a relationship that requires you to pay for the privilege of franchising and the advantages you get every month, every year.

Finally, if the franchise firm has business reverses, through no fault of yours, you have to live with the results of their actions. Everything they do reflects on you and your operation.

It's Not All Roses

Articles in business publications and franchisors who are anxious to sell you, indicate that buying a franchise is a guarantee of good fortune. Amazing success rates of 95 percent to 99 percent have been reported. Even the government seems to support these figures. Although franchising is the most foolproof way of getting a business going, there are still failures; nothing like the rate of failure for independent small businesses but enough to keep potential franchisees on their toes.

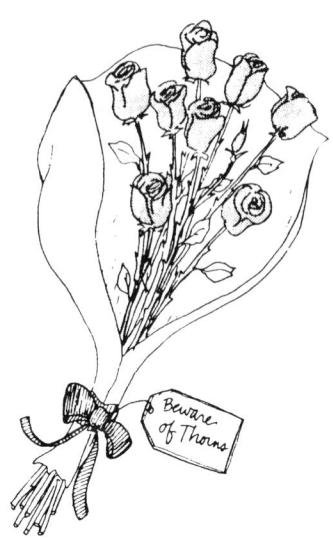

You know what they say about liars figuring and figures lying. The statistics don't tell you about the franchisee in Des Moines who invested $100,000 in a business and eventually had to to sell it to someone else for $15,000 because that was all he could get. The business is still in operation and it's included in the success statistics - the $85,000 loss however, is not shown anywhere.

Franchisors aren't very anxious to report failures within their system. Some buy back failed franchises either at the original cost or at a loss to the franchisee. Others attempt to sell their distressed operations. A few hope their failures will simply go away and still others carry a franchise on their records even though it's been closed for months. When a franchisor states they have 250 operating units, there may only be 200 actually open for business. Fifty have been closed and are up for sale.

One man, anxious to get in on the franchise bonanza was contacted by a company that offered him not only a franchise but three existing company-owned locations. To complete the deal he was required to pay, in addition to the royalty fees, for the buildings and the equipment.

It wasn't until after he had signed the contracts and had been in business for months that he discovered the restaurants he had purchased were sold by the owners because they hadn't made a profit in three years - while they were being operated by the franchisor. What's more he found that the used equipment he had purchased could have been bought new, on the open market, for less. It can't be emphasized too much - as in any venture, it's best to beware of who you're doing business with.

By and large franchising is the safest form of independent business ownership, but you should never think franchising is a sure thing. You can't give a franchisor a check and automatically expect instant success. Consider franchising with the same thorough eye you would any other investment.

If you look on a franchise as a guardian angel that won't let you fail, no matter what, you are unlikely to succeed for two reasons: A good franchisor who gets the idea that you're not likely to work hard at making it a success probably won't let you buy in.

Second , even the best franchise in the business cannot prevent lack of ability from causing failure. A franchisor may finally help to save an unsuccessful operation to preserve the franchisor's reputation and keep a store open, but you still carry the burden of success or failure. At worst you could lose your franchise and your investment - and your store may go on to another franchisee who could make a success of it without you.

How to Finance a Franchise

Once you've decided to go into business and have settled on the franchise you want to deal with, the next step is to round up the financing. Most franchisors won't go any further with the transaction if you don't have solid financial backing ready to complete the deal. However, even if you don't have the money available to invest, there are a number of ways to finance a franchise investment.

One is the franchising company. About one out of five franchisors has a financial assistance program for franchisees. Some of these can provide financing for the entire investment including real estate, inventory and working capital. Others will finance only the initial franchise fee.

Some of the source books listed later in this chapter will give you information on franchisor company investment.

OTHER SOURCES OF FINANCING

The Small Business Administration

Many franchise operations are started with assistance from The Small Business Administration. To qualify for an SBA-guaranteed loan, you must first have been turned down by at least three other sources, usually banks or savings and loans.

The loan is actually made by a bank in your trading area, but the SBA backs it by guaranteeing to fulfill your obligations in the event of a default.

The SBA particularly favors franchises because of their higher likelihood of success. The best strategy for obtaining an SBA loan is to contact a local loan officer whose bank has experience in SBA-guaranteed financing. Often, independently owned banks have the best SBA departments.

SBIC Investments

Another possible financing source is a licensed Small Business Investment Company (SBIC). This supplier is an independent venture capital group subsidized by the government to invest in small businesses. An offshoot of this organization is the Minority Enterprise Small Business Investment Company, or MESBIC, which specializes in loans and grants to minority-owned businesses.

Many SBICs and MESBICs are particularly interested in helping franchise businesses get off the ground.

Venture Capital

If you plan to open several franchises or to sub-franchise, it may be possible to obtain financing from a professional venture capital group. Each year, venture capitalists invest about $12 billion in more than 50,000 new businesses. Venture capitalists expect a high return on their investments, for example two hundred to three hundred percent. Moreover they expect to receive the payout in a short period of time.

When you raise money from a venture capitalist, you must be willing to give up a share of your ownership in the business. The investors will own shares in your company, entitling them to a portion of your profits. Usually you would also agree to buy back the investor's shares at some point, at a guaranteed price.

Independent Investors

Besides the professional venture capital groups, there are also small independent investors who seek select startup opportunities. Many of these investors are retired executives or military officers. Like the venture capitalist, the independent investor is looking for an attractive payoff and a share of ownership. The two best sources of independent investors are small business brokers and the classified section of your daily newspaper. Another way to go about it is to take your business plan to a business broker - he or she may already know a client looking for the kind of opportunity you offer.

Advertising for a partner in the classified section of a newspaper is permitted in most states; however it's not usually legal to advertise just for money. It's *always* absolutely illegal to offer to sell securities - such as stock in your corporation. The best advice is to advertise for a "general manager" with "partnership possibilities."

THE GOVERNMENT'S ROLE

It wasn't too long ago that franchising had earned a bad name because there were so many so-called franchisors offering businesses in which the chances of success ranged from poor to almost nonexistent. The situation has changed for the better, due to government regulations and the work of industry associations that have demanded higher ethical standards. With today's complex regulations, franchisors must observe a long list of disclosures and requirements.

After the Federal Trade Commission introduced sweeping franchise reform in 1980, more than half of the self-styled "franchisors" then in business quickly disappeared.

The first of the "full and accurate disclosure" laws governing franchise opportunities was passed by the California legislature in 1971. Since that time other states have passed similar laws to regulate franchising. Franchisors who offer or sell franchises in regulated states must comply with a standard form for disclosing significant information to prospective franchisees. A similar requirement is now enforced by the Federal Trade Commission for all franchisors and potential franchisors operating in the U. S.

THE UNIFORM FRANCHISE OFFERING CIRCULAR

The disclosure format is called the Uniform Franchise Offering Circular or UFOC. The UFOC is a document designed to inform potential franchisees about the background of those offering the franchise and the mutual obligations involved in the franchise contract. In some states, this information must be filed with an agency responsible for monitoring franchises. A state regulator may have to approve the offering before it can be promoted to prospective franchise buyers.

The FTC requires franchisors in every state to provide a UFOC to prospective franchisees before the contract can be signed or any payment can be made. If a franchise salesman asks you to pay a deposit before the required time period has ended it may be a violation of state or federal law.

In most states with specific franchise laws, franchisors must also comply with the opinions of state-employed regulators. Such authorities have almost unlimited power over who may (and may not) do business in their states.

Even in unregulated states, a franchisor must follow the FTC's rules for full and accurate disclosure in the form of a UFOC prospectus. A potential buyer may not be compelled, persuaded or tricked into signing until all the facts have been disclosed and clarified.

Although the UFOC is intended to inform you about the proposed franchise investment, it *does not* completely shield you from possible fraud.

The responsibility of verifying a franchisor's background and credibility remains with the franchisee.

So don't rely on the UFOC alone. If any gaps appear in the information provided you are entitled to ask for a complete resume of each of the principals, covering their entire business history.

The Federal Trade Commission requires all U. S. franchisors to disclose a precise list of information to the public. However, wherever a state law or regulation is stronger than the FTC rule, the local restrictions take over.

As of today, there are 14 states that regulate franchising. In most of these states, the regulations are considerably more strict than those of the FTC. Most of these states require the franchisor to apply for registration, then wait for approval from a state authority before beginning to offer franchises. The laws also apply to out-of-state franchisors who do business in the regulated states.

The states currently with franchise regulations are:

California
Connecticut
Illinois
Indiana

Maryland
Michigan
Minnesota
New York
North Dakota
Rhode Island
South Dakota
Virginia
Washington
Wisconsin

STATE FRANCHISE REGISTRATION

In states with franchise regulations a franchisor, no matter where his company headquarters is located, must register in that state before offering or selling franchises there.

What if your franchised outlet will be in a different state than the one in which you live? As a resident of a state which requires registration, the franchisor must still comply with your state's laws even though you may be planning on opening the outlet out of state.

If the outlet will be located in a different state which also has a registration requirement, the franchisor must register in that state, as well.

FRANCHISING IN A NON-REGULATED STATE

But what about franchisors headquartered in one of the states that do not require registration? When they offer or sell franchises to people who live in unregulated states, they still have the legal responsibility of preparing a UFOC and complying with the FTC's required waiting period.

Although the UFOC is intended to shield you, as a prospective investor, against fraudulent business practices, *no official regulatory body checks the accuracy of the information.* Even in states with strict regulations, the franchise authorities have neither the staff nor the budget to verify the contents of the thousands of UFOCs which come to them each year.

Unfortunately, many prospective franchisees believe the government actually approves the information from franchisors. It doesn't. For instance here's the wording you'll find contained as part of the disclosure material:

To protect you, we've required your franchisor to give you this information. *We haven't checked it, and don't know if it's correct.* It should help you make up your mind. Study it carefully. While it includes some information about your contract, don't rely on it alone to understand your contract. Read all of your contract carefully. Buying a franchise is a complicated investment. Take your time to decide. If possible show your contract to an advisor, like a lawyer or an accountant. If you find anything you think may be wrong or anything important that's been left out, you should let us know about it. It may be against the law.

There may also be laws on franchising in your state. Ask your state agencies about them.

Federal Trade Commission
Washington D.C. 20580

SOURCES OF ASSISTANCE AND INFORMATION

Regulated States

State agencies can be substantial sources of help and information as you consider buying a franchise. In a regulated state disclosure statements and detailed information about the franchise are kept on file with the proper state agency. They must be given to any prospective franchisee before he or she signs a contract and pays any money to the franchisor.

Non-Regulated States

If you do not live in one of the regulated states, you can check out the available information on any franchise within your state by contacting the secretary of state, a securities commission or division, a banking division, or the office of attorney general. These offices should be able to direct you to any information they have about a particular franchisor's activities in that state.

The state attorney general's office should also be able to discuss any legal difficulties a franchisor is having in that state. But knowing that, you should check out the complete details before you jump to any conclusions. Sometimes dissatisfied franchisees, who expected too much and did not succeed in the way they thought they should, try to make up their losses by taking advantage of the legal system to punish a franchise company.

Of course, you should also write the regulatory agencies in the state where the franchise is incorporated and find out the available details about who is behind the franchise and how the company has conducted its business with franchisees and the public.

Organizing The Search

Whether you start with a specific franchised business in mind or are just exploring the general franchising area be sure to use all of the information and help you can get. It's better to be safe than sorry when you are preparing to invest thousands of dollars.

Whichever approach you use, better results will be gained by doing a little comparison shopping. Be extremely selective and allow plenty of time for your search. There are hundreds of franchisors to choose from, and there are many franchises within any given area or category. The first rule is not to hurry. People who are in a hurry tend to make mistakes and let their emotions overcome their reason.

Once you have decided to systemize your search, there are a number of resources available to assist you with your search for the right franchise. A selected few are listed below.

Finding the Opportunities

How do you locate current franchise opportunities? The directories and magazines we have listed can give you a good head start.

Ads for franchise offerings appear every day in business and financial newspapers. *The Wall Street Journal* and *U.S.A. Today* have classified advertising sections devoted specifically to franchise opportunities.

Local newspapers carry franchise advertisements in their classified and business sections.

Periodicals such as Inc., *Money, Entrepreneur, Success, Income Opportunities, Business Opportunities* and *Venture* also run franchise ads.

To save your time and avoid wasted effort you should read franchise offering advertisements with care. If they look too good to be true they usually are. Many ads will ask you to call a long-distance number at your own expense. Still others, have a toll free number that you may call.

It's also a good idea to seek out franchise trade shows which travel around the country. It's even worthwhile to go to a city where a franchise trade show is being held. These exhibitions, which include information booths of numerous franchisors, provide a concentrated showing of various opportunities and give you the opportunity to talk face to face with representatives of the organizations.

NON-GOVERNMENTAL SOURCES OF ASSISTANCE AND INFORMATION

Better Business Bureaus

Council of Better Business Bureaus, Inc.
1515 Wilson Blvd.
Arlington, Va. 22209.

Files on many franchise firms are maintained by Better Business Bureaus. A summary report for a specific company on which a Bureau has a record can be obtained free of charge from the BBB in the area where the franchising company is headquartered.

If you can't locate the address of the local BBB, send a postage paid, self addressed envelope with the name and address of the company for which you want information to the Council of Better Business Bureaus. The Council will either refer your request to, or provide the address of, the appropriate Bureau.

International Franchise Association

International Franchise Association
1305 New York Avenue, NW
Suite 900
Washington, D.C. 20005-4709

IFA, founded in 1960, is a resource center for both current and prospective franchisors and franchisees. IFA has been responsible in the drafting of legislation that regulates franchising, and has testified on behalf of programs that encourage women and minorities to become more involved in the business community through franchising.

IFA offers many valuable publications that are available to the general public, including *Franchise Opportunities Handbook,* the IFA membership directory and *Franchising Opportunities World,* a bimonthly magazine sold by subscription and at newsstands. IFA also produces audio and video tapes on subjects relating to franchising. A free list of publications can be obtained by calling 1-800-543-1038.

The U. S. Department of Commerce and Small Business Administration advise prospective franchisees to check whether a franchisor is an IFA member.

National Alliance of Franchisees

National Alliance of Franchisees
P.O. Box 75416
Washington, D.C. 20013
(301) 386-3377

Franchise Education

Franchise Studies Program
School of Business Administration
University of Nebraska
Lincoln, NE 68504

Joseph Mancuso, Executive Director
Center of Entrepreneurial Management
83 Spring Street
New York, NY 10012

Federal Government Agencies

The Federal Trade Commission
Bureau of Enforcement
Sixth Street & Pennsylvania Avenue NW
Washington, D.C. 20580

Franchise Directories and Guides

Source Book of Franchise Opportunities
Published by Dow Jones-Irwin
P.O. Box 12488
Oakland, CA 94604

Franchises Unlimited Directory
Published by Excel Progressive Publications
1925 Pine Street
Niagara Falls, N.Y. 14301

Franchise Opportunities Handbook
Published by United States Department of Commerce
Superintendent of Documents
U. S. Government Printing Office
Washington, D.C. 20462

The Franchise Handbook
Published by Enterprise Magazines, Inc.
1020 North Broadway
Suite 111 Milwaukee, WI 53202

Franchise and Business Opportunities
Published by Franchise Business Opportunities Publishing
    Company
Suite 205
1725 Washington Road
Pittsburgh, PA 15241

Directory of Franchising Organizations
Franchise Investigation & Contract Negotiation
Published by Pilot Books
103 Cooper Street
Babylon, NY 11702

Quarterly Franchising World
Published by International Franchise Association
1305 New York Avenue, NW
Suite 900
Washington, D.C. 20005

Franchise 100
Published by Venture
521 Fifth Avenue
New York, NY 10175

Franchising Directory
Published by Entrepreneur
2311 Pontius Ave.
Los Angeles, CA 90064

Books on Franchising

Handbook of Successful Franchising
by M. Friedlander
Van Nostrand Reinhold
115 Fifth Avenue
New York, NY 10003

The Source Book of Franchise Opportunities
by J. Bond
Richard D. Irwin, Inc.
1818 Ridge Road
Homewood, IL 60430

Magazines on Franchising

Franchising Opportunities World
International Franchise Association
1305 New York Avenue, NW
Suite 900
Washington, D.C. 20005

Franchise Update
101 Church Street
Suite 19
Los Gatos, Ca. 95030

Canadian Franchise Directory

Franchise and Dealership Guide
OPPORTUNITIES CANADA
2550 Golden Ridge Road, Unit #42
Mississauga, Ontario L4X 253

*From Franchising Opportunities World

<table>
<tr><td>**Chapter 21**</td><td>

Computer
Applications

</td></tr>
</table>

PUTTING THE COMPUTER TO WORK
FOR YOUR SMALL BUSINESS

The Importance of Computers to Small Business

The experts say, "Don't get left behind." In this chapter you'll discover just what all computer owning business people know and why they'd rather give up their Mercedes sedans than their desktop personal computers. You'll learn how much a computer can mean to the success of your small business, how a personal computer works, and what to look for when you buy one.

During the 1950s, when expensive mainframe computers were introduced, big businesses quickly discovered how much a computer could help in almost every area of their operations. Then, when minicomputers came along a few years later, they were snapped up by medium size businesses. Now there are personal computers that can do as much as the old mainframes and minis, and are so inexpensive they can be put to work by even the smallest small business. Computers are not just for big business. They're for every business, especially for small and home-based businesses.

First of all you should know that the personal computers available today are powerful, dependable and inexpensive – becoming more affordable every day. When they're used for word processing, accounting, cost projection, inventory control and other key areas of business, a personal computer will pay for itself in less than a few months. A computer is the most effective basic tool for managing your business and adding to your efficiency.

It's no more necessary to know the ins and outs of how a computer works than it is to know how your car's engine operates, or what's really going on inside your television set. Most computers are now simple enough to operate that almost anyone can use one. A few helpful technical terms will be explained, mostly to help you choose a computer or upgrade your system.

So what exactly does a personal computer do to make your operation easier to run and to be more productive? Most important of all, it helps you control your business. As a small business you need every bit of help you can get. You need to keep tight control of your finances, income and expenses. You need to keep track of your inventory – when and what you'll need to reorder to keep things running smoothly. Your computer can be a compact storehouse for all your business figures. And you need to communicate.

A computer is a work horse of communication. Letters, memos, flyers, brochures, email, faxes, sending and receiving files, self-help programs and tutorials, music, art, drawing and drafting, a computer can communicate your data or ideas in a way that no other tool in history has.

L a b o r saving is what the computer does best. It speeds up every function that is repeated on a regular or irregular basis.   It can reduce the number of employees you need to keep your business running smoothly.   It's much easier to write letters and notes and work up billing on your computer. And, if you have to make changes or corrections, you can do it much faster than working at a typewriter or even by hand. Keeping track of and calculating business numbers is simpler on a computer spreadsheet than using pencil and paper.   Some computer programs are so helpful it's like having a consultant right in your office, ready to give you answers to difficult questions.

What a Computer is All About

There are two parts to any computer system: The machine itself, and its components, are called Hardware, and the computer programs are called Software. The computer is like a record player. The programs are like the records you put on the player. The programs will turn your computer into a number handler, letter writer, database filing system, mailing list manager, bar coding or fax machine as well as many other helpful functions.

As a filing system, your computer can store all your vital business information in a way that makes it easier to find when you need it. Paperwork and filing cabinets are reduced to a minimum.

Using a computer may mean learning to operate a familiar but, to many people, a foreign machine. The main thing that keeps most people from getting into the computer world is fear of the unknown. Actually, running a computer is just one step more involved than using a typewriter and in some ways is easier to use than a VCR. Computers and computer programs have come a long way. These days they work with you in a very logical way. It's like the difference between operating a Model T in the early days of automobiles and the ease of jumping into your Pontiac and driving away now. Most computer systems use simple on-screen menus that take you from function to function in a painless manner.

Some people shy away from the keyboard. They react with confusion and sweaty fingers. But you don't need to learn how to "type" like an expert. You can use two fingers and when you type an "a" you'll see an "a" appear on your computer screen. You quickly get the hang of it and within minutes you can start feeling comfortable and go on to learning the fine points of computer operation.

Printers

Your computer's main connection to the outside world is the printer. This is the device that takes what you've produced on your computer screen and puts the image on paper. There are various kinds of computer printers, and as you'd expect, important differences from one type to another. The two basic types are the ones we'll compare here – a laser printer or ink jet printer.

Ink jet printers shoot tiny drops of liquid ink onto the paper to form the printed image. Ink jet printers are economically priced. They are a major improvement over the old dot-matrix printers for quality output, quiet and speed, but not quite up to the precision of lasers. Ink jets generally use single sheets and can print envelopes easily. For a small office that needs mostly correspondence, flyers and other marketing media, labels and spreadsheet printouts, ink jet printers are the answer.

At the high-end, laser printers are the more expensive. They produce the highest quality reproduction, almost equal to commercial printing. Laser printers are also quiet and fast. Lasers use single sheets stacked in a tray and also print labels and envelopes.

If your new business needs color output, the ink jet is probably the way to go. Color laser printers are priced higher than color ink jet printers. Thus, most small business owners lean toward a color ink jet printer. However, because of the rapid technological changes taking place in printer design and development, the cost for color laser printers may soon come down appreciably.

Software: What Kinds of Programs Will I Need?

An important consideration before buying your computer is to determine for what it will be used. First ask yourself: do you want to write letters? Email? Track inventory? Perform financial analysis? Organize customer information? Invoicing? Create flyers and other marketing materials? Want access to the Internet? Share information between employees and customers and suppliers? What you'll need is software. Software is also called a program or an application. Software programs come in all shapes, sizes, and prices. For example: there are over two dozen accounting programs, many word processing programs, handfuls of desktop publishing programs, and several business plan software packages.

Finance

The speed and efficiency with which personal computers handle the accounting needs of small to moderate size companies is the answer to a businessperson's prayer. Personal computers work best for any information that is figured, re-figured and moved around. A computer can make general ledger books a thing of the past.

Accounting programs are designed to keep a close and highly organized account of your business's financial situation - including payroll and inventory. Most accounting programs are capable of writing checks, can manage bank accounts, credit cards, track investments and loans, and reconcile with your bank account online.

To get an idea of how an accounting program works, consider what you have to do when you write up an invoice. To do the job manually means a certain amount of calculation, looking up information, and repeated typing. On a computer the figuring and looking-up happen automatically, and excess typing is eliminated.

For invoicing, you assign an identification code (a name or number) to each customer and set up the account with any relevant information. When you create an invoice you just enter the identification code and the computer can place the customer's name and address, other shipping information, discount schedule, payment terms and sales tax, in the proper places on the bill form.

Each item in your inventory is assigned a code. To add the article to your invoice, just type in the item's code and the quantity of pieces ordered. A description of the item, retail price, extended retail price, and discounted price are displayed. You continue entering codes and amounts until the invoice is complete.

The invoice is calculated with the click of a key, taxes and shipping are added if needed, and a grand total is calculated. A packing list and shipping label can be printed along with the invoice.

But that's just the beginning. The various accounting modules (accounts payable, accounts receivable, invoicing, inventory, general ledger) are linked together, and the time saved is impressive. When computer programs work together and share information, they are known as interactive.

Accounting software is usually a complex program and the quality varies. Take your time selecting and buying accounting software. There may be accounting software written especially for your kind of business. Sometimes they're advertised in trade journals that cover your business, or you might check with your national trade association.

Financial Record Keeping

It's absolutely necessary for any business to maintain accurate financial records in order to track profit and loss and to preserve financial information for tax obligations. To be successful every business must be up to date on its accounts receivable, accounts payable, inventory, payroll and checking accounts. When you use an electronic financial record program, you don't have to be a trained accountant or bookkeeper to handle these jobs easily and efficiently.

For a small business, you may not even need complete professional accounting software; an inexpensive personal finance program might do all your company demands. Professional accounting programs require that you thoroughly understand accounting principles. So the time and effort it takes to understand the software, and the mistakes you make while learning will be more costly than the benefits you would gain.

The whole point of any financial management software is that it collects your transactions into specialized compartments so, whenever you need to, you can sort expenses by category. Like database programs, financial software allows you to recover and group transactions in different ways. The major benefit of all electronic bookkeeping is that you don't have to write each entry in two or more files. If you pay an expense, the software will automatically debit a particular category.

Financial programs, just like spreadsheets, permit you to figure and re-figure according to various formulas that are already in place, or that you type in. So if you want to check on how much money you have coming in at any time, hit a couple of keys and the computer adds all the entries in accounts receivable. Of course a simple addition like this can be done by hand, but a computer does it much faster and is more dependable for accuracy. The larger your business, the more time and effort you'll save.

The kind of financial management program you choose is a personal matter. General purpose database or spreadsheet programs take some effort to get going. You have to set up the categories and formulas yourself. Financial management programs are generally all set up and are ready to go as soon as you have filled in the blanks with your own list of accounts and expense categories.

Check writing, personal finance, and small business accounting programs carry out many of the same functions. All three cover the major necessities of business financial management; writing checks, recording deposits, grouping expenses and income by category, keeping tabs on credit card expenses and managing bank accounts. They are all basically accounting programs and the major differences are the extra functions each publisher adds into them.

The simplest approach for many small businesses could be using a good check writing program and having an accountant or bookkeeper come in from time to time.

The next step up, a personal finance program, might be better for a small business owner who wants to track both business and personal finances, including investments. Some business owners may also use this kind of program to track inventory.

The company with more than five employees probably needs a more complete accounting software.

Inventory

Inventory modules are often included, or can be purchased separately, with your financial accounting package. With a module from your financial package the inventory is integrated with the other modules: invoicing, purchasing, and accounts receivable.

A less efficient way to keep track of inventory is to set up a file on your database or spreadsheet program. Just fill in the blanks with the item names and any other information you want related to them. You can have columns for your purchase price and your selling price. Or you can put in the purchase price and set up another column that multiplies your cost by the markup percentage and have the program do the calculation for you. Many retail businesses or manufacturing firms set up their databases to signal when it's time to reorder particular items.

Word Processing

Every business that deals with people needs communications, so the words you use and how you use them can make an important difference in how successful your business will be. Word processing is a powerful tool for any writing you do: letter writing, memos, even desktop publishing.

With a word processing program the words you type into the computer are displayed on the video screen and can be moved, changed, deleted or added to. One important difference between using a typewriter and word processing is word wrap. As you type into your computer you don't have to think about hitting the return key to move down to the next line, just keep typing and the machine does it for you.

Only after the text has been corrected or revised – the way you want it – do you send it to your printer. Then if the printed copy still doesn't satisfy you, make your changes and another copy can be printed.

Look at it this way – with a typewriter, the addition or deletion of a single word means retyping an entire document. The addition of a single paragraph on page 3 of a 20-page report generally means retyping pages 3 through 20. With a word processor, everything after the added paragraph is moved down and the whole report is perfectly reformatted. The document change takes place in seconds. The printer prints a new copy in minutes. This is one of the most important time and work savers your computer can perform.

Word processing makes you a better writer and leads to better correspondence. Small mistakes, which might have been considered too troublesome on a typewriter to correct, can be easily corrected on a computer. Afterthoughts and clarifications can be added more freely.

Good writing comes from editing. Going over what you've written, making changes and alterations, such as replacing one word with a better word, is so easy it becomes a habit. This is the difference between acceptable work and more accurate writing. Word processing gives the writer complete control of anything he or she writes.

Word processors these days come equipped with the tools that make good writing easier and help you write more forcibly. Functions included with the word processor most often are: a spell checker, grammar checker, thesaurus, glossary, outliner, and mail merge.

Spell Checker

Good word processors include a spell checker. The spell checker goes through your document looking for any misspellings. It offers you the correct spelling. You press a key and the spell checker substitutes the correction in place of the incorrect spelling. Of course you have to know some differences in words like "their" and "there" and "its" and "it's". A grammar checker may even help you with those. Some spell checkers will point out doubled words, like "but but" that you have mistakenly typed. It will then ask you if you want to delete one of the repeated words.

If you make typing mistakes (who doesn't?) or are unsure of spellings, you can just type away, finish the document and put it through the spell checker. You may be amazed at how good the program is at picking out and correcting your mistakes. An added benefit is that you can add specialized business words or jargon to the spell checker's list.

Grammar Checker

A grammar checker works in much the same way as the spell checker. When you finish your document you run the grammar checker and it checks the document for you. It knows how sentences are constructed and looks for possible mistakes and often offers constructive suggestions to improve your grammar. Who doesn't occasionally type an incomplete sentence or put a comma where it's not suppose to go?

Thesaurus

If you're ever at a loss for a word, or would like to strengthen a statement with a better word, a thesaurus that maintains a list of synonyms is a great (vast, enormous, immense, huge, excellent) help, especially when it is built into your word processor. You simply indicate the word you want to look up. A small screen pops up and gives you a list of alternative words. You select the one you want, hit a key and it replaces the old word automatically. If your word processing program doesn't include a thesaurus, you can buy a separate program that will work with it.

Glossary

Most word processing programs include a glossary. With this feature you can file away words that you use often -- long words, scientific terms, anything you want. Then instead of having to type them out every time you want them, you just type in a few letters, press a key and the word you want appears in your document.

Outliner

Half the job of writing is organizing your work. One feature you might want to consider, even if it isn't included in your word processor, is an outliner. It allows you to set up an outline of headings and subheadings that can help you organize your work and avoid missing major points. You can place topics or headings anywhere in the outline, anytime you think of them and you can rearrange them at any point and add or eliminate points as you like.

When you have the outline arranged as you want it, it's a simple matter to convert the outline into a regular document and make the changes that will make it into a letter or report.

Mail Merge

From time to time you'll want to send out personalized letters to a number of customers or prospects. Word processing programs generally include a mail merge function that allows you to create mass mailings in the simplest way. The mail merge feature will combine a letter written in your word processor with names, addresses, and other details you enter into a data base.

You've received mass mailings with your name and even individualized details like "You're one of our preferred customers in Golden Valley," entered perfectly into the body of the letter. It's certainly more impressive than "Dear Customer," or "Dear Friend." Well, a mail merge program is what they use. Once your mail merge system is set up you can print out these kinds of letters to as many customers or prospects as you want with only a few keystrokes.

The mail merge function is also handy for sending bills, past due payment notices, new product or service announcements. You can even use the same setup to print the envelopes or mailing labels.

Word processors often come bundled in "Works" or "Office" packages. A works program is usually a scaled down version of the typical retail software package. It also includes a scaled down version of a spreadsheet program and a scaled down version of a database program. Works packages have few bells and whistles and are not usually sufficient for most businesses. Office packages are geared specifically for small businesses. They are the full retail version of the word processor and spreadsheet programs, and include other applications like a Personal Information Manager and a Presentation program. The Office Pro version will also include a full version of the database program.

Spreadsheets

A spreadsheet consists of rows and columns and has been designed to perform mathematical functions. The use of spreadsheets has been an essential part of making financial decisions for decades. Today an electronic spreadsheet on a personal computer is an excellent organizer and analyzer of information, especially financial data. It can reduce to seconds the hours, sometimes days, it took to figure out financial decisions with a pencil and paper.

If you were figuring a profit-and-loss statement by month, each month's figures (sales, cost of goods, overhead, etc.) would be a vertical column. The individual items would be horizontal rows. Some items in each row would be fixed costs, such as rent, and some would be variables, such as commissions.

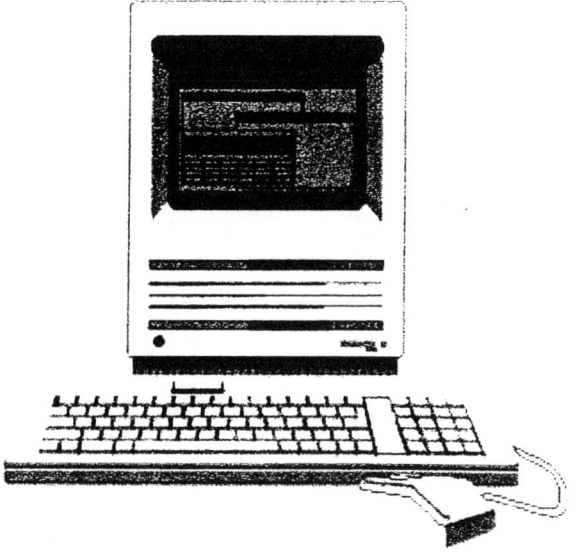

Once you enter these figures into a computer, the program will answer all kinds of "What if?" questions: "What if the new product we just introduced continues to sell at the same rate as it did in the first two months?" "What if sales go down by 10%." "What if the cost of goods increased by 2% but sales increased by 4%?" And so on.

Electronic spreadsheets are helpful when deciding at what point a project will become profitable. "How many gizmos will we have to sell before the improvements we are going to make are paid for?"

The spreadsheet program can also create charts that are graphic presentations from your spreadsheet data into area, bar, column, line, pie, radar, xy (scatter), combination, or 3-D formats.

A spreadsheet analysis, database or charts can be used in numerous ways to support points in a business letter or report. It can also be used for creating invoices, financial statements, tables, estimates, bills, catalogs and price sheets. It's easy to move data generated by your spreadsheet into word processors, presentation graphics programs and desktop publishing software.

Integrated word processors provide links to spreadsheets so that information you change in a spreadsheet will automatically change in the linked word processor document.

Databases

A computer database is like an electronic filing cabinet. It stores information in a chain of records. Each record is like a file folder for storing related information about any particular topic. A record contains information you want to keep relative to a specific person, company, transaction, inventory item, anything. For example, a doctor's office might keep one record for each patient, while a store might use one record for each invoice.

Within each record are fields or cells. Each cell contains a specific piece of information, such as a company name, amount billed or a transaction date.

In addition to establishing a structure for storing your information, a database gives you the flexibility to display and print information in any form you need.

With a database you can find, update, rearrange, or print any group of records you want. You can sort records into groups, and have the database summarize the data for each group. You can choose to view records one at a time, or to look at many records at the same time.

Databases that have been professionally compiled are often available online. These professional databases offer specific information to their subscribers. Like a database on your personal computer, an online database holds certain kinds of information. For example, Dow Jones News/Retrieval, CompuServe Delphi and GEnie all offer stock quotations. Dun and Bradstreet's Financial Records includes financials of thousands of public and private companies. Standard & Poor's Online has earning and income estimates of companies. TRW Business Profiles covers the credit rating of any company that has ever applied for credit. Wall Street Journal articles are available on the DIALOG data bank that also includes specialized databases on such subjects as finance, medicine, electrical engineering, physics, electronics and demographics.

You get access to this world of online information by using a modem, which is a device that connects your personal computer to a telephone line so that two computers can communicate with each other. To access a given database, you need a subscription to the information service that carries it. You also have to pay for the amount of time you use the service.

Income Taxes

As a business owner you can expect to pay much higher income taxes than a wage earner. At the same time, the more successful your business is, the more likely you are to be audited by the IRS.

But there's a bright side; you're entitled to a bundle of deductions salaried people can't take. Every business purchase, meal, trip and office equipment purchase can help lower your tax debt. As an entrepreneur you have to become familiar with business tax matters. You soon learn that keeping up-to-date records is essential, and there's nothing like a computer for helping you do that.

Experts will tell you that keeping track of your business deductions throughout the year is the surest way of getting more back at tax time. It's simple enough to set up tax-deductible categories in a check writing, a personal finance program or in a spreadsheet, to track business expenses.

Even if you don't prepare your own taxes, good records help your accountant or tax preparer concentrate on saving money on your taxes and should hold down the time spent and cost for your tax preparation.

Once the numbers are in your computer, you won't have to retype them into lists of totals for tax preparation. In fact, the expense records you keep all year long can be transferred into certain tax preparation programs.

Tax Preparation Software

There are tax preparation programs that will take you, line by line, through the appropriate forms and schedules. Most of these software packages contain all the income tax paperwork likely to be needed for individual or business taxes. Modules for state tax returns are sold separately by some publishers. Don't expect a tax program to organize your records; for that you need a checkbook, finance or accounting program.

Every tax preparation program offers help in guiding you through the sometimes involved requirements for filling in the blanks. Some include IRS instructions for each line of a schedule or form. Some come with complete tax preparation manuals. They all perform addition and multiplication functions, such as adding up totals you've entered for business or medical expenses and calculating how much you can deduct. They also save you the work of entering the same information twice by automatically copying figures they've calculated from various schedules directly to the proper lines on your basic 1040 form.

Most also use on-screen replicas of the IRS tax schedules and forms. You fill in the blanks just as you would on paper, and in many cases, you can print out these computer forms as legal tax returns. You should check on any program you are thinking of buying to be sure you are getting what you want.

According to the IRS most mistakes on tax returns result from tax payers' calculations. This is one more problem that a good tax preparation program will eliminate. Business tax payers are faced with complex mathematics calculations and many chances for mistakes to creep in. With most tax programs, you simply enter the figures called for and let your computer do the work of figuring.

A useful feature in most tax programs is that they run a constantly updated tab of your tax bill. As you add deductions or change figures, you can actually watch your tax balance go down. You can determine how much a Keogh or IRA contribution, or higher mortgage interest payment, would affect your overall taxes.

Some programs work like having a tax advisor in your computer. They ask questions that prompt you to fill in information that is then sent to the proper line on the tax form. For example, the screen might ask you to type in business loss amounts, and when you do, the figures are sent to the proper line on the proper schedule.

Then there are the complex calculations such as deductions allowed for business use of an automobile, a home office, business travel or equipment purchase. The program's tax advisor will figure how much you can claim as a deduction or a depreciation on capital equipment, according to your particular situation.

There are tax programs that compute three different ways of filing: joint return, married filing separately, and single, so you can decide which gives you the lowest tax bill.

Publishers update their tax programs every year to match changes in the tax laws. The updates are generally offered at a special low price to owners of the previous year's programs. Tax preparation programs are, of course, tax deductible.

Tax preparation software may not save you money but they will certainly save you time and effort and mistakes. The programs will handle calculations and help to prevent costly errors. If you do go to a tax preparer, the software will do much of the organizing that you would otherwise pay for. Consider the costs and decide for yourself which approach would be most beneficial.

Electronic Tax Filing

If you are filing as an individual, and are entitled to a tax refund, there is a quicker way to get that money back from the IRS and many state government tax offices. Electronic filing by modem speeds the refund to you in days rather than weeks. Of course, if you're not getting a refund, there's no point in filing electronically. Also, if your return requires supplementary data, or you're married and filing separately, you have to file on paper.

To take advantage of electronic filing you can go to an IRS-approved tax preparation firm; or find an accountant or tax preparer who is set up to file electronically. For a small fee, they will forward your return to the IRS by modem. The IRS checks the return for accuracy and acknowledges acceptance or rejection, usually within 12 hours after it has been transmitted. Electronic filing is so popular that, by the mid-1990s, half of all tax returns were filed electronically.

The Business Plan

One of the most important things every small business should have is a business plan. It is a road map that is designed to take you where you want to go and is the connection between your goals and managing plans for the business.

There are too many people in business who know what they are doing, their products and their market, but who don't know how to write a good business plan.

The very act of preparing a business plan is an activity that will help to focus your attention on where you are now, where you want to go, and how you can get there. It will help you understand the risks, rewards, and requirements of your business. The business plan is an ongoing document that includes specific goals and the steps needed to achieve them.

Word processing and spreadsheet programs can be very helpful in creating your business plan. The business plan involves describing your company and product or service, analyzing the market and the competition, outlining your operations and management and generating a financial forecast far enough in advance to show a break-even point. However, if the idea of working out a business plan, facing the complex math and many pages of text stop you in your tracks, you're not alone.

Fortunately there are business plan computer programs that will help you get the job done. They will walk you through the process and point out areas you might not otherwise have considered.

There is a wide range of financial planning software available, some good, some not so good. True business plan software covers sales and marketing forecasts, break-even analysis, cash flow, and cash balance sheets. The better software includes outlines and prepared text to help you with the written portion of the plan.

Business plan software programs can take you step by step through the writing process. The software and the manual that comes with it bring up questions and give you ideas. It's almost like having a business consultant at your side as you work. They provide an excellent way of looking closely at your goals and comparing them with the practical problems you'll face in starting or growing your business. Writing your business plan is the first and most critical step in creating a business that has the greatest chance for success.

Good business plans provide for several different spreadsheets, and they cover two and three year periods. The three principle spreadsheets statements are Profit and Loss, Balance Sheet, and Cash Flow. Each of these are important for the business owner, prospective investors, and last, but not least, your friendly banker.

A business plan software package that is offered by The American Institute of Small Business, is **How To Write a Business Plan**. The package covers products or services involving retail, wholesale, manufacturing, research and development, consulting, and nonprofit organizations.

It includes the primary financial forms and provides all of the necessary elements for creating a business plan on your computer. The easy to follow instructions clearly and easily lead the way through each form to eliminate guesswork. It provides exact language choices and alternatives for each section of your business plan. You can also insert your own language or change the suggested copy to fit your needs.

Financial Planning

You might have a healthy cash flow for a given period of time but be losing money annually, or vice versa. If you know how to write a financial plan and how to operate a spreadsheet, you're on your way. If you need help in either area, a specialized program with preset pro forma profit-and-loss and balance sheets will be more helpful.

There are computer programs that are designed to let non-financial and non-computer experts apply the basic techniques of small business finance.

Some are exclusively for specific businesses and are very complete. Personal finance and accounting software also generate balance sheets and profit-and-loss statements.

Some financial planning programs are tailored to specific styles of businesses such as real estate, professional services, manufacturing and retail -- as well as personal finance. The labels and formulas are set up to calculate revenue forecasts, income statements, balance sheets, cash flow statements, projected break-evens, and budgets for your industry. You only need fill in the numbers that relate to your finances.

Another kind of specialized program is the financial calculator, which is a kind of mini-spreadsheet with the necessary formulas already in place. They give you the tools and practical knowledge to handle compound interest calculations, retirement planning, college planning, investments, rental property, mortgage refinancing, buy/rent/lease decisions, loan analysis and depreciation scenarios. They can also contain a form 1040 screen that's useful for estimating your tax liability.

Project Planning and Managing

You work on project planning every day. You make decisions about which jobs come first, what goals you have to meet, and what kind of timetable you have to work with.

Too many business people don't take the time to plan ahead in detail. They know what results they want, they know generally how to get the jobs done, but they figure they'll solve the specific problems when they get to them. Sometimes this approach works, often it doesn't.

There are too many ways to go wrong and only a few ways to go right. It is always best to take some time at the beginning to work out all the details: Set schedules, plan routines and designate who will do the work and what they'll need to get the tasks done.

Project management software can be used to organize details and help many business activities work out on budget and on schedule. What kind of tasks are they good for? Specialized project management programs can be used to bring a product to market, to handle maintenance on a machine, to accomplish a sale, or to keep track of a service project, such as expanding the size of your manufacturing plant.

Project management programs make initial planning easier and more effective by helping you divide the work into smaller sections and designate the people, equipment, materials or subcontractors needed for each task.

Then, after the project is going, they help you track results and reorganize work and assets to meet changing needs. The software warns you of conflicts within a project or among several projects. It traces ongoing and total costs, a big help when bidding is involved.

The major benefit of project management software is that it keeps you in control. A good project management chart illustrates all the connections between a project's tasks and shows clearly how various parts of a project depend on each another. Like a battlefield commander you can see your projects develop on-screen when you enter information.

The high quality reports and charts created by project management software can help explain or sell your projects to customers or associates.

Using a Spreadsheet for Managing Projects

Sometimes you'll be more interested in controlling cash flow in a project than managing jobs or dealing with resources. Although it's not as complete a project management tool, a spreadsheet can do a good job in helping you manage money.

A spreadsheet with columns for income and expenses will give you a good picture of how the money is moving within the project. As the operation develops and you make changes, you can easily spot how an alteration in any one column will affect the whole project.

Desktop Publishing

Every small business needs some kind of regular promotion and publicity. Flyers, brochures, business cards and other promotional media can be conceived and printed out using desktop publishing. Another economical, yet effective, method of advertising is to put out a newsletter. Your computer makes the job easy enough to do it yourself, and since you send your newsletter to only a carefully selected list, it helps keep down your marketing costs.

A good newsletter can open the way to new business because, like a newspaper or magazine, it provides interesting, timely and worthwhile information for a particular target market. Most important, a newsletter fosters a continuing relationship with customers or prospects because it helps establish you as a qualified expert.

To publish a newsletter, you need one of the more complete word processors or a desktop publishing program. To do the job right you also need a computer with plenty of memory and a good supply of hard disk storage space.

Pictures, borders, cartoons, and fancy swirls are called clip art or graphics. Clip art is used to lighten up, or dress up, the appearance of your newsletter. Imagine a page of text – nothing but text. It can be daunting to read; but liven it up with an attractive border, put the text into columns, and add a couple appropriate images, and your text becomes appealing to the eye, and inviting to the reader.

Copyright free clip art can be purchased on CDs at most software retailers. Each compact disk may hold thousands of images. A handy reference book is often included so you may easily locate the image you want. Also, professional online databases of millions of clip art images are available on the Internet. These databases are offered to their subscribers for a monthly fee.

Be prepared to put some extra effort into this project. Publishing a worthwhile newsletter takes some basic understanding of writing, layout design and maintaining a mailing list. If you need large quantities of newsletters, you'll soon learn something about the printing business too. There are plenty of desktop publishing firms ready to help if the production work becomes too much trouble.

Don't worry about getting fancy. Remember that some very fine newsletters are just two sides of a single page, signed by the writer, like a letter. You can publish weekly or monthly, or come out only two, three, or four times a year.

Desktop Publishing With a Word Processor

If all you want to set up is a simple one-sheet, two-sided newsletter, a good word processing program will probably be fine for your needs. So, it's a good idea to look carefully into what you can do with the word processor you already have before investing in a high power desktop publishing program. Just be sure it permits multi-column formatting and is able to wrap text around illustrations.

Desktop Publishing Programs

If you plan to do more than an occasional promotion piece, a desktop publishing, or a page layout program, will offer you more control over the total look of your work. Basically you'll get more professional letter spacing, fancier graphics and spot color. You can type text directly into a desktop publishing program; they all have text editing and spell checking capabilities. However, it's more efficient to handle the actual writing on a word processor.

There are two basic ways to produce your newsletter. One is to print out copies on your printer, but using a printer to turn out large numbers of copies can be costly and a wasteful way to treat a printer.

Another way is to print a single copy of your material, paste up a mechanical, and take it to a print shop. A mechanical is the final layout version with type and artwork, or spaces for artwork, made ready for professional printing. Actually when you do desktop publishing, you're really preparing mechanicals for your typesetter and printer.

Some newsletter publishers cut costs by having one master copy printed and then making photocopies.

Personal Information Managers

A Personal Information Manager (PIM) keeps track of your scheduled meetings and events, contact names, customer names, addresses, phone numbers, birthdays, or whatever information about people you don't want to forget. It replaces tiny scraps of paper, on which you've jotted information. PIM software is also on small hand-held computers, and is often included in Office software bundles.

Employee Management

Human Resources database applications can keep track of personal information, medical, and other benefits, training, skills, and evaluation reports. Professional pre-formatted reports let you monitor critical HR issues and control wages, bonuses, qualification, and equal opportunity issues. Layout your entire organizational needs with jobs, skills, managers, training, projects, and pay scales, or import data from any ODBC database. Build a resume file from applicants, then use the program to scan the documents on file to find just the skills you need. Organize training for your staff, and document it. Find information on tenure, review dates, benefits, and more. Track time spent on various projects and generate invoices for various tasks and projects, with a complete view of workers and supervisors assigned. You can even document costs for company properties. From recruitment to benefits, training, personal growth, time sheets, and more, HR software tracks every phase of an employee's job history to provide you with the big picture, regardless of the length of employment. It might just be all you need to run a first-class HR department, regardless of how large your company grows.

Computer Aided Design

A Computer Aided Design (CAD) program is a drawing tool. CADs are used to draw floor plans, render 3D models, make mechanical designs and schematic drawings, ray tracing of still images, and walk-through animation; anything that needs to be designed and manipulated. If your small business is in the mechanical arts, you probably already know the value of a CAD. The CAD is a precious and precise drafting tool.

Vertical Markets

Vertical market programs are applications written specifically for your type of business. Whether you're a portrait photographer, real estate agent, or a church secretary, there is an application written for your niche. They often include template letters and database information for keeping track of your clients, customers, and contacts.

Inspiration and Creation

Several software programs, which exercise your thoughts, are available. They are hoping to inspire you or to help you create ideas. It's hard to explain how each of them works, but basically, they ask you questions, and from your answers, the program organizes your thoughts and correlates them to similar ideas in its database. The output it gives you makes you think of the problem in a different way – a brain calisthenic. The ideas generated by these programs are your ideas that are organized and viewed from a different perspective. Creative and inspirational software are visual thinking tools that you and your employees can use to develop ideas, plans, and business processes. They feature integrated diagraming and outlining environments to let you quickly generate ideas, create diagrams, organize information, outline proposals, and more. If your business depends upon your creativity, or you want to come up with innovative ideas to operate your company, these programs can be not only helpful, but a lot of fun.

Internet Software

The Internet is a very important marketing tool for the small business owner. On the Internet, a software program is called a client. Don't be confused by the term. Email clients transmit electronic mail at near instantaneous speeds. Browsers allow you to view web pages. Chat clients are a way of having real time conversations with other people; those people may be thousands of miles away, or in the building next door. To act as your gateway to the Internet you will need an Internet Service Provider (ISP) or an Online Service. If you plan on creating your own web page, you'll need an HyperText Markup Language (HTML) editor.

Email clients, browsers, chat clients, ISPs and Online Services, HTML editors, are discussed more fully in Chapter 23.

Optical Scanner

Some businesses, such as legal offices and design studios, need to copy information from papers or publications into computer files for editing or re-use. The optical scanner takes pictures or text from printed sources and converts them into computer usable documents so you can revise and merge them into your own work. There are many kinds of scanners that can be used for the recognition of characters and graphics.

Scanners come in a variety of shapes and sizes; luckily the prices have dropped considerably since they were first mass marketed. Hand-held scanners digitize a four-inch-wide strip (about half a normal page). These are the least expensive models. Sheet-fed and flatbed scanners offer advanced features for digitizing graphics and optical character recognition. These are larger and more costly than the hand-held models but usually produce a much clearer image.

Optical Character Recognition (OCR)

An OCR is an optical scanner software or device that recognizes typewritten or printed characters and converts them into digital code. So the material you scanned on the printed page is transferred to a document that you can rewrite or edit on your computer screen.

Fax Modems

Almost every business these days needs a facsimile (fax) machine as much as it needs a telephone for electronic on-paper communications with clients and suppliers. But if you want to fax a document stored in your computer, or receive a fax to use in your own document, using a standalone facsimile machine can be a time-wasting problem.

A practical solution is to use a fax/modem, which sends text and graphics directly from your computer to any fax machine and receives fax transmissions as a computer file. Fax/modems, which can also work as communication modems (to send files computer to computer), attach directly to your computer.

With a fax/modem you don't have to print out a word document or spreadsheet before you fax it. In addition, the faxes you send from your computer are sharper at the receiving end, since they haven't been scanned into a fax machine.

Which Computer Should I Choose?

There are two primary types of personal computers marketed to the individual and small business: IBM-compatible (often called the PC) and Apple Macintosh.

The advantage of the PC for many years was mostly their lower cost. Thus, within the business community, there are far more IBM-compatible machines in use. More programs are available and more add-on components are offered by many independent companies. The fastest PCs are faster than the fastest Macintoshes, although, for most business applications, the differences are insignificant.

The Macintosh was generally considered easier to learn and easier to use. Almost all programs, such as word processors and spreadsheets, use essentially the same commands, so once you feel secure with the Macintosh you can use more programs more quickly. In addition, the Macintosh allows you to mix, match and move items between one program and another more easily.

The Windows operating system, installed on most IBM-compatible computers, followed Macintosh's use of graphics to make Windows software easier to learn and use, and for moving items from one application to another.

Deciding which type of computer to choose depends on the computing power you need and how much money you want to spend for ease of use. Don't expect the cheapest machines to perform all the functions you'll want. It's better to choose a computer with more capacity than you think you'll need because as you become familiar with what a computer can do, you will find that you'll probably want to add more functions. Later it will cost more or be impossible to upgrade with add-ons.

All brand name computers are dependable and there is plenty of useful software for each. The decision is finally a matter of your preferences. It's best to check out both kinds of computers at a dealer, by running the kinds of programs you will be using most.

The significant differences in new computers is that of speed, storage, and memory. Most applications will not demand the most state of the art computer. In this computer age, technological changes take place every minute of every day. What is current and top of the line today, can be mediocre or outdated in a few months. Yet, this should not delay your choice of a new computer. Know what software applications you want to run, and then choose a computer that runs those applications well. Your computer will then serve your company for many years.

Computer Jargon

There are basic technical terms you should know in order to make an intelligent computer choice. Some of the more common terms that you will hear from a computer sales person include: CPU, ROM, Megabytes, Hard Disk, Disk Drive, and Memory. Each of these terms are clearly explained in the glossary of computer terms found at the end of this chapter.

CPU

The Central Processing Unit of the computer is usually referred to as its "brain." Technological advances means that newer, faster, better CPUs are released a couple times a year. Again, this is not something you need worry about. As long as you're buying a new computer, the CPU should be a current standard.

Memory

The computer needs four kinds of electronic memory to store data and instructions in order to operate; they are:

Read only memory (ROM). This is the permanent memory that cannot be altered. It holds a program that checks out the computer's system and prepares the computer to do its work. A power outage will not erase the ROM. The Read Only Memory is on a chip inside the computer.

Random access memory (RAM) holds information that can be changed or erased. It's a temporary memory. Just like your desktop can be likened to a temporary file cabinet while you're working on papers, RAM is the memory the computer uses while working in a program. The size of the RAM is one of the items that makes one computer more efficient than another; the bigger the RAM the greater amount of information it can read or write to operate. If your computer has enough RAM you'll be able, for example, to use a word processor and a spreadsheet at the same time. The RAM loses all memory when computer power is turned off. Most computers can have their RAM size increased by adding additional RAM chips.

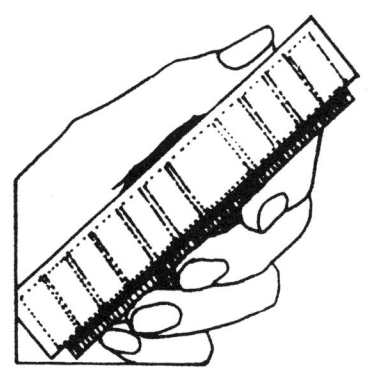

To illustrate how RAM works, let's say you wanted to revise a letter, the computer would read the original letter from a disk, where it was saved, into the RAM. All the changes you make also go into the RAM. The revised document would then be saved back to a disk.

The third type of memory is the hard drive in your computer. The hard disk is a sealed magnetic device which stores very large amounts of information on which your work can be recorded, erased and used over and over again. Most computers today measure their size in Megabytes. (A Megabyte is a million characters. A Byte is a single character). Hard drive size has grown tremendously over the years, and at the same time, the prices have dropped. One or more additional hard disks can be easily attached to your computer. The size of hard drive needed to run your business is based on what type of information you need stored on your computer. Graphics and sounds are huge memory hogs. Normal correspondence and accounting information is not.

Computers also use removable diskettes for storage. That's the fourth type of memory used by computers. Floppy diskettes are the little 3.5" hard plastic gizmos you've seen people stick in personal computers. They hold 1.44 megabytes of data. Larger capacity removable storage is available in the form of Zip drives, Jaz drives, and tape drives.

Not only do hard disks hold a great deal more information than diskettes, but information is read and written faster on hard drives than diskettes.

Technical Support

Service after the sale is an important consideration. Even the most experienced computer user will be stumped from time to time, especially at the beginning, with problems that will require expert help. Some dealers are very helpful in answering computer and software questions by phone. Some don't offer any help. When it comes to difficulties with using software programs, most publishers have telephone help lines that offer expert advice. The best time to find out which dealers and publishers are most helpful is before you buy.

***

A DECISION YOU CAN MAKE WITH CONFIDENCE

In this chapter you have become familiar with the computer and some of the most common computer software. The truth is, very few businesses are run these days without a computer, and those that are, could be managed more successfully if they used the available technology. Most businesses can function fine with just a couple software packages – a financial package and a wordprocessor. But computers are marvelous machines that can do much more to make your business successful and more rewarding. It's been often said, tongue in cheek, that a computer is a "toy." It's the most important toy of the twenty-first century! Most of us find working on the computer a joy; so don't be afraid of the computer or technology. Learn more about it and use it. You'll be ahead of your competition.

A GLOSSARY of common computer terms

Application
A software program written for a particular purpose such as word processing, database management, spreadsheet, accounting or tax preparation.

Baud rate
Used mostly for modem communication. Baud rate is the speed of transmission of characters between two computers. One baud is a bit per second.

Byte
A single character. A grouping of adjacent binary digits operated on the computer as a unit.

Central processing unit (CPU)
The "brain" of the computer; a microprocessor that performs the actual work of computing.

Character
Letters, numerals and punctuation marks on the computer's keyboard.

Chip
See integrated circuit (IC)

Clock Calendars
Computers have a built in clock calendars that update time and date automatically.

Command
An instruction by the user that causes the computer to perform an action. Commands are usually typed in from the keyboard or chosen by using the mouse and its pointer on the screen.

Communications
The exchange of information between two computers.

Data
Numbers, characters and symbols which can be used by a computer.

Database
A database stores information in a chain of records. Each record

contains related information about a company, transaction, person or any other topic.

Default or default value
A standard setting or action. In word processing defaults can be line width, lines per page, characters per inch and tab settings. Many defaults can be modified by the user.

Digital
The basic technology behind computers is digital storage and transmission. By converting information to a binary code which represent words, numbers or graphics, the computer system can accept, use and store them. Digital code can be copied over and over again by a computer without losing accuracy, unlike analog signals used for sound and television recording.

Disk drive
The mechanism that holds a disk, retrieves information from it and saves information to it. All computers contain at least one built-in drive.

Diskette
A flexible or hard disk that is used to store information.
> A flat magnetic disc, in a plastic protective case, on which information can be recorded in the form of small magnetized markers. The system works in much the same way sounds are recorded on tape.

Document
Any file created with a word processing, spreadsheet or other application.

Fax or facsimile
A fax machine reads any form of writing or drawing information from paper and transmits it to another fax machine using a standard telephone line.

File
Computer files can contain programs, data, or text. A file document is produced when you create text or graphics on the computer screen, give the material a file name and save it on a disk. Only data or text files can be read from, written to and edited by the user.

File Name
The identifying name assigned to every file.

Graphics

Graphics are pictorial symbols or illustrations displayed on the computer screen.

Hard disk
A disk made of metal and permanently sealed into a drive or cartridge. A hard disk stores very large amounts of information and operates much faster than a floppy disk.

Hardware
Hardware is the physical equipment that makes up your computer system. Hardware includes such items as video monitors, printers, disk drives and keyboards. See Software.

Integrated circuit (IC)
An electronic circuit contained entirely in a single piece of semiconducting material, usually silicon. Also called a chip.

Interactive
When computer programs work together and share information they are interactive.

Menu
A computer menu is similar to a restaurant menu. It shows a list of actions and asks you to choose the one you want by pressing a letter or number key or by using the mouse and pointer on the screen.

Megabyte
A millions bytes i.e. a million characters

Modem
A modem (short for MOdulator/DEModulator) is a device which allows computers to communicate over telephone lines.

Mouse
A small hand-held device, connected to the computer, that controls a pointer on the screen to control various functions. When you move the mouse on a flat surface, the pointer moves.

MS-DOS
MicroSoft Disk Operating System. This is the operating system for IBM compatible computers.

Operating system
A program that organizes the internal operations of the computer and

its related devices. An operating system performs basic tasks such as moving data to and from parts of the system and managing information in memory.

Peripheral device

A piece of hardware such as a video monitor, disk drive, printer, or modem - used with a computer and under the computer's control.

Program

A set of instructions that tells your computer how to perform a particular task such as word processing or accounting. Programs are also called applications, or software.

RAM

Random access memory (RAM) is where the computer keeps information that can be altered or erased while you're working with it. The larger the RAM the more work it can do, such as using a word processor and a spreadsheet at the same time. Most computers can have their RAM size increased by adding additional RAM chips. When power to the computer is turned off, the RAM loses all memory.

RGB monitor

A type of color monitor that receives separate signals for each color (red, green, and blue).

ROM

Read only memory (ROM) contains permanent instructions that checks out the computer's system and prepares it to do its work. ROM can be read but not altered. A power outage will not erase the ROM program

Software

Computer software, also known as programs and applications, are sets of instructions, stored on a floppy disk or hard disk, to be executed by a computer to perform a task. The term "software" distinguishes these programs from the actual equipment, or hardware. See Hardware.

Text

Text is information stored on a computer which can be read on the screen. A program executed by the computer is not considered text.

Chapter 22

Internet Opportunities

AN OVERVIEW OF THE INTERNET
AND ITS USES FOR YOUR SMALL BUSINESS

What is the Internet?

The Internet is a vast network of linked computers. They are linked by cables and phone lines; a cooperatively-run collection of computer networks that span the globe. Computers store information; so mostly, the Internet is information – a mammoth source of information – and information is power. The Internet surfer is like a grain of sand on the beach, and the information on the Internet is like the ocean.

However, the Internet isn't just about data. It is an international community of people who share information, interact, and communicate. From the point of view of its users, the Internet is a vast collection of resources – people, information, and multimedia.

The Internet isn't run by any organization, and it isn't owned by any organization. Instead, people grow the Internet when they build computer networks and link their network to others. The resulting patchwork of Internet worked computers creates a global system of communication.

The Internet isn't just one function. The most publicized aspect of the Internet is the World Wide Web, but there's also email, ftp, usenet, telnet, and IRC. Nor is the Internet static, but constantly evolving with new protocols and functions. Technically, the "plumbing" of the Internet is based on a set of rules for data exchange called the TCP/IP protocol suite. But, as with the computer, you don't have to know how it works, only that it works, and how you can use it.

Should you be online?

There is not a single enterprise (business venture) that could not benefit from being online. The change from traditional to WWW publishing is changing the way we conduct business. The volume of sales generated on the World Wide Web in 1995 was around 436 million dollars. It increased a hundred fold in just a few years.

The ironic thing is that many web sites are not profitable. How can that be? At this time, the lion share of Internet profits are divided amongst only one percent of the advertisers. Why then should you be online? Because more than 30% of Americans own computers, and that figure is growing. Another growth figure is the number of consumers searching for information first on the Internet. If someone wants information on a product or a company, they'll search first on the Internet for that data.

Business on the net

Back in old days, before 1990 or so, there were no markets in the virtual community. If you wanted to buy a book, you still had to jump in your car and drive to the nearest bookstore. This was because, in those days, the Internet consisted mainly of a series of government-funded networks on which explicit commercial activity was forbidden. Today, much of the Internet is run by private companies, which generally have no such restrictions. Many companies have begun experimenting with "online shops" or other services. In fact, a majority of the websites are now commercial or corporate websites.

Many of the shops on the net are run by manufacturing firms, software engineering companies, booksellers, and newspapers, while the services provided on the Internet range from delivery of indexed copies of legal documents to an online stock broker that hopes to entice you to subscribe to any of several economics publications (of the electronic or printed-on-paper variety). A number of companies also use "Usenet newsgroups" to distribute press releases and product information.

Total commercial activity on the Internet and on other networks, such as CompuServe, with its Electronic Mall, or Prodigy, with its advertisements on almost every screen, is phenomenal. Companies are increasingly becoming aware of the potential of the web and investing large sums in website development. According to analysts, an organization typically spends between US$ 100,000 and US$ two million to develop a Web site, and up to half a million dollars a year to maintain the information and keep it up-to-date. That's the big guys. The advantage to being a small business on the Internet is that you can move more quickly. Update your page, offer those sales, keep your page current.

Many customers do not like the idea of sending a credit-card number via the Internet (an e-mail message could be routed through several sites to get to its destination). These concerns have largely disappeared as Net users turned to such means as "message encryption" and "digital signatures." Shopping is relatively safe on the Internet.

An Internet timeline:
1969: UCLA graduate student Jon Postel began tracking computer network addresses for the Defense Advanced Research Projects Agency's (DARPA) Arpanet project.
1970s: Postel moved to USC's Information Sciences Institute and continued his work. He also developed a list of technical parameters that became the Internet Assigned Numbers Authority (IANA).
1980s: DARPA continued funding the early Internet, mostly for federal scientists.
1987: IBM, MCI and Merit developed NSFNet, a national high-speed "backbone" network that supported 4,000 research and educational institutions.
1991: The National Science Foundation took over coordination of the early Internet's nonmilitary functions.
1992: Congress gave the NSF authority to

allow commercial activity on the Net. NSF signed a cooperative agreement with Network Solutions Inc. (NSI) of Herndon, Va. to track Internet addresses. Only 7,100 addresses existed.

1995: NSF allowed NSI to charge $50 per year for Internet addresses ending in .com, .org and .net. NSI put 30 percent of this revenue into a federal Intellectual Infrastructure Fund for future Internet research.

1996: IANA called for additional top-level Internet addresses ending in suffixes such as .store or .firm.

1997: As part of a larger e-commerce strategy, President Clinton directed the federal government to get out of the Internet business. By now, roughly 90 percent of 1.5 million Internet addresses were commercial sites.

1998: The Commerce Department issued a plan for a revamped Internet-address system. It called on scientists, business leaders and others worldwide to form a private, nonprofit corporation to oversee the Internet.

WWW stands for World Wide Web

The World Wide Web allows you to see words and pictures. The WWW project, started by Tim Berners-Lee while at CERN (the European Laboratory for Particle Physics), sought to build a "distributed hyper-media system." In practice, the web is a vast collection of interconnected documents, spanning the world.

These documents are in HTML, HyperText Markup Language. The advantage of hypertext is that in a hypertext document, if you want more information about a particular subject mentioned, you can usually "just click on it" to read further detail. In fact, documents can be and often are linked to other documents by completely different authors – much like footnoting, but you can get the referenced documents instantly!

To access the web, you run a browser program. The browser reads documents, and can fetch documents from other sources. Information providers set up hypermedia servers from which browsers can get documents.

The browsers can, in addition, access Internet files other than WWW files. Other access methods include FTP, NNTP (the Internet news protocol), gopher, and an ever-increasing range of other methods. On top of these, if the server has search capabilities, the browsers will permit searches of documents and databases.

The documents that the browsers display are hypertext documents. Hypertext is text with pointers to other text. The browsers let you deal with the pointers in a transparent way -- select the pointer, and you are presented with the text that is pointed to.

Hyper-media is a superset of hypertext; it is any medium with pointers to other media. This means that browsers might not display a text file, but might display images, or sound, or video, or animations.

What is a web page?

That's the page you see on your monitor. When you click on colored text or a graphic and it takes you somewhere else you have moved to a new web page. A web page is the representation of a document which resides at a remote site. This is key to understanding what the web itself is and the implications.

A web page has the wonderful feature of allowing embedded references (or links) to other pages.

Please, let me explain by example.

When you "visit" a web page, you are instructing your browser to go get a copy of this page from whatever computer in the world it is stored on. The computer then uses the telephone wires to request a copy from the remote site. That machine sends back the copy and viola, there it is on your screen. If the page were to be modified this evening and you came back tomorrow you would see the new web page.

So what?

So . . . in essence you are "looking over the author's shoulder." When he makes a change, wherever he is located, you can see it as soon as you load the page. Because of this, web pages are often called "live documents." Wouldn't it be neat if documents (books, magazines etc.) with time sensitive material could update at any time? It "is" neat and it's called a web page.

You should be excited right about now if this is the first time you are realizing this. Each web page puts you in contact with the author. So if you visit the Database of China Law and Taiwan Law (Li & Partners) web page you are getting a page from a computer in Taiwan. That is what the "tw" means in the URL of the page (http: //www.law.com.tw). The Law web page is maintained by folks who live in Taiwan. There is no middle man to interpret for you. No news anchor to tell you what Taiwan Law is. Hear it is from Taiwan itself.

And because of the availability of "cyberspace" virtually anyone can put up a page saying anything. A soap box to the world if you will. Makes the world seem cozy and warm doesn't it?

The implications and applications of this are:

> A weather page - updated every hour with current weather reports. Stock tickers - stock prices which are updated every 15 minutes. Store fronts - go to Amazon and buy a book from the largest book store I know of (2.5 million titles) without having to go to Washington state (USA). Oh, and you don't have to browse if you don't want to. Just type in the name of the book you want on the Amazon page and they will tell you the price.

The web, and specifically web pages, provides a new medium where anyone, anywhere, can publish. The web allows participants to interact with one another and contribute via email, chat rooms and store fronts. This instrument will change social interaction of folks everywhere. Imagine a medium where you could send the author a message if you liked the document, or didn't.

Differences between the WWW and Traditional Media

1.Geographical reach:

WWW:

The web provides literally worldwide access. It enhances globalization of a company by instantly globalizing the company's markets. When your company has a web page, suddenly, it's available to anyone in the world to read, and your products or services are offered to those readers.

Traditional:

With traditional publishing media, your access is always geographically limited to where you decide to distribute or air your message.

2.Cost of access:

WWW:

The web provides year-round, 24-hours a day, access to your company by your customers and business partners. The cost of reaching additional parties is zero. There is no additional cost to a "second printing and distribution" of your message.

Traditional:

With traditional media, you pay for extra printings, extra airings, new billboard locations, etc.

3.Flexibility:

WWW:

The web provides for dynamism of your message content: It is easy and relatively cheap to update information as the needs of the company or the content of the corporate message changes.

Traditional:

The traditional media is static: It is costly and more difficult to revise the content of your printed or aired message.

4.Interactivity:

WWW:

The web is interactive. The web page dynamically responds to different target viewers' interests by providing them the information they need.

Traditional:

The traditional media are non-interactive. The message is a priori set in print or video. And the message must be fixed for a given target market.

How many hits do web sites get?

When a reader visits a web site, it's called a hit. In the U.S., corporate sites get anywhere between 1,000 to 1,000,000 hits per month. Smaller sites of interest to geographically or topically limited market segments may end up getting as few as 1,000 hits per year. A manufacturing firm with worldwide markets falls into the first category while a local "bed & breakfast" facility falls into the second category. The number of hits is proportional to how much the web site is promoted.

Regardless of the target markets, the number of hits depends on: the relevancy of the information the web site content offers, how interesting and organized it is to attract first comers, whether it is maintained and updated regularly with relevant information to make the visitors come back for new information, and on how heavily the presence of the web site is publicized. With the millions of web sites on the Internet, promotion is the key to any successful web site.

How companies use the WWW

The following are some examples of how companies with a successful Internet web presence use the web:

1. Advertising. Showcasing the company's product lines and services.
2. Public Relations.
   a. Promoting affiliation with the company through: Online corporate partnerships. Customer support pages. Showcasing

innovative, solutions-oriented product uses/applications. Accepting public submissions to online company magazine. Online raffles, drawings, and contests. And direct, topic-specific e-mail notices to interested customers.

b. Making product announcements

c. Distribution of press releases to "usergroups"

d. An online corporate annual report

e. A virtual tour of the company

f. Event support: Special pages for events participated in by the company or organized by the company.

3. Direct sales. Secure, online purchasing opportunities for wholesale and/or retail customers. Product catalogs. Automated online price quotes for complex projects. Product specifications. Warranty/quality/safety information.

4. Operations Management

a. INTRANET applications: "Internet" within the company provides all documents to all (authorized) staff or customers instantly, under security. Inter-company video conferencing and mail technologies

b. EXTRANET applications: Distribution/Logistics/Inventory applications: where suppliers and/or wholesalers/distributors access and/or update company databases. Forecasting support applications (for "Bottom-up" sales forecasting - driven by distribution/logistics feedback from wholesalers), Training & Certification applications for training personnel or distributors away from company headquarters. Typically, organizations make use of architectures based on Three-Tier "Intranet" Designs to implement direct sales and operations-related applications. And increasingly, companies are setting up their own private Corporate "Extranets" for EDI (Electronic Data Interchange) with their trading partners.

Is WWW a passing fad?

No. To answer this question, let's look at some variables that are reliable measures of the growth of the Internet and the World Wide Web. The number of hosts on the Internet has roughly tripled in the time from January 1994 to January 1996. The WWW has grown very fast. In fact, the WWW has grown substantially faster than the Internet at large, as measured by number of hosts. The rate of the web's growth has been and continues to be exponential, but is slowing in its rate of growth. For the second half of 1993, the Web had a doubling period of less than three months, and even today the doubling period is still less than six months.

Browsers

The favored browsers are Netscape, Internet Explorer, and Opera. Many others are available, but they're less popular for one reason or another. Browsing the Internet is also referred to as "surfing the net." Browsers are the software that allows you to view the files of, or "move about" the World Wide Web. Thus, the term "browsing."

To look at a Web page, just choose the desired icon (small picture) or "link." Links are colored text, graphics, or pictures. Usually the brighter or darker colored text is for new links, and the duller or lighter colored text signifies you have been to that Web page before. (It all depends on the author of each individual Web page.)

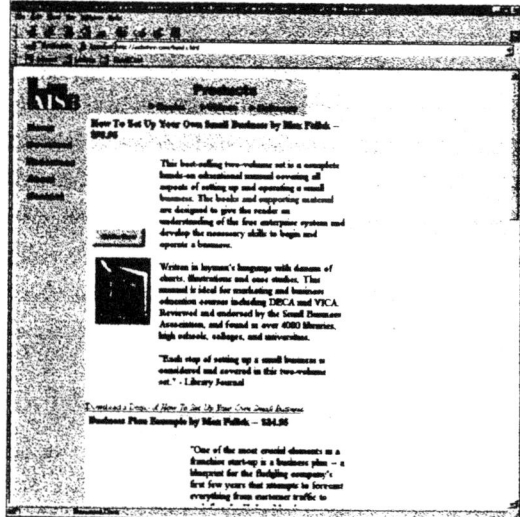

Links can be underlined, depending on your browser options. When you highlight a link (or put your mouse pointer on it), the browser will display a URL (Uniform Resource Locator = address) at the bottom of the browser screen. They usually begin with the "http://" (HyperText Transfer Protocol). (More URL protocols: "gopher://", "ftp://", "news://", "file://")

When you follow a link, you can choose the "back" button of your browser's toolbar to return here. (Or right click the mouse and choose back.) You need to click "back" for each time you clicked on a link. If you get lost, you can type the URL in the text box, under the toolbar, where your browser says "Location:", "Go to:", "address:", or something similar; or choose "history" on the Explorer toolbar (on Explorer 4, choose the small down arrow just to the right of the back button), "go" on Netscape's toolbar, then choose the URL, or page title. The URL for the American Institute of Small Business is: http://www.aisbofmn.com

The easy way to shorten your return, is to "bookmark" the web page. To do this for Netscape, you choose "bookmarks" from the toolbar, then choose "add bookmark," or you can right click the mouse and choose add bookmark ("favorites" for Explorer). Any time you wish to return to a web site choose "bookmarks" for Netscape, or "favorites" for Explorer. Then choose the title of the page or URL.

What is an ISP and what is an Online Service?

An Internet Service Provider is a local or national service that is a gateway to the Internet. You pay a certain fee each month, for that you can call into the service, and through them, access the Internet. They provide a number for you to call to access the Internet, they assign you an email account, and sometimes they provide some software.

Examples of Online Services are AOL, CompuServe, and Prodigy. An Online Service is a computer service you dial into, that has its own utilities, such as email, chat, and resources. They provide you with access software that connects your computer to their service. And also they may provide a gateway to the Internet.

What is email?

Email is the means by which messages, or letters, are sent and received from one computer to another through the Internet. These messages are sent and delivered virtually instantaneously. It is also possible to attach files and photos. Email allows you to send messages to people around the world. Many people are getting email addresses because it is such a cheap and fast way to communicate. No stamp. No envelope. No running to the mailbox in the rain. Here are some examples of Internet email addresses:

joel@solutions-4u.com
president@whitehouse.gov
someone@unbc.edu
jmm@grfn.org
someone@freenet.vancouver.bc.ca

Notice that all of the letters in the email address are in lowercase. This is usually done for simplicity. However, the computer does not care.

Email addresses usually consist of a name or initials followed by the at symbol (@) and then the name of the domain, the ISP the recipient has their Internet account on. The last portion of the address (e.g., com, gov, edu) tells you what classification the domain is.

Com stands for commercial.
Gov stands for government.
Edu stands for education.
Org stands for a nonprofit organization.

Why Is Email Different?

Electronic communication, because of its speed and broadcasting ability, is fundamentally different from paper-based communication. Because the turnaround time can be so fast, email is more conversational than traditional paper communications.

In a paper document, it is absolutely essential to make everything completely clear and unambiguous because your audience may not have a chance to ask for clarification. With email documents, your recipient can ask questions immediately. Email thus tends, like conversational speech, to be much sloppier and more ambiguous.

This is not always bad. It might not be a worthwhile expenditure of energy to slave over a message, making sure that your spelling is faultless, your words eloquent, your grammar beyond reproach, if the point of the message is to inform the recipient that you are ready to go to lunch.

Granted, you should put some effort into keeping your subjects agreeing with your verbs, spelling correctly, avoiding mixing metaphors, and so on. But if The Rules that Mrs. Grundy laid down in seventh-grade English get in the way of effective communication, throw them out.

However, because of the lack of vocal inflection, gestures, and shared environment, email is not as rich a communication method as a face-to-face or telephone conversation. Your correspondent may have difficulty telling if you are serious or kidding, happy or sad, frustrated or euphoric. (Sarcasm is particularly dangerous to use in email.) Thus, your email messages should be different from both your speech and your paper compositions.

Mailing Lists

Discussion groups use mailing lists to contact the interested membership. Each person's email message that is sent to the mailing list gets routed to every person who is a member of the particular list. It's a cross between email and Usenet newsgroups. You need only to request to be included on a mailing list.

Topics of mailing lists are wide-ranged: From Animal Liberation, to Daily Jokes, to Genealogy, to Zoroastrianism. At present, there are more than 7,000 active mailing lists. But be careful, some mailing lists spawn hundreds of email messages each day.

What is File Transfer Protocol?

File Transfer Protocol (ftp) is used to send files to your computer. Many universities and businesses have computers that offer software over the Internet to anyone who wants it. They usually do this through the File Transfer Protocol.

Web browsers (such as Netscape) can access ftp sites. This has the advantage of presenting the files in an easy-to-use interface. To do this you must have a basic understanding of URLs. What are URLs?

Universal Resource Locators

URLs are basically the addresses of Internet resources, usually World Wide Web pages. They look complicated at first but if you break them down they become quite easy to understand.

Here are some example URLs:

http://www.solutions-4u.com/
http://www.microsoft.com/
ftp://ftp.somecompany.com/somefolder/somefile
telnet://solutions-4u.com/

The first part of the URL tells you (and the computer) what type of service you are contacting. "http" is used for World Wide Web resources, "ftp" is used for File Transfer Protocol and "telnet" is used for Telnet.

The first part is always followed by "://".

The next part is the address of the machine that you are connecting to. This is followed by the information that shows what page you are going to, on the computer you are connecting to.

URLs are usually given all in small letters for simplicity however the computer does not usually care.

What is Usenet News?

Usenet News allows you to talk with people around the world. It's like a bulletin board at your neighborhood grocery store. Messages are posted for all to see. Usenet is divided into many different topics called Usenet Newsgroups. By many, I mean tens of thousands of newsgroups. So, it's like a bulletin board at your neighborhood grocery store if your neighborhood grocery store had a bulletin board the size of Minnesota.

Based on the topic, some groups tend to be very good for having clean content and the others whole purpose is the discussion of more a controversial nature. Many newsgroups are monitored so no one can post messages off the selected topic.

There are dozens of newsgroups specifically for promoting your web site, or hawking your products or services. And, if you're offering online technical support of your products, a newsgroup is a great place for your customers to come to ask their questions and receive the solutions.

Netiquette

The Internet has set up its own rules of proper behavior, frequently called Netiquette.

Rule 1: Remember the Human. The golden rule your parents and your kindergarten teacher taught you was quite simple: Do unto others as you'd have others do unto you. Stand up for yourself, but try not to hurt people's feelings.

Rule 2: Adhere to the same standards of behavior online that you follow in real life

Rule 3: Know where you are in cyberspace. Look before you leap. When you enter a domain of cyberspace that's new to you, take a look around. Spend a while listening to the chat or reading the archives. Get a sense of how the people who are already there act. Then go ahead and participate.

Rule 4: Respect other people's time and bandwidth

Rule 5: Make yourself look good online

Rule 6: Share expert knowledge

Rule 7: Help keep flame wars under control. "Flaming" is what people do when they express a strongly held opinion without holding back any emotion. It's the kind of message that makes people respond, "Oh come on, tell us how you really feel." Tact is not its objective.

Does Netiquette forbid flaming? Not at all. Flaming is a long-standing network tradition (and Netiquette never messes with tradition). Flames can be lots of fun, both to write and to read. And the recipients of flames sometimes deserve the heat.

But Netiquette does forbid the perpetuation of flame wars -- series of angry letters, most of them from two or three people directed toward each other, that can dominate the tone and destroy the camaraderie of a discussion group. It's unfair to the other members of the group. And while flame wars can initially be amusing, they get boring very quickly to people who aren't involved in them. They're an unfair monopolization of bandwidth.

Rule 8: Respect other people's privacy

Rule 9: Don't abuse your power

Rule 10: Be forgiving of other people's mistakes

Finding Things on the Internet

Many people discover that the Internet is so large that it is hard to find what they are looking for, because there is so much out there, and no central index. This is just as true on the World Wide Web. This section will help you find how to look for information on the Web. It is important to note that the "find" button at the top of the screen in your browser will find a word in the page you are viewing ONLY. It will not search the Internet.

Search Engines and Directories

A Search Engine is a tool for locating information on the Internet. There so many search engines on the WWW, but the most notable are: Altavista, Excite, Hotbot, Infoseek, Lycos, and Webcrawler. Yahoo! is a directory. Generally speaking, a search engine is an automated "card catalog" of web sites. You enter a key word and it searches a database it has compiled and then it lists the most likely web sites to find the information you're searching for.

There is something else that is important to note. There are two different search types:
1. an "AND" search,
2. an "OR" search.

An "AND" search allows you to search for everything that has the word "food" and the word "drink." An "OR" search allows you to look for all documents that have the word "food" or have the word "drink." Most of the search tools use these searching capabilities. It's called a Boolean search when you use "AND" or "OR."

A directory is similar, except it is usually maintained by people – actual humans doing work – cataloging the information on web sites. You click on categories until you come to the information you seek.

After developing your web site, it is very important to submit your URL (the address of your web site) to all the search engines and directories. That is how your potential customers will find you.

Viruses

Many people and worried about getting viruses from the Internet. There is only one way that you can get a virus from the Internet: that is, to download a program and run it. If you don't even know what that means than you are not at risk. You can't get a virus from the following activities:

Browsing the World Wide Web
Getting email
Downloading pictures
Chatting with other Internet users

What is IRC?

Internet Relay Chat. Where people meet to "chat" live, also referred to as "in real-time." There are several networks for IRC.

IRC or Internet Relay Chat was developed by Jarkko Oikarinen of Finland in 1988, and since has been used in more than 80 countries. A multi-user chat system, IRC enables people to meet on channels, which are like virtual rooms where they may converse in text, in groups or privately.

Participants may join several channels simultaneously, conducting different conversations in multiple windows, and even maintain private conversations while separately involving themselves in group discussions in other windows.

Thousands of channels exist, public and private, professional and social, temporary (unregistered) and permanent (registered). Channels have names prefixed by a # (such as #IRChelp), and are easily created. You join a channel by typing /JOIN #channel, with #channel representing the channel name.

All channels have a channel operator, whose nick (IRC name or nickname) is preceded by an @ symbol. A channel operator has administrative rights, such as conferring operator status on other participants, making the channel private, or kicking out offensive members. In registered channels, when the operator is away, the channel is managed by a computer program known as a BOT.

Participating in an IRC chat involves only downloading the free software, filling out the configuration screens, connecting to a server, and learning the few basic commands that will enable you to join a channel and converse with other participants.

Making a web site

In building a web site, you must decide if you're going to design your own or hire someone. A professionally designed web site can cost in the thousands. Fortunately, for those companies less wealthy, there are a preponderance of students of the Internet who'd love to design your web page for mere hundreds of dollars, instead of thousands. From these budding entrepreneurs, don't expect high tech/cutting edge/state of the art HTML designed web pages. Expect a simple, straight to the point, attractive web site. Also, don't expect that they'll offer high maintenance and support. They'll probably design your page, you pay them, end of deal.

Design it yourself: HTML Editors

Several free, easy-to-use programs are available for building simple Web sites. Netscape's Communicator comes with one, called Composer, and Microsoft offers its Internet Assistant, which can be used with Word . Microsoft Publisher and Adobe PageMaker also come with Web-authoring tools. And if you're an America Online member, you can use AOL's Personal Publisher (key

word: personal publisher). All of these programs let you create Web pages without knowing HTML, the source language in which all Web pages are written. Instead, you can use icons and menus to get the job done. Once you've created a site, you'll have to upload ("publish") it to a Web server before it can be viewed on the Internet. AOL and most other Internet service providers give you free space on their servers, plus instructions for uploading your pages.

Retail HTML Editors are also available in abundance. A couple advantages of purchasing an editor are:

First, technical support; as a registered user you'll be able to call the company when you have questions. Second, more options and ease of use; these programs have been specifically designed to aid the new user; they often include a function called a wizard. A wizard walks you through the process, step by step, of developing a simple web site.

Relatively, developing and designing your own web page is easy, but time consuming. If you're unprepared to spend the time learning a new software program, or your time is best spent elsewhere, then spending the money to have someone else design your web page is the answer.

Promotion, Promotion, Promotion

Once your web page is designed and is resident on a server (accessible to the Internet), the next step is to promote your web site. Promotion on the Internet is like any other form of advertising in that it's an ongoing process. Plan to spend a few hours each month in getting your site noticed. The advantage of Internet promotion is that most of it is free.

You know what search engines are. It's important that the search engines know about your site. Every search engine had a simple process of submitting your page for inclusion. The same with directories. The submission form will ask for the URL of your site, a contact person's name, sometimes a phone number (but this is not part of the listing – it's not displayed to the searcher), and sometimes a brief description of your site.

Classified Ads are also free. They're like web bulletin boards. You submit a description of your site, or your products, and the URL of your site. Classified ads web sites are usually specific to a certain topic, like "women-owned business," or "auto-parts."

Usenet Newsgroups, like classified ads, can be utilized for advertising your company, products and services. The same newsreader client that you use to read the newsgroup messages can be used to submit postings to the groups. Make sure you don't post off-topic or you will be flamed; non-flattering email will be sent to you.

A popular form of advertising on the Internet that is not free is the Banner Ads. Banner ads are graphic ads that advertise a company, product, or service, and when the reader clicks on the ad, their browser takes them to the web site of that company. Advertising on a search engine, where you're ad could be seen by a million people in a month, could cost you tens of thousands of dollars. A site receiving fewer hits, of course, costs less; perhaps a couple hundred dollars for three months.

The site where you're advertising will supply you with the specifications on the size of the ad. There are limitations to file format, dimensions and size of the graphic. Graphic programs, such as Jasc's Paint Shop Pro, can be used to create banner ads. However, for an additional fee, the site will also design your banner ad for you. Costs for this service are usually in the hundreds of dollars.

A word of caution on banner ads. Know your market. Make sure you are advertising where your dollars are doing the most good. This statistic is reported by the Institute of Cosmetic Surgery, advertising on a popular news site: Although their banner ad appeared 55,000 times in six months, the click-through rate (the number of times someone actually clicked on their ad for more information) was 298 times. And no customers and sales were achieved through that banner ad.

TO CONCLUDE:

The Internet is a tremendous force to be mastered. A business MUST be on the Internet, and it MUST promote. It has been called, by financial experts, "The future of business." Every business will have an Internet presence.

Making a web page is not a one time shot. It's your advertisement to the world, and it's the world's window into your business. It must be updated constantly to be kept current.

The hype surrounding the Internet can be intimidating. When television was first implemented people said it was overrated and just a passing fad. You should not make that same mistake about the Internet.

Chapter 23

Creating a Business Web Site

YOUR SHOP ON THE INTERNET

Does every business need a web site? No. Does your business need a web page? Possibly. Do you want more customers and do you want to provide better service to your existing customers? Definitely.

The importance of having a web page for your business is directly related to what you are selling. The more rare or unique your product or service, the more likely your web site will be a success on the web. And by success I mean the more it will stand out and be visited and create more sales for you. What's available at your local mall does not make for good merchandise on the web (unless you can substantially sell it for less). If you provide something that is hard to come by, the web is a perfect place to hawk your wares.

There are two basic business web sites. Those that contain information important for your customers – a promotion site. Or those that are specifically set up for transacting business – an e-commerce site.

A Few Reasons We Can Think of to Put a Business on the Internet

To establish a presence. Globally, approximately 50 million people have access to the World Wide Web. Quite simply, there are few businesses that can ignore a market of this size. In the near future, having an e-mail address and web site will be like having a phone number and business card — crucial to even small companies.

To network. By linking your pages with those of your networked contacts, you are referring clients back and forth. If, for instance, your product complements, is used within, or uses a product from another manufacturer, a potential client can get a complete package of information with just a few clicks of a mouse.

To provide availability advertising. There's little doubt that the most used resource directory is the Yellow Pages. Imagine a book of Yellow Pages that covers the globe—all a client would need to do is tell it what he or she was looking for, and it would automatically open to your listing. That's exactly how the www works.

Not only can you list basic information (your business expertise, location, hours, how to contact you, methods of payment, and so on), but you can update this information instantly (time-sensitive specials, current interest rates, announcements, and press releases). You can even have an entire catalog, including full-color photographs and graphics, available for instant viewing and ordering.

To augment traditional advertising. Imagine including a brochure with every business card, piece of letterhead, print or broadcast ad, and even in your telephone's on-hold messages. By including your www address, that's exactly what you can do. A www address, such as www.buyfromme.com, is small enough to fit anywhere, yet it provides instant access to your entire line of products or services. Furthermore, an instant e-mail response can be built into web pages to get and give feedback while the questions are still

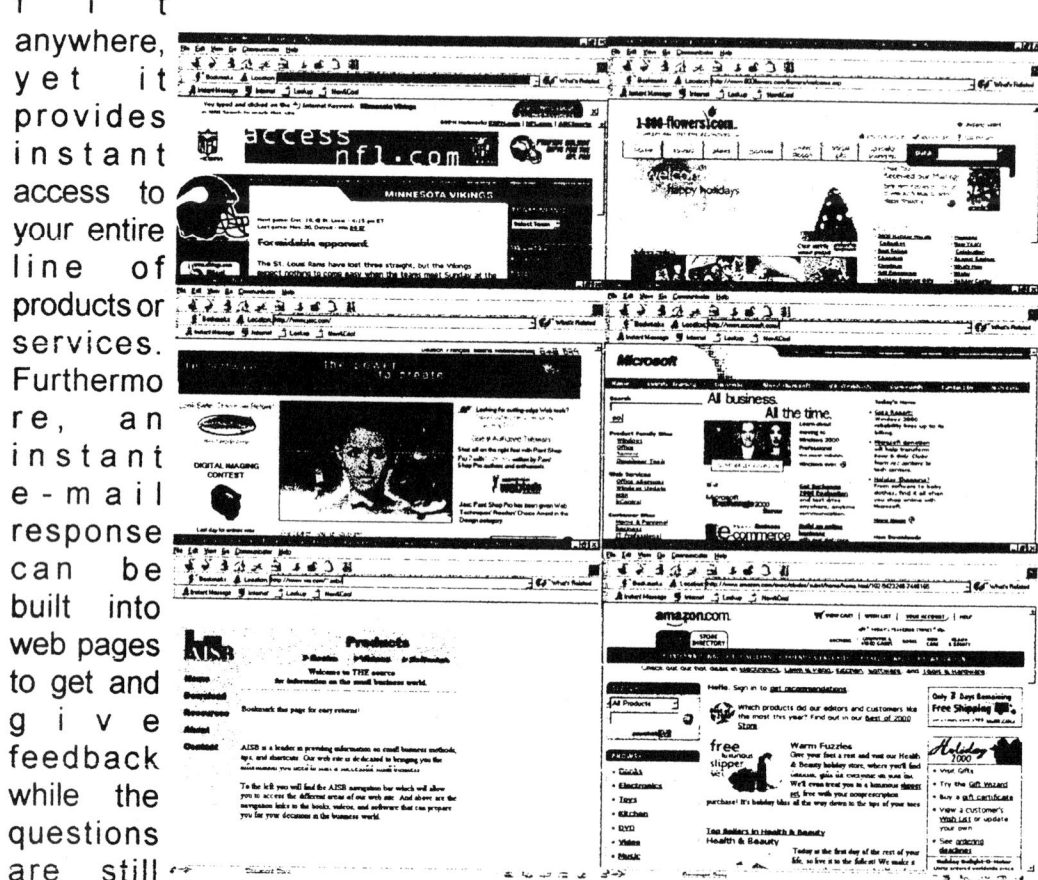

fresh in your customer's mind, without the cost and lack of response of business reply mail.

If you read any of the nation's largest magazines and newspapers, you'll notice more and more www addresses printed within advertisements. The reason for this is simple: The www allows a much higher degree of communication for the advertising investment — more bang for the buck.

Customer service. Wise people have often said that it's easier to keep an old customer than to get a new one. Keeping an open line of communication is one of the most important ways to serve your customers. Via the www, you can post information, offer troubleshooting tips, and request forms and the like that will enable you to "keep your finger on the pulse" of your customers.

Publicity. The media is perhaps the most advanced profession today in regard to electronic communication, since their main product is information and they can get it more quickly, cheaply, and easily online. Because of this, online press kits are becoming more and more common. Most pressrooms have gone digital in the past decade so it is much easier for them to simply take a press release and photos from a web site than it would be for them to strip-in hard copy. The easier you make it for the press, the more likely you are to have your press releases turn to articles in a timely fashion.

To open international markets. As the United States is discovering, digital information has little respect for international boundary lines. Because of this, markets that may have once been too difficult to approach can now be very profitable.

With a web site, you can open up a dialogue with international markets as easily as with the company across the street. We'll go so far as to say that you should decide how you want to handle the international business that will come your way before you start a web site, because it is a good possibility that your online marketing will bring international opportunities—whether it is part of your plan or not. Information about your old car for sale could be read by people around the world.

To test market new services and products. The advertising costs of rolling out a new service or product can be enormous. Many times, because of the cost of printing and mailing, companies hold off releasing new products until the next generation of their catalog. On the web, new products and services can be released globally and instantly; updating a web page to include a new item costs a fraction of what it would to print a new catalog. The Internet's two-way communication also enables you to receive immediate feedback from your markets.

To reach a highly desirable demographic market. The demographic of the www user is probably the highest mass-market demographic available. College educated, high income, credit card holders (most ISPs require credit card deposits) — it's no wonder that magazines that deal with the Internet are easily able to get high-revenue ads on a regular basis.

To reach the specialized market. Thinking of selling nude photos of George Bush? With millions of Internet users, even the most narrowly defined interest group will be represented. And, because of the search capabilities of the www, your potential customers will be able to find you.

To provide 24-hour, 7-day accessibility. A fax may come in from Tokyo at 2:00 in the morning. By the time someone comes in to open the office, the sale is lost. By accessing your www system, however, the same potential client could have surveyed your brochure and placed an order — for less than it cost to send the fax.

To save money. Say your company prints 10,000 copies of a brochure. You send 2,000 out via the mail, give 2,000 to the sales staff, and put 6,000 in a warehouse for later use. Over the next few months, you add new products/services, or you move offices, or you add partners. You now have thousands of outdated brochures.

One of the main reasons that so many of the largest corporations in the world have rushed to the www is to try to contain print and print-storage costs.

To sell. Obviously, sales is the most important part of any business — so why didn't we make this the first item on the list? Because a good businessperson will have seen that all of the other points listed add up to increased sales. The www is perhaps the most powerful marketing tool ever devised, but it is only a tool. Even the most perfect promotional system can't make up for a poor product or service, inept staff, or any of the hundreds of intangible stumbling blocks that lie in the way of successful sales. However, with the powerful communication tools and enormous market available in Internet marketing, there's far less of a gamble.

The fact is that clients can find you; review your information in text, pictures, and even sound and video; contact your sales staff; and place an order from their own desks within a matter of minutes, 24-hours a day. No other form of business communication provides this degree of sales support.

What Makes a Great Web Site?

What are the essential traits of great web sites? When you visit a site and find yourself staying awhile, what makes you stay? A sense of humor helps. Flashy graphics are nice. But the fundamental traits that make a site work are more elusive. This chapter will break down the essential characteristics of great web sites into some easily followed rules of thumb.

Most of these guidelines are just plain common sense, which seems to be a scarce commodity on the web. Stick with standard HTML and your pages will look good on all browsers that support it. Give away something valuable: information, software, advice, humor, and people will flock to your site. Original content is the most important trait of a great web site.

Here are the web site guidelines. Web sites should:

Provide credible, original content in as many forms as possible. Original content is the most important trait of a great web site.

Provide valuable, timely information to the user, not lots of data web sites should be updated regularly. Stale web sites say "been there, done that." For the information to be valuable it should be well-edited. For external links include only the best sites with concise descriptions. For internal content be like a magazine editor, don't rush to publish mediocre or incomplete articles.

Customize and target your content/site to your users. Think "one-to-one" web sites. Custom-tailor the information to customer's preferences.

Be responsive on a 56 kbps modem (the typical Web user). Use graphics sparingly to convey information. Each graphic takes another trip to the server. Consolidate neighboring graphics or use table cells with background colors to speed display. Size graphics to fit in a typical user's window (a maximum of 465 to 532 pixels wide [i.e., the default Netscape screen to a printed page], or for max screen space viewable on all platforms use a max of 580 pixel wide tables to fit on Mac screens). It's easy to see if a site's been designed on only a PC, the page is too wide on a Mac, typically 620-640 pixel wide tables fit a PC's monitor but are too wide to display on a 14-15" Mac monitor.

Break up your tables vertically for a cascading load to appear more responsive. One huge table takes much longer to display content than stacked smaller tables which display one at a time. Microsoft's IE5 has a fixed table width feature that speeds table display, unfortunately this is proprietary and does not work on Netscape's browser.

Optimize graphic file size for web display (a maximum of 20 KB per graphic). Use jpegs where possible and appropriate (continuous-toned images) and minimize the color palette of gifs to optimize file size. The majority of graphical web browsers in use today can only view .gif and .jpg files without launching helper applications. If you ask your viewers to obtain a different helper application, you will shut out a large portion of your target audience. Because of the amount of time they take to load, graphic files can detract from the usefulness of your page. Minimizing file size should be considered when incorporating graphics in your page. Loading time depends on the size of the file, not the size of the picture. Compare the size of your file in .gif or .jpg format and select the smallest file size providing the best picture size and quality on the screen.

Picking between .gif and .jpg: Use .gif with solid colors and sharp contrasts or lines between solid color areas. .gif is best used with cartoons, clip art, text diagrams and charts. Use .jpg (or jpeg) with photographic quality, continuous blends of color   ranges. .jpg tends to blur sharp edges or contrasts. Provide text alternatives to graphics for low-bandwidth users, the blind, and for speed. ALTernate text tags for images should be functional, not descriptive. If the graphic has no function, use ALT=""

Optimize your HTML by removing excess spaces, comments, tags and commentary, especially on your home page, to minimize file size and download time. Products like Mizer and HTML Turbo automate this process by removing excess characters. These products are drag and drop, and should be used as the last step before you upload your page (the files are harder to read after many of the returns are removed). After optimization your pages will appear to snap onto the screen.

Be easy to read. Make your pages as easy to read as possible. Black text on a white background (just like this page) is the easiest to read. There are some nearly impossible to read pages that use backgrounds the same shade as the text (dark text on a dark background and vice versa). If you use a background, stick with the lighter shades and let the text stay black.

The second most important trait a web site should have is interactivity. Be interactive; good interactivity engages the user and makes your site memorable. After original content, the second most important trait a web site should have is interactivity. The web is an interactive hypermedia communications medium that your web site should reflect. Sites that involve the user and have a sense of fun or adventure will get more hits, and can charge more for ad space.

Users equate poor organization with poor site design. Be well-organized. Balance the number of levels with page length to minimize scrolling and display time.

Designing pages so important content is "above the fold" is a good idea, though some sites take this maxim to an extreme and cram everything into a cramped mess. Where possible, place your pages' important content to fit into the typical user's screen (465 pixels wide by 340 pixels high for a 15" monitor). Web pages should be at most two 8.5 x 11 pages in length.

Part of having a well-organized site is providing multiple ways of easy navigation. Supply both text and graphics for buttons. And users feel more comfortable if you maintain a consistent look and feel throughout your site.

Build it, and they will come?

A common misconception companies new to the web have is that if they put up a page, people will visit it. If you set up a retail business in your basement, how will people across town know where to find you? Advertise and Promote.

In order to have a popular site, you've got to offer something to the user:

information, interactivity, fun, freebies, something more than an 800 number. Original content is important. Users may come to your site once, but to keep them coming back you've got to have fresh original content.

Sites that offer freebies get noticed. Free software, services, databases or electronic newsletters will attract users like a magnet.

The web is an interactive, dynamic, and rapidly changing new communications medium that your web site should reflect. Well-organized, edited, and timely original content set in an attractive, interactive, and consistent format are some traits of great web sites.

Steps to Creating a Web Site

Creating a web site is best accomplished in steps. These steps are: plan, design, code (HTML), upload (FTP), test, promote, and maintain. Each step has a clear objective and definable outputs.

Step 1 - Plan Your Web Site

To plan your web site you must:
1) Define its purpose
2) Define your intended audience's interest, values and knowledge
3) Assess your available resources
4) Determine the start date and update frequency
5) Select your hosting service
6) State why you are developing a web site.

To develop a plan for your web site create a word processing document and answer the following questions:

Who?

Who is your target audience? Study your target audience. Clearly, a site meant for an older, conservative group would not be interested in flashy graphics and blaring audio. Try to picture yourself in your audience's shoes. What would they like? Now, write down your intended audience. Not sure? Look at some of your competitors! Check out their sites to see how they appeal to their target audiences. What are they doing right? What are they doing that needs improvement? List your audience background, their interests, skills, values and knowledge.

What?

What's the purpose of your site? To educate, entertain, provide unique help or information to others, or a combination of these. As you plan your web site remember each web page should have an objective, but within the constraints of the web site's purpose. If you aren't sure how to proceed look at other web sites on the Internet for ideas. Look at the categories in some of these search engines for examples of audience interests.

When?

When do you want to start your site? How often do you plan on updating your site -- daily, weekly, twice a month, or monthly?

Where?

Where is your site going to be hosted? Choosing the right hosting service depends on your individual requirements. Before you sign-up for any hosting service (free or commercial), make sure you can get the features you need.

Your existing Internet service provider (ISP)? If you have an existing Internet account chances are your ISP will provide you free web space and allow you to create a personal web site. But, if you want to create a site for your business you will probably have to pay your ISP to host it.

What about free hosting service? These sites will host your web site for free. Some allow you to host your business or non-profit organization, some host only personal web sites. With over 50 sites listed you should be able to find one that meets your requirements. Commercial hosting service? Commercial web space providers are plentiful - but, they are not free. There are hundreds of hosting companies to choose from. You have to be careful who you select to host your web site.

Why?

Why are you developing a web site? To inform your customers or to sell products and services?

How?

You can hire someone to create your site or do it yourself. How will you create your web site? How do you plan on researching material for your web site?

Your Web Site Plan is dynamic in nature and should be updated as you learn more information about the above six questions, your web site design, receive feedback from your readers, change your focus and/or technology changes.

Step 2 - Design Your Web Site

You should focus your design on achieving the results stated in your Web Site Plan. Don't include something just because it is cool or fun. Always keep your target audience in mind - ensure your design is based on their knowledge, needs and values. Outputs from this step will be:
1) A Design work folder and sub-folders for your site.
2) Web design tools downloaded.
3) A sentence outline for each of your web pages.
4) Links, images, and sound files to be used for each page.
5) A standard header, footer and navigation scheme.
6) A hand drawn organizational chart of your site.
7) A text file for each of your pages.
8) The colors you plan to use for your background, text, link, and visited link
9) Web site style (basic, table or frames).
10) An updated Web Site Plan.

When writing for the World Wide Web, you may have to adjust your writing style. Web usability studies show that web readers tend to skim over information rather than read it. Why? 1) It's hard on the eyes to read much on a computer monitor. 2) The reading speed on a screen is about 25% below reading the same material on paper. The solution? Get your message across as quickly as possible.

When designing your web site you should keep the following design principles in mind. A site should be useful. A site should have a purpose. A site should operate quickly, each page should download within 15 seconds. A site should be structured to allow visitors to navigate with ease. Graphics should be kept to a minimum to allow fast loading of your web pages. Use standard headers and footers for each of your web pages. Use the same background color throughout your site. (White is most common color) Use the same color for your text throughout your site. (Black is most common color). Use a common font size and color for specialized text segments. If you are developing your first web site, don't worry about the font tag. Establish site wide consistency rules. Keep it simple.

Web Site Design Tools

Carpenters, electricians and auto-mechanics all need the right tools before they begin work. Well, so do webmasters. It's called software. Some software you already have, others you can download as freeware or shareware. You can have your site built before the shareware programs expire. Your ISP's web site might provide software for creating web pages. And there are many sites on the Internet that provide downloadable software. www.download.com is one example.

The use of colors, consistency, content, graphics, navigation and web style all work together toward creating an effective web site. Learn about web site design and you will be able to answer these questions: How do you want your site to look? Do you want to use frames or tables? Do you want your navigation on the left or right side, the top, or the bottom. What colors do you want to use?

Using the guidance above, the information you developed during the Planning step, create a text file (.txt) sentence outline for each page of your web site.

Links

The real beauty of the web is that files can be linked. These files can include documents, images, movies or sounds. Links also called hyper-links or anchors, they may be external to your site or internal (links to other pages within your site).

To create a hyper-link you must know the file's URL. A URL (Uniform Resource Locator) is the address for a resource on the World Wide Web. For example, the URL http://www.yahoo.com/index.html, or just www.yahoo.com. When you create a link whatever text that appears between the opening and closing HTML tags will become underlined and colored. If you click

on the underlined text it will send the browser to that URL. Don't worry about HTML tags yet. Time to start collecting all the external links you plan to use for your site. Place them in a text file called "my- links" and place them in the "links" sub-folder you created for your web site.

Images

With a careful selection of icons, bullets, and bars you can give your site a personality all its own. But, if you overuse graphics they can seriously slow down the page's loading time and clutter design. Start collecting your graphics now! Copy your images and place them in the "images" sub-folder you created for your web site. Make sure these files are offered freely by the webmaster, some may ask you to provide them a link back. Do not link directly to any external graphics.

Free graphics and animations can be obtained from many sites, like www.fg-a.com. Buttons, bullets, flags, gifs, animations, horizontal lines and more are free for your personal or business site.

Sound

Just because your computer has a sound card, and the Internet is a multimedia environment, doesn't mean you have to incorporate sounds on your business web site. A lot of web designers believe that midi files or other audio files should not be used with a business web site because the tune is repeated and quickly become irritating. However, if you wish to download a sound file to your site, right-click directly on the midi or wav graphic or link and select "Save Target As" from the pop-up menu. If you do use sounds, do not "loop" it. Have it play once, not indefinitely.

Banners, Logos, Headers and Buttons

To maintain consistency, your headers, banners, logos and buttons should look the same on every page. The header is the first line of text, banner or logo you want readers to see at the start of each page.

Footers

Footers should contain at least the following information: URL of your site. Author of the site. Author's e-mail address. Date the page was created/last updated.

Navigation

Design your site so that users can easily navigate through it. If the visitor to your site needs to scroll down for information, always include a "Go to top" link at the bottom of each page so that users can easily return to the beginning of the page.

Feedback

Developing methods for users to interact with your site is essential for creating a good web site. User feedback is a very important to improving your site. At a minimum provide your e-mail address so that users can provide you their comments, suggestions and opinions. Make sure this is included on each page.

Encourage bookmarks; add a note to your pages reminding visitors to bookmark your site. It increases the chances that your visitors will be back.

Organizational Chart

Draw an organizational chart by hand of your site. This should show you how the pages are grouped and how they are linked to one another.

Now it's time to go to work! Develop the actual text that will be used for your pages and save them in separate text files (.txt) for each page. Update Your Web Site Plan. Update the "How" paragraph of your Web Site Plan to reflect: 1) The links (URL), images, and sound files to be used for each page. 2) Location of your standard header, footer, navigation scheme and text files for each page. 3) The colors you plan to use for your background color, text color, link color, and visited link color. 4) The web site style (basic, table or frames) you plan to use.

Step 3 - Create HTML Code For Your Web Site

To create HTML code for your web site you can use an HTML wizard, HTML templates, HTML editors, manually create your code or a combination of these methods. Outputs from this step will be: an HTML document for each of your web pages, which includes: your text; links; images; sound files; with a standard header, footer and navigation scheme.

What is HTML?

HTML is the acronym for Hypertext Markup Language. HTML is the language used to tag various parts of a web document so browser software will know how to display a document's text, links, graphics and other media. HTML documents have a file extension of either .html or .htm. To view an HTML document, right click your mouse button, then select View Source.

Create Your Web Site

As mentioned above, there are four ways you can create a web page:
1) Use an HTML wizard.
2) Use pre-made HTML templates.
3) Use an HTML editor.
4) Use a text editor such as Notepad to write your HTML code.

For newbies to the web you can download the Home Page Wizard. The author Alexey A. Popoff lives in Moscow, Russia. It's also free and can be downloaded here: http://members.xoom.com/myhood/hpw_122.exe

After you have downloaded the wizard, create some web pages and study the code by right clicking your mouse and select View Source.

Web site templates. Don't have the time to learn HTML? Why not use HTML templates? With a template, the bare page is filled in by you. You insert your text and graphics, then save the page and upload it.

HTML Editors. To assist the novice, as well as the expert with creating a web site, HTML editors are available. Many of these editors provide tool bars, buttons and icons that insert the necessary tags for you. But watch out, some HTML editors are more complicated than learning HTML from scratch. Want to use an HTML editor? Download one or more of the freeware editors from www.download.com.

Manual HTML. To create HTML manually you will need to use a text editor such as Notepad. If you own a PC and use Windows chances you already have Notepad installed. To locate Notepad on your PC, click on Find, select Files or Folders, enter Notepad.exe, then click on Find Now. Mac users can use SimpleText. See Appendix H for some simplified HTML coding.

Cut and Paste Time. After you have created your code for each of your pages, copy the header, navigation bar, and footer you created during the Design step and paste them on each of your web pages. Double check everything. After you have created .html (.htm) files for each of your pages. If your web site is hosted on a UNIX/LINUX system, check the case of your file names. UNIX/LINUX host are case-sensitive (the file index.html is different from one named Index.html). In addition, html files on a UNIX/LINUX host must end with an .html extension, not .htm. Click on your home page, navigate through your site and ensure that all internal links and navigation buttons work.

Spell check your web pages using an automated spell checker. If you don't have a spell check capability, wait and perform this check during Testing. Individual browsers may support specific tags in different ways. It is a good idea to view your page with different browsers to see how your tags are translated. Printout and carefully proofread your pages. Although you may have checked your pages using a spell checker, watch out for mistyped works (words) - see what  I mean. Also, have someone else proofread a copy of your pages. Correct your errors. Make all the required changes on your files.

Step 4 - Upload (FTP) Your Files

To upload your files to your host computer you need to determine your FTP address and password. Complete the pre-FTP checklist. Next, select and download your free FTP software. Setup your host profile. Learn to FTP a few test files. Then, upload your web site files to your host computer.

FTP is the acronym for File Transfer Protocol. FTP allows you to send and receive files to and from computers.

Pre-FTP check.

1.Determine your host FTP procedures. Check with your web site hosting service and determine your URL, obtain their FTP instructions - FTP address, user name and password. Record and keep this information for future reference.

2.Select FTP software. If you don't have an FTP program, you will need one. Here are a few popular programs.

FTP Explorer - PC FTP Explorer is a file transfer protocol client for Windows 95 and NT 4.0, that looks and acts very much like the Windows Explorer. Free for home and educational use.

WS_FTP - PC Offers a side-by-side display of the local and remote sites directory. LE version free for non-commercial home users. Download LE Version

Fetch - MAC For Macintosh computers. Easy to use. Free to users affiliated with an educational institution or charitable non-profit organization. Information and download

More FTP Programs - PC There are scores of free FTP programs available, if you don't like the three above, try one of these at download.com.

How does FTP software work? FTP requires a client (FTP program) installed on your PC to connect to your host, or server. Once you are logged in, you are presented with a directory. If files already exist on your host you can select the download to option and pull files off the FTP server to a specified directory on your computer. If you select the upload option, you must also select your PC directory that contains the files you wish to upload. The files are then copied from one location to the other. It's like copying files from one directory or folder on your PC, except that one of the folders could be on the East coast and the other folder on the West cost.

After you obtain an FTP program spend some time learning how to use it. Each FTP program is different. Read the instructions first. Setup your FTP software to access your host computer. Enter the FTP host address you obtained earlier. If Anonymous is already selected on your FTP software screen, click on the Anonymous checkmark to deselect it. Enter your User ID and Password. If you see an option in your FTP program for a file type of either ASCII or binary, use ASCII when transferring HTML files, and binary when transferring graphics files. Or, if the option is available select auto-detect, and your program will automatically do this for you. Most FTP programs are setup to use Port 21. Don't change this unless your hosting service indicated to use a different port. In most cases you can ignore other entries on your FTP screen such as Use firewall, PASV mode, Description, etc. - unless your hosting service indicates otherwise. Check your folder and file names.. Make sure they are all in lower case letters. Otherwise, they will not work on UNIX based hosts. Don't use spaces or special characters in your folder or file names. Don't use more than one extension in your file name.

Next, create two test folders on your PC - Upload and Download. Select some test files and copy them to the Upload folder. Run your FTP software and logon to the Internet. Select the upload option on your FTP program and your PC folder Upload. Select the test files to transfer (FTP). Once uploaded, the test files should be viewable in your FTP window. Now select the FTP download option and download a few files to your Download folder. Continue to upload and download test files until you feel comfortable using your software. Delete all test files on your host before you begin uploading your files.

Prepare files for uploading. Move all the files that you plan to upload to the same folder/directory on your computer. Double check to ensure they can be viewed locally with your browser using your navigation scheme.

FTP your files. Access your FTP software and transfer all the files (html, gif/jpeg and mid) in your PC folder to your web site folder. Check to see that each of the file names you uploaded are viewable in the download window.

Did the FTP work? Start your browser, go to your URL. Explore your site.

Step 5 - Test Your Web Site

To test your web site, test each HTML file using a free an online HTML and spell checker. Check each of your files one at a time. Correct your errors off-line and FTP the files back to your site. Re-validate your files. Continue until all spelling and HTML errors have been corrected. Also, check to ensure that all your links - internal and external are active. Determine the download time for each page. As a final check ask your friends to visit your web site and provide comments.

Before you advertise, promote or make your web site available to the public, make sure you thoroughly test each file.

HTML validation

Before you validate a web page, you need to add a Document Type Definition (DOCTYPE) as the first line for your HTML page. For example: <!DOCTYPE HTML PUBLIC "-//W3C//DTD HTML 3.2//EN"> This specifies the syntax (grammatical structure) of a web page. Next, you need to select a free on-line validation service to use. An example is:

Dr. HTML - Performs spell checks, image analysis, hyper-link testing and HTML syntax tests. Plus, it provides you the time (in seconds) it takes to load your page using a 14.4k modem. www2.imagiware.com/RxHTML

Or, you can download SpyGlass and validate your HTML documents off-line on your own PC. It's free. Spyglass has discontinued maintaining the HTML Validator. But, it is still available for you to download free.

More than likely using an HTML validation service will not be a pleasant experience. You may receive dozens or even scores of error messages. It's a troubling, deflating experience. A common first encounter will be the error message, "too many errors to continue". Don't panic, give up or surrender. Spend some time reading the rules, correct as many errors as you can, upload your page and re-validate your page. Continue to do this until you have corrected all of your errors. If you are about to give up because you don't understand the errors, try another validation service - some are very picky.

Broken links. Search your web site for broken links.

Spell check your site. Make sure you check all of your pages for misspelled words.

Download time. Determine your download times using modem speeds of 14.4k, 28.8k, 56k, ISDN 128K and T1 Link 1.44 Mbps. Ideally, try to keep your download time for your home page size under 20 seconds (sites that take more than 20 seconds to load lose up to 50% of their visitors), all other pages under 12 seconds using a 28.8 modem.

"Fat" graphics are the leading cause of slow-loading web pages. The site www.ZDNet.com will also identify which graphic files you need to reduce and you can use their free image optimizer to slim-down the graphics on your web page. There are many factors outside your control that may affect your download time: (1) your host hardware and configuration, (2) Internet traffic and (3) time of day. Remember, factors you can control to affect your download time include: (1) size of each page, (2) number of images on each page, and (3) the size of each image.

If possible, testing should also be done with a variety of browsers using various computers.

You can simulate the testing of your web pages using different screen resolutions and window dimensions at this site.

Update your files. Based on your testing results, make all the required changes and FTP your new page to your host computer.

The final test. Ask other people to evaluate your web site: Ask several of your friends and family members to evaluate your web site and provide you their recommendations to improve it, make sure they give you specific details. Consider their recommendations carefully and make the required changes, spell check your files again and FTP all changed pages to your host computer. Re-validate and spell check all the files you changed. Make a backup copy. Download all your HTML, image and midi files to your computer and copy these files to a diskette. Label this diskette as "Backup for My Web site".

Step 6 - Promote Your Web Site

To promote your web site you need to add your web page title, meta description and meta keywords. Create a text file containing your promotion data. Select your search engines and directories. Add your URL. Maintain records of all your promotion actions. Promote your web site off-line. Promote your web site as often as possible.

Web Site Promotion

To ensure that your web site gets the attention it deserves, you have to promote it. To do so, you will have add a few more lines of HTML tags to your web pages, plus fill in some online forms to register it with the various search engines and directories. Fortunately, there are Internet sites available to do most of the work for you for free. Plus, there are numerous sites willing to provide you valuable information about promotion.

Promotion. Your first step in promoting your web site is to learn how search engines work and about Internet promotion. Start by:

Add meta data to each of your pages and FTP the new pages to the site hosting your pages. But, that's no sweat you can FTP in your sleep by now!

Measure twice and cut once. Before you spend a lot of time trying to register your site, make sure the meta data on each page is correct and double check everything else.

Visit META Tag Analyzer (www.scrubtheweb.com/abs/meta-chec k.html) to check your Meta data on each page. They will check your title tag length, check your meta keywords and description for size, check to ensure you have not exceeded the repeat limit for keywords and check for multiple title tags.

23-17

Visit the Site Inspector (www.siteinspector.com) and double check the design of each page. They will check the following: HTML design, browser compatibility Netscape and Internet MS Internet Explorer), hyper-links, spelling, search engine readiness and load time.

Make all the required changes off-line and FTP the changed pages to your site.

Registration. Now let's register your site with the top search engines. Access your text file that you created for the meta data and add the following information to it: your URL, your name, and your e-mail address. Use this information to cut and paste the required registration data with the search engines. Each search engine is different and may not require all of this information. Register your site with: AltaVista, Anzers, AOL NetFind, Infoseek, Excite, HotBot, Lycos, NorthernLight, REX, WebCrawler and What-U-Seek using the forms on this page.

Multi-submit Sites. Since getting listed on the major search engines is so important, we do not recommend that you use any multi-submit site to register with Alta Vista, Excite, HotBot, Lycos, InfoSeek, WebCrawler or Yahoo. Multi-submit sites are very useful for your registration with the lesser known search engines, directories and free for all (FFA) links. A favorite multi-submit site is Selfpromotion.com. Here you can promote your site with search engines, indexes, and directories (over 100). Return when you receive an e-mail message indicating your promotion is complete, and see the results. The service is free.

Keep good records of your promotion actions. Create a database containing your online promotion actions. At a minimum include the following: the name of search engine/directory/link exchange; date of registration; lead time for registration; a code verifying that your site is registered; month verified; and any reciprocal link requirement. For the major search engines, also include your primary keyword phrase(s), search engine position and date.

The waiting game. After you have registered your site with the top search engines, don't expect to see your listing within the next hour or even day.

Read the latest search engine news. Based on a survey conducted by Credit Suisse First Boston Corporation and @PCData, 5,300 web surfers were asked which search engine they preferred to use. Participants preferred Yahoo by more than 2:1.

More registration sites. While you are waiting for some of the slower search engines to register your site, here are a few more places to promote your site:

Jayde Online Directory..
EZResult.
Linkmaster
Magellan
Nerd World
Media One
World Plaza
Search King
Starting Point
What's New Too!

Take your time. You don't have to do all the search engines in one day. Work for about an hour then take a break. More things to do. Promoting your web site through the Internet is only part of the job. You should also promote your site off-line by:

Telling all your friends/family members and ask then to link to your site. Including your URL in all your correspondence. Add an e-mail signature file. A signature file acts like a return address. At a minimum your signature file should contain the following: Your name, your e-mail address and web site URL address. Include your URL on anything that leaves your office: stationary, business cards, invoices, return address labels, business checks, telephone answering machine message, news releases, all advertising (brochures and other sales literature), billboards, Yellow Page listing, and even on the sign in front of your business. Also, make sure you inform your employees of your URL address and encourage your employees to mention your web address to your customers. Create a list of all the actions you have taken to promote your site off-line. Read, try to discover new ways to promote your site and share your knowledge with others.

Step 7 - Maintain Your Web Site

For your web site to be a success you must maintain it. If you expect visitors to return, you must provide them with something new, correct errors and keep your site up to date. In addition, you must continue to monitor your search engine ranking, continue to promote your web site and find out who is linking to your site.

Maintenance of a web site is actually only a repeat of the 6 previous steps: plan, design, HTML code, test and promote -- done on a smaller scale. Why maintain? Maintenance of a web site is performed for several reasons. These include: To enhance and/or improve the design. To update or add additional information. To respond to visitor's comments/recommendations. To correct errors and design problems. Static web sites soon die from lack of interest! The average life of a web page is 75 days.

General maintenance guidelines: Web sites should never be static. Keeping a web site current isn't a gimmick, it keeps your site popular. If your site is not updated regularly, visitors will not bother to return. If you don't occasionally offer new information or resources, you're not giving visitors any reason to return. No matter how well publicized your site is, if you don't maintain it, it will decline in popularity.

Keep it simple. Creating new and complicated web pages, will only mean more work for you.

Be reliable, If you promise monthly updates, make sure you live up to your word. Do not offer anything that you can not deliver.

Take any feedback you have received seriously and reply as soon as possible, and thank the visitor. If the feedback contains ideas on improving your site or correcting errors, evaluate each one. If you plan to add the suggestion, send an e-mail to the person who suggested it and indicate that they should return to your site on (specify a date) and see their idea in action.

A "What's New?" page can keep your return visitors up to date on what has changed since their last visit. You should also place a small "new" graphic next to items that have recently been updated, or added to your site.

Develop a web site maintenance plan. Include in this plan the frequency for updating your site (update your site on a regular basis); a sentence outline of items that you will include during your next scheduled update due to: errors; design problems; enhancements; new information and your visitor's comments/recommendations. Keep this plan current and at update time, maintenance becomes a snap.

Proof read your changed pages before you upload them.

Test all changes. If you make a change to a page, no matter how small, always validate your HTML code and spell check it.

Check your internal and external links regularly. Web sites are always changing, check you internal and external links at least monthly. Net Mechanic (www.netmechanic.com) will check your entire site and e-mail you the results free. Also, periodically check your links manually yourself.

Always develop your new pages on your local computer, and then upload them to your web site, add updated or new pages to your web site only after they have been tested, validated and work correctly.

Always retain a backup copy of your web site on a diskette, as well as your hard drive.

How Often? How frequently should you update your site? It depends on what you have to offer your visitors.

Maintenance Tips. When it's time to maintain your site consider these tips.

Content Is King. One of the biggest problems any web site owner has is finding good content. Content is what brings your visitors to a site in the first place. If your pages aren't updated and new content isn't added, your web site will become ineffective. These sites will provide you free content for your web pages.

Monitor your web site host. If your site is unreachable, call your hosting service immediately and find out why and when it will be again available.

Future Enhancements. After your web site is operational for a few months you might want to consider adding enhancements and new features, such as: a guestbook, counter, graphics, free banners, logos, buttons, a personal search engine and a web poll. Check out this page for some ideas.

Increase Your Knowledge. If you own a web site you must continue to learn.

Continue to Promote. Submit your main page (index or home page) to as many web directories/search engines as you can. Every time you browse the web and come upon a new directory/search engine, use it. Check out this page for some new promotion sources.

Continue to Monitor Your Position. Your search engine placement will change over time, so it is important that continue your placement. Often this is time-consuming and frustrating, but it has to be done!

Make sure you are registered with the major search engines. Continue to check your URL ranking

Re-register your site. Register your site again with the major search engines if you: Change your URL. Change the title of your listing. Change the content of a web page. Change the description and/or keywords of your listing. Require additional or different categories for your listing. Change your e-mail address, if it is associated with your listing.

Nominate Your Site For An Award. You need a reward after all your hard work!

Site Links. Find out who's linking to your site.

Get Your Own Domain Name. If you are a serious about your business, a domain name is the best investment you can make. You can now register domain names up to 67 characters in length, including the .com or .net or .org extensions. You are no longer limited to 23 characters for your domain name! Registering a domain name involves filling out a form and paying a registration fee. Network Solutions is no longer the only game in town.

A few almost final words. Remember, people are more likely to return to your site, if you keep it tidy, spell checked, validated and up-to-date.

Internet commerce is growing quickly. The experts predict it to continue to grow exponentially. They also predict that all successful businesses will be a part of that astounding growth. The Internet allows people throughout the world to visit your web site and see your products and services.

In this Chapter you've learned that doing a web site for your business is a large project that should not be rushed, but you can break it down so it's manageable. You've learned the steps to take to create a Web Site Plan, and to help you do it yourself. Appendix H will even teach you some simple HTML coding.

The experts tell you to Do It. Hopefully this chapter has taught you to Do It Right.

On the Road to Success

Chapter 24

Pack your own bag

"You are what you eat," say nutritionists. Motivators could say, "You are what you think."

Your thoughts determine your success in a new business enterprise at least as surely as financial and marketing preparations do.

By firmly **believing** that you will succeed, you improve your chances for success. It's as foolhardy NOT to believe that you would succeed as it is to start a business with the firm belief that you would fail.

A number of attitudes and beliefs -- call them "points of view" -- promote this faith in success.

OTHERS HAVE DONE IT, SO CAN I

"The greatest barrier to achievement is lack of adequate self-esteem to support it," says Dr. Nathaniel Branden, a psychiatrist and best-selling author.

If you don't have self esteem, you'd better find some. Just deciding that you have as much right to self esteem as anybody else helps you develop it.

Self esteem activates faith that the outcome of your efforts will be what you intend them to be.

"Faith," said Leo Tolstoy, "is the force of life."

Believe in yourself. Here, at the beginning of your grand enterprise, you have a crucial choice to make. You can choose either faith . . . or fear. One of these two emotions will dominate your life and determine whether you will succeed or fail.

You must make a conscious decision -- right now -- to let faith lead you to success.

Choosing faith in success is a logical move from one point of view. It is ILLOGICAL to choose failure -- but some people think and act as if that's what they've done -- so, practically speaking, they **have**.

Fear of failure is not going to help you reach your goal. That's the best reason to just ignore it. Fear is counterproductive: Fear is not a constructive thought. When you find yourself swept up in it, remember Roosevelt's famous World War II admonition: "The only thing we have to fear is fear itself."

You want to reach your goals and fear is not going to help you get there; so don't allow it to influence your thoughts and actions.

Choose FAITH.

Faith was just about all that David Schwartz had going for him. And it was **enough**.

He was operating a one-lot used car dealership in West Los Angeles in 1978 when he discovered a niche in the car rental business between one-day rentals and fleet rentals. The niche was a hidden demand for long-term rentals of used cars in good condition. The demand is created by people who are between cars, who are on vacation, whose cars are in the shop. People who've been transferred to a new job in a new city sometimes need a car for a week or more.

Schwartz began renting his used cars, sometimes for months at a time, and then went into franchising the business he called "Rent-A-Wreck." His prices were half what the big three in the rental business charged, one of the main reasons for his success.

By 1983 he had more than 200 franchises in the U.S., Australia and the Bahamas. In that year **Venture** magazine rated him one of the 10 fastest growing franchise operations in the nation.

Schwartz didn't hire a management consultant or conduct a marketing survey before he began. The success of Rent-A-Wreck was a result, he says, of "luck, timing and a wild idea."

But, Schwartz wasn't reckless or foolhardy. He knew the risks. And he didn't let them stop him. He considered them carefully; then set out with determination to make his idea work. Once he got started, he did everything by the book to make sure that his success would continue.

Schwartz, whether he knew it or not, lived by a precept of Henry David Thoreau: "If you have built castles in the air, your work need not be lost; that is where they should be. Now put the foundations under them."

Faith. Schwartz had it.

Believe, as David Schwartz did, that "My best WILL be good enough."

Expect wonders from yourself.

Believe! The tide WILL turn. A miracle WILL happen.

John Wallace, an unemployed tow truck driver in Seattle, down to his last $100 with a family to feed, had total faith in himself and his idea.

He knew from experience that 90 percent of tow truck calls were for minor problems that could be repaired on the spot, where the vehicle broke down. So, in 1979, he started Auto Medics of America, using his old pickup truck.

His early goal was 30 mobile repair vans operating in the Seattle area. Later, he started a highly successful preventive maintenance program for fleet operators. He now sells parts for less than auto parts stores and still makes a 50 percent profit because he buys directly from the factory.

If John Wallace hadn't believed in himself and in his idea, he wouldn't be the big success he is today.

If you really believe that you are going to succeed, as Schwartz and Wallace did, you are actually using auto-hypnosis -- hypnotizing yourself to act in a way that promotes the success you visualize and dream of.

Dr. Norman Vincent Peale, who introduced the phrase "positive thinking" into our language and into our collective psyche, says in his book **You Can Win** that, "Faith is stronger than will."

"You can pre-condition your mind to success," says Dr. Peale. "This is the basic principle of positive thinking. You can actually forecast what your future success will be from your present type of thinking."

Take Chances

To do great things, it is necessary to take chances, as Schwartz and Wallace did.

But, take CALCULATED chances.

The story is told of Captain Eddie Rickenbacker, the first air ace in U.S. history. He won the Congressional Medal of Honor in WWI. At a boisterous celebration after the war in a 12th floor room, the war hero was moved to display his bravado by standing on his head on the window ledge.

Later, somebody asked him why he had taken such a risk - 12 stories above the sidewalk.

Exhibiting the self-confidence that was an essential ingredient in his bravery, Captain Rickenbacker pointed out that there is a big difference between "calculated risk" and "foolhardy risk." He had taken a well-calculated risk. He KNEW that he could stand on that window ledge on his head without falling.

If all entrepreneurs were as confident, there would be fewer business failures.

You are not taking a foolhardy risk if you have studied the chapters in this book. You learned in Chapter 5, for example, how to prepare a Loan Proposal. It would be risky indeed to approach any lender without such a comprehensive proposal. Your GREAT IDEA could die on the vine, and that is the ultimate calamity for any new business. On the other hand, by applying what you learned, you are taking a well-calculated risk.

Be Willing to Sacrifice

Besides being willing to risk, be ready to sacrifice.

If you have any qualms about making sacrifices to succeed, remember this: Whatever you sacrifice should be less important in your life than what you sacrifice FOR. If it isn't, you've made the wrong choice about how to earn a living.

This is NOT a recommendation to abandon family life. The strength you derive from a rich family life is vital to success.

At the same time, don't sacrifice so much that all that remains in your life is work. To do so is another example of counterproductive behavior. Eventually, when all you have left is work, even that will begin to suffer.

Dr. Robert H. Schuller, famed TV evangelist and proponent of "possibility thinking," tells this story about sacrifice and self confidence: A super successful California multimillionaire started his manufacturing and marketing business by selecting a small team of bright men.

He explained the tremendous opportunity in his idea to them. He promised them good salaries, the opportunities to be creative, and shares in the financial success of the company. He offered all this on one condition -- that they invest all their money in the new company.

One of the men objected. So, the job for which he'd been selected wasn't offered to him. The others went along -- and became millionaires.

When we refer to sacrifice, remember, we're talking about TOTAL DEDICATION.

Don't fool yourself about the degree of sacrifice required to qualify as "total dedication." (You'll know it when you're doing it.)

And don't overlook the effectiveness of dedication, either.

A famous inspirational speaker on the subject of motivation says: "Show me a man with a consuming dream coupled with a deep, unshakable faith and I will show you a champion -- a mountain mover."

Michael Korda, in his best-selling book **Success**, writes: "Desire, determination, and a good sense of timing are common denominators of success -- of far more importance than any other factors."

Tommy Van Scoy, a small-town jeweler, became a mountain mover. He had operated a jewelry store successfully for 25 years. But, he wanted to grow. To do so, he knew he needed to sell better merchandise for less money -- like the chain stores.

So, he decided to increase his volume, buy in larger quantities, and then obtain greater discounts from suppliers so he could sell for less -- like the chain stores.

In 1977, he began specializing in diamonds, built up his capital, and used it to buy diamonds directly from importers in New York for half the price he had paid his wholesalers. Volume increased -- and soon, the importers were coming to HIM. He was approached by a representative of Israeli diamond cutters, and eventually, he bought all his diamonds directly from the Israeli diamond cutters for one-fifth what he had paid the wholesalers.

John H. Johnson, editor and publisher of Johnson Publishing Co. (who publishes several magazines for the black community), and board member for many large corporations, says this:

"Success in business is a time-honored process involving hard work, risk taking, money, a good product, a little bit of luck, and, most all, **a burning commitment to succeed**."

Johnson says that at first Ebony magazine was all he had. If he did not succeed with it -- he thought -- failure would destroy his life. From this belief, he acquired a total commitment to success.

To be dedicated, you must be motivated. Some people "multiply the levels of motivation," as professional motivators say, to keep themselves going, constantly pointing out the benefits to themselves of doing something essential and worthwhile.

BENEFITS

Rewards of Dedication and Sacrifice

In his book Korda writes: "If we are going to work at all, and most of us have to, we might just as well become rich, successful, and famous in the process."

Sy Merns, son of Russian immigrants, took his company public in 1983 and cashed in $35 million of the amount he received from selling personal stock. He had spent many grueling years guiding his company, Syms Corp., a Lyndhurst, NJ, off-price apparel chain, to its successful public offering.

In 1983, 302 entrepreneurs made more than $10 million each when the value of their stock soared after they took their companies public.

By the way, don't let yourself envy the dedicated, successful people in your field who reap the rewards of their dedication. Instead, TRY TO BE LIKE THEM and you will improve a hundredfold the chances that you, too, will be successful.

If you've got the best team, you'll win, too. With preparation, persistence, knowledge, follow-through, hard work, character, good physical and mental condition, self-esteem, faith, and enthusiasm on your side, you won't have to worry about losing in the end.

Sure, you may lose some games. You may get knocked down by a big linebacker once in a while. But, if you pick yourself up and hit into the line repeatedly, you will win in the end.

Even though you don't win every game, you WILL win the seasonal championship. And that's what counts – **who's ahead at the end of the season**.

One very successful entrepreneur is fond of saying that he doesn't mind losing nine out of ten times. He has learned from experience that he wins big enough that 10th time to more than balance his losses from the other nine attempts -- a result that he credits to perseverance.

PERSISTENCE

"Victory belongs to the most persevering," wrote Napoleon. He knew.

Henry David Thoreau, who lived alone at Walden Pond in Massachusetts for two years, expressed the spirit of persistence somewhat crudely, but his meaning was clear: "Do what you love. Know your own bone; gnaw at it, bury it, unearth it, and gnaw it still."

"Gnaw your own bone." Perhaps that admonition, applied to entrepreneurs, means one should take up a business that he is familiar with -- or GET familiar with, fast.

Thoreau, by the way, gave a lot of guidance to entrepreneurs in his famous book, Self-Reliance. In that book he wrote: "...if one advances confidently in the direction of his dreams, and endeavors to live the life which he has imagined, he will meet with a success unexpected in common hours."

Apply Thoreau's principles, and winning will simply be the logical result of continuous effort. If you continue to TRY, one day you'll look up and the goal line will be right there under your nose -- and you will SCORE.

Ed Lowe of Cassopolis, Michigan, was selling sawdust and dried clay to garages for soaking up oil when he got a multi-million-dollar idea -- Kitty Litter, a product name that he coined. His first bags of Kitty Litter were mistaken for a new cat food, though, causing mass feline indigestion. And, pet shop owners laughed: After all, cats had always been let out the door to scratch in the sand.

But, Ed Lowe persisted.

To shop owners who scoffed at his Kitty Litter he said: "So, give it away."

They did. Soon, customers were coming back.

He'd call on pet shops with a box of Kitty Litter under his arm and a shot glass in his pocket. He would poke a hole in the Kitty Litter with his finger, pour a shot glass of water into it, and deliver his sales pitch while the liquid soaked in.

Lowe would leave the box and shot glass behind so the pet shop owner could put on the same show for HIS customers.

He spent many days at cat shows doing nothing but cleaning out cat boxes and replacing contents with Kitty Litter, in return for a free booth. (THAT's dedication.)
Even with his creative salesmanship, Lowe's first-year sales amounted to only $500.

Later, he was caught napping when a giant company came out with a kitty litter made of alfalfa pellets. He lost most of the market.

But, he persisted.

Now he has 43 percent of the market in a $250 million industry. He lives in luxury on a 2,600-acre Michigan estate and winters at a home in Sarasota, Florida.

Persistence is next to greatness.

Persistence is magic!

Patience and persistence are the marks of a champion -- a winner.

Fate seems to be impressed by persistence. When life is darkest, the protagonist plods on, shoulders hunched in a fighting posture. He is often flabbergasted by unexpected and sudden success. The help he needs, the person he needs to help him, the idea that's essential to the solution to a major problem, a stroke of luck -- it seems to happen as if on cue.

The cue is persistence.

Consider this sorry record of a persistent man who eventually triumphed:

Failed in business, '31.

Defeated for legislature, '32.

Failed in business, '33.

Elected to legislature, '34.

Suffered nervous breakdown, '36.

24-8

Defeated for speaker, '38.

Defeated for elector, '40.

Elected to Congress, '46

Defeated for Senate, '55.

Defeated for Vice President, '56.

Defeated for Senate, '58.

Elected President, '60.

This man who suffered repeated failure was . . . Abraham Lincoln.

Many a successful person has achieved success at precisely the moment that he or she was sure that failure was certain . . . because he or she **persisted**.

Thomas Alva Edison tried 10,000 combinations of ideas and materials before he found the combination that made the first successful light bulb.

Successful people persist until they succeed or until they realize that the cost in terms of time, energy, and money of pursuing a goal is more than success would be worth.

Stubbornness

One form of persistence is stubbornness -- coming back for more even when it looks as if you're beat. It's as if you were one of those life-size, blow up clowns with the weighted bottom: You whack it, it falls to the floor, but it springs up again, every time . . . smiling!

Winston Churchill, the inspirational bulldog Prime Minister of Britain during WW II, was like that. He propped up the morale of a nation with attitudes such as the one expressed when he said: "Never give in! Never give in! Never, never, never, never -- in nothing great or small, large or petty, never give in except to convictions of honor and good sense!"

Dr. Schuller says: "You **never** quit, you simply **adjust**. You may revise your time schedule. You may scale down the size of your plans. You may rearrange your resources. But you will **NEVER** quit!!"

Stubbornness. It's not always bad to be stubborn when you have a good idea and you are certain that you are the best person to make it work.

Persistence and stubbornness often are justified because you are never defeated **in your own mind** until you QUIT. There is no hopeless situation -- just people without hope.

To buoy your hope, to motivate yourself to be persistent, wear a coat of armor as you fight life's battles. Wear a strong ego.

The slings and arrows of disappointment aimed at you will bounce off.

Ed Lowe believes that lack of persistence is the MAIN cause of failure in business.

"Unless you happen to hit a bonanza," says Lowe, "a business will take six or eight months just to reach the breakeven point."

"To get a business like a small manufacturing plant or a retail store over the hump, and to start making an annual income in the $25,000 to $100,000 range, takes four to five years, usually.

"You've got to have faith. Oh, brother, do you have to have FAITH!" Lowe says.

Make that "Persistence"

Persistence precedes the spring. The winter was long and lonely. Your mood was sometimes black, and you couldn't even visualize sunshine and green grass anymore. But then the first warm day dawned, the black cloud became a pink cloud of joy; and you couldn't even remember being gloomy. When you raised your head you could see FOREVER.

Wouldn't it be a shame to quit just before the first rose of springtime?

If You Refuse to Quit, You Can't Be Beat

Even if you fail occasionally, you can turn failure into success as long as you do not admit defeat. NEVER admit defeat.

Some of the business ventures of Ed Lowe, the Kitty Litter King, failed. ("Actually," says Lowe, "the businesses just └didn't succeed'." Lowe never admits defeat.)

"There's nothing wrong with failing," he says, "as long as you've got the guts to go on."

The moral is: **Do your very best every day**, as your daddy taught you, and you'll be able to hold your head up high, no matter WHAT happens. What may happen, by the way, may well be success.

Barbra Streisand, singer and actress, has apparently inexhaustible energy. She has a reputation for going to the limit in everything she does.

Barbra's been known to work 24 hours straight to prepare a one-hour television show. The benefit, she says, is the satisfaction that she has given the best performance she was capable of.

INSPIRATION follows PERSPIRATION

Remember that success is just the flip side of failure. Try long and hard enough and failure often BECOMES success.

Try, try again.

There's a lot to be said for the idea that says to succeed, you've got to fail. The more often you fail, some say, the closer you get to success.

To keep your chances alive, just make sure that you learn from your failures. A fairy tale Indian said: "White man fool me once, shame on white man. White man fool me twice, shame on Indian."

Says Korda: "Failure has its positive points. It provides you with a pause during which to assess your motives, your abilities, and your opportunities. Failure teaches you far more than success ever can, if only because failure sharpens the survival instincts and forces you to learn your business in depth and detail.

"Failure is the best school for success. There is nothing like it for hardening the will and maturing the personality."

Joel Sugarman is a big success now. He is the president and creative driving force behind JS&A Products. He began the business in his basement and it now occupies a new building in suburban Chicago.

But, there was a time when he couldn't even sell a mousetrap. Here is the story. He took literally the old adage: "Build a better mousetrap and the world will beat a path to your door." He BUILT A BETTER MOUSE TRAP -- a trap that zapped mice with a laser beam, yet.

However, the world did NOT beat a path to his door.

He placed a quarter-page ad in the Wall Street Journal. But, he didn't sell a single mousetrap. He DID learn a lot that he applied to future endeavors, however -- as proven by his present success.

Failure is part of life. It certainly is part of selling. Good salesmen learn to take rejection (failure) in stride. They aren't afraid of calling on prospects just because the customer might say "No." They hear that all the time; but they aren't paralyzed by fear. Rejection, to them, is part of the job, as it should be for any entrepreneur.

Failure is only a temporary setback for a persistent person.

Enthusiasm

Enthusiasm is the spark for persistence.

Successful entrepreneurs almost glow with confidence and enthusiasm. They project a positive self-image. They believe that they are winners, so they usually are -- an example of a type of self-fulfilling prophecy.

They act like winners, and others **expect** them to be winners -- so they are treated like winners.

Be ENTHUSIASTIC. If you don't feel enthusiastic sometimes, well . . . ACT enthusiastic. It's a way to **generate** enthusiasm.

Enthusiastic people enjoy life. They enjoy their jobs, their families, their recreational activities. Whenever they tackle something, they tackle it with gusto. They enjoy whatever they do whenever they do it.

To whip up enthusiasm for your business, set reasonable, realistic goals -- long-term and short-term goals. Once you achieve them, then set new goals. Goals are motivational.

One female entrepreneur, in writing her goals, wrote: My long range personal goals are to achieve a position of power and authority through my business with which I can make an impact on my community."

In their book, **Minding My Own Business**, Marjorie McVicar and Julia Craig wrote: "Goals are the essence of success. A written goal is the passport that sends you on your way. Without a goal, your movement is sideways. You shuffle to the left, shuffle to the right, always waiting until . . . "

An entrepreneur's goals should incorporate the **reason** that she or he wants her/his business. Why not work for somebody else? A clear answer to that question can be very motivational. In fact, the satisfaction and pleasure that one derives from doing exactly what he wants to do working for himself or herself is the entrepreneur's SECRET WEAPON -- an advantage over people who work for somebody else.

To emphasize the importance of goal-setting, one business motivator gives an annual Christopher Columbus Better Leadership Award to failures. He chose the name of the award by reasoning that Christopher Columbus was a man who started out not knowing where he was going, didn't know where he was when he arrived, and couldn't describe where he'd been upon returning.

THE ADVENTURE OF ENTREPRENEURING

Entrepreneuring is exciting. The possibilities that lie before you are limited only by your imagination.

Making a real, day-to-day experience out of a dream: That's exciting! Reaching a goal that, in your private moments, you had, sometimes, for just an instant, despaired of ever reaching -- that is exciting!

Starting a new business is one of life's most stimulating challenges. Succeeding is one of life's most satisfying accomplishments. THIS is what you are fighting for. It is a worthwhile endeavor.

A very good case can be made for the assertion that challenge is what makes life worth living. The pleasure and satisfaction that come from doing the difficult, from achieving goals that few can achieve, is what makes life more than just a survival game.

Many a successful person has said that life was never so stimulating as when challenge after challenge was being met and overcome.

William J. Benzick of St. Paul faced such a challenge and won. He started Best Food Services in 1975 with no customers. Now his food service management and catering firm services forty locations and employs 285 people. In 1983 he was named Minnesota Small Business Person of the Year.

Self Confidence: A Result of Meeting Challenges Successfully

Accepting a challenge, then proving to yourself that you have the character needed to cope with it, is a great confidence builder.

Another way to develop self confidence is to take chances, and to succeed.

It was hard at first, and far from a certain success since neither one of them had experience in mail order, but Claude and Donna Jean Jeanloz of Miller's Falls, Massachusetts, enjoyed working together and making tangible progress every day.

They took a chance. They committed $50,000 to the printing of a catalog of hard-to-find household fixtures, hardware and ornaments. They mailed it to 27,000 prospects.

From 1978 to 1982 they grew to 93 employees and to sales of $5 million.

The Excitement of Challenge

Many entrepreneurs find day-to-day challenges exciting in themselves. So, maybe they can't point to a significant success every day. But, they get a thrill out of just DOING the daily "chores" for **their own business**. The thrill stimulates them to perform at peak efficiency. What's more, knowing that they are functioning well is a thrill in itself.

Charles Dickhoff of Eau Claire, Wisconsin, starts new businesses just for the challenge in it. When a new business becomes successful, he often sells it and uses the proceeds to start another business.

Why?

"I enjoy the challenge," he says.

Korda feels that the key to success is to feel that your work is "play." You are doing it because it is the best game in town -- the only one at which you can get paid for doing what is fun.

"Your chances of success are directly proportional to the degree of pleasure which you derive from what you do," he says, unequivocally.

"Success is a game," says Korda. "You play it with deadly seriousness at first. But, once you are on your way, you have to stand away from it from time to time to see just how much fun it is. You get relaxed about it when you do. There's a moment when it becomes purely a game. And when you reach that moment, you've made it, and nothing can stop you!"

IT IS HONORABLE TO TRY

Clench your fist, grit your teeth and refuse to take "No" for an answer -- even when you harbor a little doubt about the outcome. That takes guts; and courage is something you can be proud of. It's also what you need to succeed in business.

When you are courageous, when you DARE to be successful -- voila! -- unshakable faith in the certainty of your success assumes control of your thinking. You feel . . . **powerful**. And there's nothing evil about power as long as you keep it working toward honorable, productive ends.

A Sense of Power

A sense of power is the gift of courage.

"A man of courage is also full of faith," wrote Cicero, the Roman philosopher and politician.

Ovid, a Roman poet born the year Cicero died, would have said that a courageous person is **justified** in feeling confident about the outcome of his efforts. Ovid wrote: "Fortune and love befriend the bold."

If you have the character to wrestle your doubts to three falls and then step over them into a dark room filled with lurking liabilities, calculating competitors, misery-making mistakes, bad luck, and economic sneak punches . . . why, then you have ALREADY WON. Faith in the certainty of success, and the cool determination that success requires, are awaiting you just beyond the lighted door.

Don't procrastinate from starting a business until the unlikely day when you will have a 100 percent chance of success. Frequently, if you hold back until you feel there is no way you can fail, that's what you'll do . . . fail.

In his book entitled **Getting Yours**, Thomas K. Connellan writes: "There is no such thing as a perfect moment. If you wait for it, you'll wait forever."

Very often, you will not succeed unless you just seize the moment and . . . try.

Sometimes, you won't learn to do something until you do it.

Of course, you should prepare. However, when you are as ready as you're ever going to be . . . leap! Jump in the lake. Chances are good that you will **learn to swim . . . quickly!**

James Walters faced far less than a sure bet when he quit his job with a huge corporation at 46 to start a new business manufacturing and selling a computerized pari-mutuel wagering system, a "totalizer" that he had built in his garage.

He quickly learned about such things as bad luck and economic sneak punches.

First punch: Financial institutions wouldn't lend him money; so he had to raise start-up capital from friends. He did it.

Second punch: He ran out of money while manufacturing computers to fill his first big order. He had to get an advance from his customer, or fold.

He got the advance.

He had to go public to raise the necessary capital to land an order from The Royal Hong Kong Jockey Club. The order, to produce 1,500 off-track betting terminals, was the largest in the history of Walters' industry. For him, it was an "all or nothing" situation.

It took courage. He knew very little about the mechanics of a public stock offering, but he gave it the old college try.

And he did it.

Now, Walters has multiplied his initial $35,000 personal investment into $2.5 million.

EXPECT SUCCESS

The mood, the mental tone that the expectation of success generates in itself **PROMOTES** success.

Practice pausing, mentally, as you prepare to leave for work each day and think: "Something wonderful is going to happen today."

The THOUGHT actually promotes the expected result.

There's a reason why "positive thinking" as a philosophy of life has hung around for so long: It works. It generates confidence and enthusiasm.

Dr. Peale, who wrote a book entitled **Positive Thinking**, described a positive thinker: "A positive thinker does not refuse to recognize the negative. He refuses to **dwell on it.** Positive thinking is a form of thought which habitually looks for best results from worst conditions . . . it is possible to expect the best for yourself even though things look bad.

"The remarkable fact," he says, "is that if you seek good, you are very likely to find it.

"Don't ever let yourself get caught in the trap of remembering all the reasons why you can't succeed. Sure, every single human on the face of the earth can come up with a list of reasons why he or she might fail. The winners among them are those who are fully aware of their faults, all right, but who disregard them and build upon their STRENGTHS -- their positives -- instead.

Of course, you can work on eliminating your faults at the same time you are busy being successful. Said St. Francis de Sales: "Do not lose courage considering growing imperfections, but instantly set about remedying them."

Make very sure that you are not unconsciously sabotaging yourself with FEAR of failure.

Korda writes about the fear of success: "...the fear of

24-16

success . . . is . . . an enormous obstacle because success implies change and change is frightening. People build comfortable, predictable lives around failure. They are reluctant to give up its assurance and familiarity much as people with a physical complaint often are unwilling to have it cured."

Are you willing to succeed?

Ask yourself that question sometime when you are finding success difficult to achieve.

Korda, in his book **Success**, writes: "You have a right to succeed. Your chances of succeeding are probably just as good as anyone else's -- and they are almost certainly better than you think they are."

"The people who succeed," says Korda, "do not, as a rule, work all that much harder than people who fail. In some cases, they work very much less hard. They have simply mastered the rules of success."

Korda says that it helps to convince yourself that what you want is OK -- that your goals are OK. Success, he says, should be considered a perfectly natural and happy condition, and you shouldn't feel guilty about it.

Tell yourself, he says, that it's OK to look out for number one. It's OK to be a winner. It's OK to be rich. It's OK to be ambitious. And it's also OK to have a good time doing it.

It never occurred to Ron James of San Diego that his custom silk-screened T-shirt business might fail, even though he started from ground zero. He spent $89 of his last $100 on a small silk screening machine, bought $6 worth of gas and set out to challenge fate.

In seven years he built his business from a first sale of two dozen T-shirts for $96.40 to a business with 5,000 clients and annual sales of $1 million. From a ramshackle 10' x 12' space in 1976, his business has grown to three retail outlets covering a total of more than 10,000 square feet.

Ron James doesn't need to be told to cultivate the habit of optimism. He already knows its value.

Visualize Success

Dr. Maxwell Maltz, famed author of **Psycho-Cybernetics**, proved a theory now being used by U.S. Olympic teams: Visualizing yourself succeeding, imagining the emotions and the actions that accompany success, is a tremendous aid in the pursuit of success -- in sports or in any other endeavor. Actually **succeeding** in your mind is identical, as far as your nervous system is concerned, to succeeding in reality.

Visualizing success, as if it really happened, promotes success by endowing you with confidence and enthusiasm.

Visualizing success gives you the attitude and the sure and steady skills of a winner.

Very often the ONLY element missing from the character of an entrepreneur who does not succeed is the unshakable anticipation of success found in the character of the entrepreneur who does.

You ARE What You Think

Remember: You ARE what you think.

"Every man is the architect of his own fortune," says an old English proverb.

If there's any truth in that proverb, then it's only smart to be the best architect you possibly can be -- and BELIEVE that you are.

"For they can conquer who **believe** they can." (Virgil)

"Whatever you can do or dream that you can do, do it. Boldness has genius, power and magic in it." -- Goethe

You Cannot Fail

There is no such thing as **failure**. One who is determined and prepared will succeed, now or later, but he WILL succeed -- unless he doesn't try hard enough. Inadequate effort is the only mortal sin of entrepreneuring and one of the few certain ways to assure failure.

Vow here and now that if you don't make it this time, it won't be because you didn't TRY hard enough!

If you prepare sufficiently, if you have strong character, if you give the enterprise your best effort, you will lose only to circumstances beyond your control -- and THAT is nothing to be ashamed of. Some of the noblest men of the ages have lost to circumstances beyond their control . . . temporarily. But, they, like Abraham Lincoln, were named "winners" by history in the end.

If something doesn't work out, think in terms of "postponement" and "regrouping." Don't use the self-defeating word "failure." THERE IS NO SUCH THING AS FAILURE FOR ONE WHO REFUSES TO GIVE UP.

To bolster your determination to succeed, try this mental exercise, visualizing each step: I am confident I have made the RIGHT decision. THIS is where I'm going to make my stand.

I have worked hard to get where I am today. I have paid my dues. I **deserve** to succeed.

No one is making this decision for me. I don't **need** to be told what I'm capable of doing. Just like I don't need to be told when to report for work, or when I can leave, or when I can take vacations, or how much money I can make.

After all, that's why I want to run my own show . . . be my own boss.

This is a decision I am making . . . for **me**, for my **family**, for my **future**.

I have considered the **cost** in terms of time, effort and commitment; and I have considered the **rewards** in terms of freedom, pride and potential wealth. Whatever the cost, the rewards are worth everything I put into my business.

I am prepared to take a few risks.

I know I have reduced those risks by studying this manual.

With so little to lose, and so **much** to gain, I am ready right now to take that step of faith onto the pathway to success.

I am determined to do my level best . . . and my best WILL be good enough.

I will not fail, because I will never quit. Never. Never! NEVER!!!!

There's no turning back. I am committed to that bright burning star in my future.

I want to be a winner. I MUST succeed.

I WILL SUCCEED !!!!

AND NO POWER ON EARTH IS GOING TO STOP ME!

SELECTED RESOURCES FOR SMALL BUSINESS AND ENTREPRENEURSHIP

APPENDIX A

Sources of Information from the American Institute of Small Business, 7515 Wayzata Blvd., Suite 201, Minneapolis, MN 55426, 1-800-328-2906

PRINT MATERIALS

FINDING MONEY FOR YOUR OWN SMALL BUSINESS: The One - Stop Guide to Raising All The Money You Will Need. 208p. by Max Fallek

BUSINESS PLAN EXAMPLE Complete example of actual Business Plan. Includes exact example of what a business plan contains including 3 years of spreadsheets for P & L, Cash Flow and Balance Sheet.

SOFTWARE PACKAGE

HOW TO WRITE A BUSINESS PLAN. For "IBM/IBM Compatible 3 1/2" or 5 1/4" or Apple MAC or Apple II by Max Fallek and Reuben Bjerke 1997. The Program includes menu of choices for each section of the Business Plan: Plan Summary, Marketing and Sales Plans, Production Plans, Key Personnel, Financing, Competition, Industry Data Research and Development.

VIDEO TAPES

YOUR OWN BUSINESS GETTING STARTED (With Study Guide)

MARKETING AND MARKETING PLANNING (With Study Guide)

HOW TO WRITE A BUSINESS PLAN (With Study Guide)

WOMEN IN BUSINESS

STARTING YOUR OWN BUSINESS FOR YOUNG ENTREPRENEURS

FRANCHISING: HOW TO FIND THE RIGHT FRANCHISE

NETWORKING FOR SUCCESS

HOW TO FIND THE RIGHT COLLEGE AND PAY FOR IT

Selected Topics by Small Business Subject Area. Reference Materials, Articles, Magazines, Books and other Publications. Topics Include:

Advertising and Public Relations

THE ADVERTISING HANDBOOK By Dell Dennison and Linda Tobey - International Self Counsel Press, Ltd., Bellingham, WA.

DO-IT-YOURSELF ADVERTISING By David F. Ramacitti - David Ramacitti, AMACOM, New York, NY

DO-IT-YOURSELF PUBLICITY by David F. Ramacitti - David Ramacitti, AMACOM, New York, NY

THE NAME'S THE THING - CREATING THE PERFECT NAME FOR YOUR COMPANY/PRODUCT
by Henri Charmasson - 1988 Henri Charmasson, AMACOM, New York, NY

THE POWER OF POINT-OF-PURCHASE ADVERTISING
by Ben Menin and Arthur E. Benning Sr., - AMACOM, New York, NY

DIRECT MAIL

A SMALL BUSINESS GUIDE TO DIRECT MAIL - BUILD YOUR CUSTOMER BASE AND BOOST PROFITS
by Lin Grensing - International Self Counsel Press, Inc., Bellingham, WA

FRANCHISING

BUSINESS OPPORTUNITIES HANDBOOK
by Enterprise Magazine - 1996 Enterprise Magazines, Inc., Milwaukee, WI

THE 2001 SOURCE BOOK OF FRANCHISE OPPORTUNITIES
by Sourcebook Publications - 1996 Sourcebook Publications, Oakland, CA

THE 2001 FRANCHISE ANNUAL - THE ORIGINAL FRANCHISE HANDBOOK AND DIRECTORY
by INFO Franchise News, Inc., INFO Press, Inc. Lewiston, NY

GENERAL

BEWARE OF THE NAKED MAN WHO OFFERS YOU HIS SHIRT by Harvey Mackay -1990 William Morrow
and Co., Inc. New York, NY

SWIM WITH THE SHARKS....WITHOUT BEING EATEN ALIVE by Harvey B. Mackay - 1988 William Morrow
and Co., Inc. New York, NY

TOMORROW'S COMPETITION - THE NEXT GENERATION OF GROWTH STRATEGIES by Mack Hanan -
1991 Mack Hanan, AMACOM, New York, NY

HOME-BASED BUSINESS

HOME OFFICE COMPUTING - Solutions for Today's Small Business published monthly by Scholastic, Inc.,
555 Broadway, New York, NY 10012

LEGAL

CORPORATE AND TRADE NAME GUIDE 1989 by Leonard Street Law Firm, Minneapolis, MN

A GUIDE FOR THE PROTECTION OF COPYRIGHTS 1993 by Leonard Street Law Firm, Minneapolis, MN

A GUIDE FOR THE SELECTION, USE AND PROTECTION OF TRADEMARKS 1991 by Leonard Street and
Law Firm, Minneapolis, MN

APPENDIX B

MINORITY BUSINESS ASSISTANCE

The number of Associations and Programs providing assistance for minority-owned businesses has
mushroomed in recent years. The following organizations can be of help in finding funds, training and other

assistance--or in directing you to other organizations that can help you with your small business. This information was compiled by Business News Magazine in the fall of 1994.

The U.S. Small Business Administration (202-205-6600) or (202-205-6410)

The SBA also has field offices around the country, listed in telephone directories under the entry U.S. Government. This federal agency oversees business development programs to assist groups that have typically had limited access to capital and credit: African-Americans, Native American, Hispanics and Asian-Americans. Any other group can qualify if it can demonstrate a pattern of repeated discrimination or economic hardship. A business that is 51% owned by a member of one of these groups can participate in the SBA's contracting program, which helps direct federal contracts for goods and services to certified firms. The SBA also offers some direct loans but more often, it provides loan guarantees through outside lenders. Other SBA programs offer management and technical assistance, free of charge, to small businesses in need.

American Woman's Economic Development Corp. (800-222-2933)

Helps women start and maintain businesses of offering courses such as accounting, marketing and law. It also obtains referrals for financing.

The Black Business Association (213-380-8803)

Technical assistance, workshops and seminars on all facets of business management, guidance on obtaining government and corporate contracts and informational campaigns promoting the interests of African-American-owned businesses.

GLOBAL - Gay and Lesbian Business Organizations Across the Lands (202-387-3388)

International network of gay and lesbian business organizations. Helps members network with corporations, provides management and technical advice and conducts seminars on issues of concern to its members.

The Minority Business Development Agency (202-482-5741)

The MBDA funds business development centers around the country which in turn provide counseling and business assistance to minority-owned firms.

National Association of Women Business Owners (301-608-2590)

Leadership training, advisory services on how to manage and expand operations, and active participation in the political process to promote the interests of women-owned businesses.

The National Center for American Indian Enterprise Development (602-545-1298)

Management and technical training, assistance with loan and grant applications and other guidance for Native Americans and tribes who own or plan to start a business.

National Chamber of Commerce for Women (212-328-1354)

Provides updated business profiles, job descriptions and pay comparisons. Three main committees are: The Business Owners Advisory Task Force for women working outside the home; Home-Based Business Committee for women working at home, self-employed freelancers, independent contractors and at-home "tele-commuters" who work for outside employers; and the Productivity Improvement Network analyzes management/marketing styles for employers, employees and consultants.

The National Minority Supplier Development Council (212-944-2430)

A clearing house for minority-owned companies and organizations that want to do business with large corporations. Maintains a database of 15,000 businesses owned and operated by Black, Latino, Asian and Native Americans and more than 3,500 corporations desiring to purchase goods and services from minority suppliers

The U.S. Hispanic Chamber of Commerce (202-842-1212)

Through its 200 regional offices this organization provides training and technical assistance for Hispanic entrepreneurs and helps members network with corporations.

The U.S. Pan-Asian-American Chamber of Commerce (202-296-5221)

Helps members to expand national and international, provides business management training and maintains a national job bank for recruitment and hiring.

APPENDIX C

SBA LO-DOC Loan Application Form

SBA Lenders Application Form For 7-A Guaranteed Loan

SBA Statement of Personal History

SBA Personal Financial Statement

APPENDIX D

US SMALL BUSINESS ADMINISTRATION ADDRESSES

ALABAMA

U.S. Small Business Administration
2121 8th Avenue North, Suite 200
Birmingham, Alabama 35203-2398

ALASKA

U.S. Small Business Administration
222 West 8th Avenue, # 67
Anchorage, Alaska 99513-7559

ARIZONA

U.S. Small Business Administration
Central and One Thomas, Suite 800
2828 North Central Avenue
Phoenix, Arizona 85004-1025

U.S. Small Business Administration
300 West Congress, Box FB33
Tucson, Arizona 85701

ARKANSAS

U.S. Small Business Administration
Little Rock Field Office
Room 600, Savers Building
320 West Capitol
Little Rock, Arkansas 72201

CALIFORNIA

U.S. Small Business Administration
2719 N Air Fresno Drive
Fresno, California 93727-1547

U.S. Small Business Administration
330 North Brand Boulevard, Suite 190
Glendale, California 91203-2304

U.S. Small Business Administration
660 J Street, Room 215
Sacramento, California 95814-2413

U.S. Small Business Administration
880 Front Street, Room 4-S-29
San Diego, California 92188

U.S. Small Business Administration
(Regional Office)
71 Stevenson Street, 20th Floor
San Francisco, California 94105

U.S. Small Business Administration
(District Office)
211 Main Street, 4th Floor
San Francisco, California 94105-1988

U.S. Small Business Administration
901 West Civic Center Drive, Suite 160
Santa Ana, California 92703

COLORADO

U.S. Small Business Administration
U.S. Customhouse, Room 454
721 19th Street
Denver, Colorado 80202

CONNECTICUT

U.S. Small Business Administration
33 Main Street
Hartford, Connecticut 06106

FLORIDA

U.S. Small Business Administration
7825 Bay Meadows Way, Suite 100-B
Jacksonville, Florida 32256-7504

U.S. Small Business Administration
1320 South Dixie Highway, Suite 501
Coral Gables, Florida 33146

U.S. Small Business Administration
501 East Polk Street, Suite 104
Tampa, Florida 33602

GEORGIA

U.S. Small Business Administration
1720 Peachtree Road, N.W., 6th Floor
Atlanta, Georgia 30309

U.S. Small Business Administration
52 North Main Street, Room 225
Statesboro, Georgia 30458

HAWAII

U.S. Small Business Administration
2213 Federal Building
300 Ala Moana Boulevard, Box 50207
Honolulu, Hawaii 96850

IDAHO

U.S. Small Business Administration
1020 Main Street, Suite 290
Boise, Idaho 83702

ILLINOIS

U.S. Small Business Administration
Business Development Office
500 West Madison, Suite 1250
Chicago, Illinois 60606

U.S. Small Business Administration/SCORE
500 West Madison, Suite 1250
Chicago, Illinois 60606

U.S. Small Business Administration
511 West Capitol, Suite 302
Springfield, Illinois 62704

INDIANA

U.S. Small Business Administration
429 North Pennsylvania Street, Suite 100
Indianapolis, Indiana 46204

IOWA

U.S. Small Business Administration
373 Collins Road, N.E.
Cedar Rapids, Iowa 52402

U.S. Small Business Administration
749 Federal Building
210 Walnut Street
Des Moines, Iowa 50309

KANSAS

U.S. Small Business Administration
110 East Waterman Street
Wichita, Kansas 67202

KENTUCKY

U.S. Small Business Administration
600 Federal Place, Room 188
Louisville, Kentucky 40201

LOUISIANA

U.S. Small Business Administration
1661 Canal Street, Suite 2000
New Orleans, Louisiana 70114-2890

MAINE

U.S. Small Business Administration
40 Western Avenue, Room 512
Augusta, Maine 04333

MARYLAND

U.S. Small Business Administration
Equitable Building
10 North Calvert Street
Baltimore, Maryland 21202

MASSACHUSETTS

U.S. Small Business Administration
155 Federal Street, 9th Floor
Boston, Massachusetts 02110

U.S. Small Business Administration
1550 Main Street
Springfield, Massachusetts 01103

MICHIGAN

U.S. Small Business Administration
515 McNamara Building
Detroit, Michigan 48226

U.S. Small Business Administration
300 South Front
Marquette, Michigan 49855

MINNESOTA

U.S. Small Business Administration
100 North 6th Street, Suite 610C
Minneapolis, Minnesota 55403-1504

MISSISSIPPI

U.S. Small Business Administration
101 West Capitol Street, Suite 400
Jackson, Mississippi 39201

U.S. Small Business Administration
One Hancock Plaza, Suite 1001
Gulfport, Mississippi 39501

MISSOURI

U.S. Small Business Administration
1103 Grand Avenue, 6th Floor
Kansas City, Missouri 64106

U.S. Small Business Administration
620 South Glenstone, Suite 110
Springfield, Missouri 65802

U.S. Small Business Administration
815 Olive Street, Second Floor
St. Louis, Missouri 63101

MONTANA

U.S. Small Business Administration
301 South Park, Room 528
Helena, Montana 59626-0054

U.S. Small Business Administration
2525 Fourth Avenue North, 2nd Floor
Billings, Montana 59101

NEBRASKA

U.S. Small Business Administration
11145 Mill Valley Road
Omaha, Nebraska 68154

NEVADA

U.S. Small Business Administration
301 East Stewart Street
Las Vegas, Nevada 89125

U.S. Small Business Administration
50 South Virginia Street, Room 238
Reno, Nevada 89505

NEW JERSEY

U.S. Small Business Administration
60 Park Place, 4th Floor
Newark, New Jersey 07102

NEW MEXICO

U.S. Small Business Administration
625 Silver, S.W., 3rd Floor
Albuquerque, New Mexico 87102

NEW YORK

U.S. Small Business Administration
26 Federal Plaza, Room 3100
New York, New York 10278

U.S. Small Business Administration
35 Pinelawn Road, Room 102E
Melville, New York 11747

U.S. Small Business Administration
100 South Clinton Street, Room 1071
P.O. Box 7317
Syracuse, New York 13260-7317

U.S. Small Business Administration
111 West Huron Street, Room 1311
Buffalo, New York 14202

U.S. Small Business Administration
333 East Water Street
Elmira, New York 14901

U.S. Small Business Administration
445 Broadway, Room 2368
Albany, New York 12207

U.S. Small Business Administration
100 State Street, Room 601
Rochester, New York 14614

NORTH CAROLINA

U.S. Small Business Administration
222 South Church, Suite 300
Charlotte, North Carolina 28202

OHIO

U.S. Small Business Administration
1240 East 9th Street, Room 317
Cleveland, Ohio 44199

U.S. Small Business Administration
85 Marconi Boulevard
Columbus, Ohio 43215

U.S. Small Business Administration
5028 Federal Office Building
550 Main Street, Room 5028
Cincinnati, Ohio 45202

OKLAHOMA

U.S. Small Business Administration
200 N.W. 5th Street, Suite 670
Oklahoma City, Oklahoma 73102

OREGON

U.S. Small Business Administration
International Trade Program
One World Trade Center
121 S.W. Salmon, Suite 210
Portland, Oregon 97204

PENNSYLVANIA

U.S. Small Business Administration
475 Allendale Road, Suite 201
King of Prussia, Pennsylvania 19406

U.S. Small Business Administration
Branch Office
100 Chestnut Street, Suite 309
Harrisburg, Pennsylvania 17101

U.S. Small Business Administration
Branch Office
20 North Pennsylvania Avenue
Wilkes-Barre, Pennsylvania 18701

U.S. Small Business Administration
District Office
960 Pennsylvania Avenue, 5th Floor
Pittsburgh, Pennsylvania 15222

PUERTO RICO/U.S. VIRGIN ISLANDS

U.S. Small Business Administration
U.S. Federal Building, Suite 691
150 Carlos Chardon Avenue
Hato Rey, Puerto Rico 00918-1729

RHODE ISLAND

U.S. Small Business Administration
380 Westminster Mall
Providence, Rhode Island 02903

SOUTH CAROLINA

U.S. Small Business Administration
Strom Thurmond Federal Building
Suite 172
1835 Assembly Street, Room 358
Columbia, South Carolina 29202

TENNESSEE

U.S. Small Business Administration
50 Vantage Way, Suite 201
Nashville, Tennessee 37228-1500

TEXAS

U.S. Small Business Administration
300 East 8th Street, Room 520
Austin, Texas 78701

U.S. Small Business Administration
7400 Blanco, Suite 20
San Antonio, Texas 78216

U.S. Small Business Administration
400 Mann Street, Suite 403
Corpus Christi, Texas 78401

U.S. Small Business Administration
1100 Commerce Street, Room 3C36
Dallas, Texas 75242

U.S. Small Business Administration
819 Taylor Street, Room 8A32
Ft. Worth, Texas 76102

U.S. Small Business Administration
222 East Van Buren Street, Room 500
Harlingen, Texas 78550

U.S. Small Business Administration
505 East Traves, Room 103
Marshall, Texas 75670

UTAH

U.S. Small Business Administration
125 South State Street, Room 2237
Salt Lake City, Utah 84138

VIRGINIA

U.S. Small Business Administration
P.O. Box 10126
400 North 8th Street
Richmond, Virginia 23240

WASHINGTON

U.S. Small Business Administration
915 Second Avenue, Room 1792
Seattle, Washington 98174

U.S. Small Business Administration
Farm Credit Building, 10th Floor
Spokane, Washington 99204

WEST VIRGINIA

U.S. Small Business Administration
District Office
P.O. Box 1608
Clarksburg, West Virginia 26302-1608

U.S. Small Business Administration
Branch Office
550 Eagan Street
Charleston, West Virginia 25301

WISCONSIN

U.S. Small Business Administration
212 East Washington Avenue
Room 213
Madison, Wisconsin 53703

U.S. Small Business Administration
500 South Barstow Street, Room 17
Eau Claire, Wisconsin 54701

U.S. Small Business Administration
310 West Wisconsin Avenue, Room 400
Milwaukee, Wisconsin 53203

U.S. SMALL BUSINESS ADMINISTRATION
INSTRUCTIONS FOR LENDER ON HOW TO COMPLETE THE SBA*LOWDOC* APPLICATION

The following directions provide assistance in completing the SBA*LowDoc* application. Each section corresponds to the same tion on the LowDoc application. If a particular section or entry is not specified in this guide, no special directions are required complete that entry. You may find it helpful to refer to the LowDoc Program Guide if there are credit policy questions. If essary, use separate sheets of paper for additional answers to each section. **ALL BLANKS MUST BE COMPLETED – USE IF "Blank" DOES NOT APPLY.**

CTION F: LENDER – If you do not have the date of the latest 750 agreement, please call your SBA District/Branch Office they will provide you with this information. The appropriate SBA District/Branch Office is based on location of business.

Name of Lender – Financial Institution.
Business Name – Applicant.
Applicant SIC Code – As listed in the Standard Industrial Classification Manual.
Lender's Address – Address of Financial Institution ****IMPORTANT**** Must be street address, all loans documents are shipped FEDEX. FEDEX will not deliver to a Post Office Box.
Telephone – Lender's Telephone Number, including area code.
Fax – Lender's Fax Number, including area code.
750 Date – Date of SBA Guaranty Agreement.

TION G: LOAN TERMS – Please complete this section as completely and accurately as possible. The Authorization for Guarantee will usually be based on the terms and conditions provided, but SBA reserves the right to amend them. Any ges will be discussed prior to approval by SBA. Accuracy and completeness will expedite loan closings.

SBA Guarantee % - Percentage of SBA Guarantee, maximum 80 percent.
Loan Amount – Amount lender has approved.
No. of Months to maturity – Loan maturity in months including interest only payments.
Payments – Mark appropriate box if payments are principal and interest or principal plus accrued interest; enter payment. If you are asking for payments other than monthly, please indicate.
No. of Months Interest Only – Only if repayment term has an interest only period.
Initial Interest Rate – Interest rate of the loan at closing and whether it will be fixed or variable.
Spread – If interest rate is variable, indicate the spread over the Wall Street Journal Prime Rate. If adjustment period is other than monthly or quarterly, please check "Other", and indicate the frequency.
Life Insurance – Are you requiring principal to obtain and in what amount?
Standby Agreement – Who will be executing the standby and in what amount?
f Start-Up or Purchase of Existing Amount – Indicate nature of source by entering the amount of the injection by the appropriate category, "Cash" is money reported on a personal financial statement. "Assets" are those assets reported on a personal financial statement. "Stand-by Debt" is any obligation which will be placed on standby. "Other" includes gifts, inheritances and other sources not already mentioned.

f Proceeds

Amount and Purpose – "Fixed Assets" includes all fixed assets financed other than real estate, such as, vehicles, equipment, furniture and fixtures. "Impact Current Assets/Liability" is amount for inventory and working capital. If "Debt Payment" applies, enter name and amount in space provided on application. Refinancing of participant bank debt is limited to 25 percent of loan request. "Other" include the balance of assets financed that are not specified elsewhere, such as, working capital, goodwill, and leasehold improvements. If purpose of loan is to purchase a business in entirety, use "purchase of business." If only assets of business are being purchased use of proceeds should be itemized by asset category.

teral

Type – Enter code for type of collateral securing loan: RE-real estate; FF-furniture & fixtures, EQP-equipment; or INV-inventory, etc.
Description – Briefly describe collateral (e.g., location of real estate, type of equipment, or description of inventory).
Market Value – Should be the lender's assessment of the current market value of collateral. (Please note that market value hould be based on prudent lending standards and values should be supported by appropriate documentation.)
Existing Lien(s) – If collateral has existing lien(s), enter the lienholder name and balance outstanding on each. (Please note: nter original loan amount if real estate mortgage/deed of trust is open-ended.)
Collateral Value – Should be the lender's assessment of the collateral's liquidation value net of existing lien(s).

SECTION H: FINANCIAL STATEMENTS

Balance Sheet – this section is a summary of the business' balance sheet. If the business is a start- up, enter a pro forma balance sheet, after application of loan proceeds (**Use Pro Forma only if startup**).

1. As of _____ - Date of the most recent fiscal year statements if within the last three months, or the date of the most recent interim statements if not more than 90 days old at the time SBA receives the application if previous fiscal year statements are over three months old (Note: the date of the Balance Sheet should correspond with the date of the Current period in the Income Statement section and the date of personal financial statements).
2. Total Current Assets – Should equal the total of Cash Equivalent, Net Trade Receivable, Inventory, and Other Current Assets. Net Trade Receivables means after deduction of receivables which are unlikely to be collected.
3. Total Assets – Must equal the total of Total Current Assets, Net Fixed Assets, and Other Assets.
4. Total Current Liabilities – Should equal the total of Notes, Trade Payable, Current Portion of Long-Term Debt (Current LTD), and Other Current Liabilities.
5. Total Liabilities – Should equal the total of Total Current Liabilities, Long Term Debt, and Other Liabilities.
6. Tangible Net Worth – Net worth after deducting all intangible assets.

Income Statement – This section is a summary of the business' previous, current and projected cash flow statement. If business is a start-up, enter two years of pro forma data in the "Current" and "Projected" columns.

7. Prior FY – For period of last year full fiscal year.
8. Current – Must be for the same period as the Balance Sheet Statement.
9. Projected – Over the next 12 months.
10. Rent (if applicable) – Discontinued rent due to purchase of asset(s) with loan proceeds.
11. Cash Flow – Must equal to the total of Rent (if this expense is being eliminated), Depreciation/Amortization, Annual Interest Expense on Long Term Debt, and Net Income. (In comments, address whether the depreciation is really available for debt service on the basis of when the depreciable asset will need to be replaced.)
12. Term Debt P&I – For the Current period, enter the total of all term debt payments including principal and interest. For the projected period, enter the total of all term debt payments for 12 month period, including the new SBA*LowDoc* loan.

SECTION I: LENDER COMMENTS – Lender's analysis of applicant's character, management abilities, financial condition of business, and repayment ability. Also, any other comment you feel necessary including whether projections are realistic. Business start-ups and purchases must discuss the amount and nature of the injection of the principal(s) into the business. Lender's comments must also address whether the projections are reasonable and attainable on the basis of the applicants capacity.

SECTION J: ELIGIBILTY – Use the SBA*LowDoc* Eligibility Checklist to assist in making and documenting the determination of the applicant's eligibility. Please keep justification for this determination in applicant's file.

following directions provide assistance in completing the SBA*LowDoc* application. Each numbered section in this guide
esponds to the same number on the SBA*LowDoc* application. Please type or print legibly. **SBA*LowDoc* uses a credit scoring
em, thus ALL application entries must be completed or use "N/A" if blank does not apply.** If necessary, use separate sheets of
r for additional answers to each section.

TION A: BORROWER

Business Name - Legal name of the entity applying for SBA*LowDoc* loan.
Trade Name - The operating name, if different from business name.
Type - Legal organizational structure of the business.
Address - Street address of business.
City, State, County, Zip - City, state, county and zip of the business.
Mailing Address (if different from street address).
Phone - Telephone number, including area code of the business.
IRS Tax ID # - The business employer I.D. number assigned by the IRS, or the owner's social security number. Please do not use
"Pending" on this line.
Business Bank - Financial Institution business is currently using for checking and/or loans.
Checking Balance - Current amount business has in checking account.
Nature of Business - Examples dairy farm, manufacture tires, wholesale shoes, retail toys, lawyer, etc.
Date Business Established - The original date the business was started
Date Current Ownership Established - The date of **the most recent change** in ownership. This includes the date that the current
owners acquired or purchased this business or the date of any change in the percentages of ownership of the current owners.
# of employees - Number of full and part-time employees on payroll for each pay period for the last 12 months averaged by the
number of pay periods.
# of affiliate(s) employees - Please note that affiliates are defined as businesses that have common ownership, common management,
or contractual relationships that give one control over the other. Calculate same as #14.
After the Loan - Anticipated number of employees that the business will employ within two years from the date of the loan.
Exporter - Mark appropriate box if business exports any product or service.
Pre-Qual - Mark appropriate box if Pre-Qualification service used.
Franchise - Mark appropriate box if business is a franchise.
Franchise name - If business is a franchise.

**TION B: LOAN REQUEST (Total all SBA debt including this application, and excluding disaster loans, cannot exceed
000)**

Amount - Total amount of loan requested by borrower.
Maturity - Number of months or years until loan is to be repaid.
Purpose - Briefly explain how the loan will be used.
Have you employed anyone to prepare this application - Check appropriate box, amount paid, name of packager, Social Security number or Tax I.D.
number of packager.

TION C: INDEBTEDNESS - Please provide the requested information on all business debts. NO personal debts should be listed
se blocks unless said debts were used for business purposes. Add additional sheet if necessary. Provide the number of scheduled
nts in a 12-month period or other terms, if appropriate, to report "Pmt. Frequency."

TION D: PRINCIPALS Complete this section for each principal. Section D can be photocopied for this purpose. **Account for
ercent of ownership. Principal includes:** 1) the owner of a sole proprietorship; 2) each partner of a partnership; 3) each
, director, and holder of voting stock of a corporation or a limited liability company; 4) any other person, including a hired
er, who has authority to speak for and commit the borrower in the management of the business. Non-owner officers and directors
ficers owning less than 20 percent complete only parts 1, 4 and 5.

NOTE: The estimated burden for completing this form is 30 minutes per response. You will not be required to respond to collection of
n unless it displays a currently valid OMB approval number. Comments on the burden should be sent to U.S. Small Business Administration,
3, 409 3rd St., S., W., Washington D.C. 20416 and Desk Office for Small Business Administration, office of Management and Budget, New
Office Building, Room 10202, Washington, D.C. 20503. OMB Approval (3245-0016).

D-1

1. Name - Full legal name.
2. Phone - Home telephone number including the area code.
3. Social Security Number - nine digit numeric.
4. Title - Position held in the business (i.e., President, Partner, etc.).
5. Address - Street, city, state, county, and zip of home address.
6. Date of Birth - Month, day, year.
7. Place of Birth - Where borrower was born, by city and state (or city and Foreign Country).
8. U.S. Citizen? - Check the proper box.
9. If No, Alien reg #. - If borrower is not a citizen, SBA must have the borrower's registration number.

D-2

1. % Owned - The percent ownership of each owner (total must equal 100 Percent).
2. Please check appropriate boxes in this section.

D-3 Personal Financial Statement

1. Liquid Assets - Include liquid assets such as checking, savings, money markets, certificate of deposits, bonds, stocks (publicly traded), cash value of life insurance, and marketable securities. **Do not** include individual retirement accounts, and similar assets.
2. Ownership in Business - Value of ownership in the applicant business.
3. Real Estate - Market value of all real estate owned.
4. Assets Other - Any assets not otherwise listed.
5. Total Assets - Total value of all assets in numbers 1, 2, 3 and 4 of this section, D-3.
6. Liabilities Real Estate - Total of all debt/mortgages on real estate owned.
7. Other Liabilities - Total of all debt excluding real estate debt.
8. Total Liabilities - Total of all liabilities in numbers 6 and 7 of this section, D-3.
9. Net Worth - Difference between total assets, number 5, and total liabilities, number 8.
10. Annual Salary - From the applicant business.
11. Other Sources of repayment - A Lender or SBA may rely upon a source of cash flow other than from operations of the small business borrower for repayment. That source must be available to the principal(s) on a consistent basis in an amount that sufficiently exceeds the individual's personal needs to permit orderly repayment of the loan over a reasonable period of time.
12. Source - Of other Source of Repayment in number 11.
13. Residence Rent/Own/Other - Indicate if current residence is owned, rented, or other (e.g., live with relatives).
14. Monthly Housing - Monthly mortgage or rent payment of residence.

D-4 - Previous SBA or Other Government Financing -

1. Please complete for all principals. Financial Institution, Agency, Loan No., Date, Amount, Balance, and Status. (Outstanding, applied for, paid in full, and any other status.)

D-5 -Eligibility and Disclosures (IMPORTANT, only one signature is allowed in this section. USE SEPARATE SHEET FOR EACH PRINCIPAL

Mark appropriate boxes, sign and date.

BORROWER

Please Print Legibly or Type (ALL BLANKS MUST BE COMPLETED, Use "N/A," If Blank Is Not Applicable)

Business Name _____

Trade Name (If different) _____

Type: Proprietorship ☐ Partnership ☐ Corporation ☐ LLC ☐ Other ☐

Address _____

_____ State _____ County _____ Zip _____

Mailing Address (If different from above) _____

_____ State _____ County _____ Zip _____

Phone _____ IRS Tax ID # _____

Business Bank _____ Checking Balance $_____

Nature of Business _____

Date Business Established _____

Date Current Ownership Established_____

Number of employees _____

Number of affiliate(s) employees _____

Total number of employees after Loan _____

Exporter? Yes ☐ No ☐ Pre-Qual? Yes ☐ No ☐

Franchise? Yes ☐ No ☐ Name _____

LOAN REQUEST

AMOUNT $_____ Maturity: _____ Purpose:_____

Have you employed anyone to prepare this application? Yes ☐ No ☐ If Yes, how much was paid? $_____ How much do you owe? $_____

Name of Packager _____ Packager's Tax ID No. or Social Security No. _____

INDEBTEDNESS: Furnish information on ALL BUSINESS debts, contracts, notes and mortgages payable. Indicate by an (*) items to be paid by loan proceeds.

To Whom Payable	Orig. Amount	Orig. Date	Cur. Balance	Int. Rate	Maturity Date	Pmt. Amt.	Pmt Frequency	Collateral	Status

PRINCIPALS: Submit all information in this section for each principal of the business. Use separate attachments for each principal.

Full Name _____ Phone _____ Social Security Number _____ Title _____

Address _____ City _____ State _____ Zip _____

Date of Birth _____ Place of Birth (City, ST or Foreign Country) _____ U.S. Citizen? Yes ☐ No ☐ If No, Alien reg. # _____

Percentage Owned _____% Veteran *: Non-Veteran ☐, Vietnam Era Veteran ☐, Other Veteran ☐ Gender *: Female ☐ Male ☐

African American ☐, Puerto Rican ☐, Native American ☐, Hispanic ☐, Asian/Pacific Islander ☐, Eskimo & Aleuts ☐, Caucasian ☐, Multi-Ethnic ☐

Data is collected for statistical purposes only. It has no bearing on the credit decision. Disclosure is voluntary.

PERSONAL FINANCIAL STATEMENT: Complete for all principals with 20% or more ownership.

Assets $_____ Ownership in Business $_____ Real Estate $_____ Assets Other $_____ Total Assets $_____

Notes Real Estate $_____ Liabilities Other $_____ Total Liabilities $_____ Net Worth (less value of business) $_____

Salary $_____ Other Source of Repayment $_____ Source _____ Residence: Own ☐ Rent ☐ Other ☐ Mthly Housing $_____

PREVIOUS SBA OR OTHER GOVERNMENT FINANCING: For all owners, principals, partners, and affiliates.

Owner Name	Name of Agency	Loan No.	Date	Amount	Balance	Status

ELIGIBILITY AND DISCLOSURES:

I. Are you or your business involved in any pending lawsuits? Yes ☐ No ☐ If Yes, provide the details as Exhibit A.

II. Do you or your spouse or any member of your household, or anyone who owns, manages, or directs your business or their spouses or members of their households work for the Small Business Administration, Small Business Advisory Council, SCORE or ACE, any Federal Agency, or the participating lender? Yes ☐ No ☐ If Yes, please provide the name and address of the person and the office where employed. Label this Exhibit B.

III. Affiliates: Do you or the applicant business have any interest in any other business as owner, principal, partner or manager? Yes ☐ No ☐ If Yes, please provide details to Lender.

IV. Are you: (a) presently under indictment, on parole or probation, Yes ☐ No ☐ or (b) have ever been charged with or arrested for any criminal offense other than a minor motor vehicle violation (including offenses which have been dismissed, discharged, or nolle prosequi) Yes ☐ No ☐ or (c) convicted, placed on pretrial diversion, or placed on any form of probation including adjudication withheld pending probation for any criminal offense other than a minor vehicle violation? Yes ☐ No ☐ If Yes to any "IV" question, Lender must submit application to local SBA Office for processing under the regular 7(a) program.

I have received and read SBA Form 1261, STATEMENT REQUIRED BY LAW AND EXECUTIVE ORDER.

If you knowingly make a false statement or overvalue a security to obtain a guaranteed loan from SBA you can be fined up to $10,000 and/or imprisoned for not more than five years under 18 U.S.C.1001; if submitted to a Federally Insured Institution, under 18 USC 1014 by Imprisonment of not more than twenty years and/or a fine or not more than $1,000,000. I authorize the SBA's Office of Inspector General to request criminal record information about me from criminal justice agencies for the purpose of determining my eligibility for programs authorized by the Small Business Act, as amended.

Signature _____ Date _____

SIGNATURE

I authorize SBA/Lender to make inquiries as necessary to verify the accuracy of the statements made and to determine my creditworthiness. I agree that if SBA approves this loan application I will not, for at least two years, hire as an employee or consultant anyone that was employed by the SBA during the one year period prior to the disbursement of the loan. I further hereby certify that: (1) as consideration for any Management, Technical, and Business Development Assistance that may be provided, I waive all claims against SBA and its agents, (2) all information contained in this document and any attachments is true and correct to the best of my knowledge.

Name _____ Date _____

Signature _____ Title _____

Corporation, Attested By: _____

Signature of Corporate Secretary

LENDER'S APPLICATION FOR GUARANTEE
Please Print Legibly or Type (ALL BLANKS MUST BE COMPLETED, Use "N/A," If Blank is Not Applicable)

F. LENDER

Name of Lender _____ Business Name _____ Applicant SIC Code _____

Lender's Address _____ City _____ State _____ Zip _____

Phone _____ Fax _____ 750 Agreement Date: _____

G. LOAN TERMS: The following section should be completed exactly as shown in the LowDoc Program Guide.

SBA Guarantee _____ % Loan Amount _____ No. of Mos. to Maturity _____ Payments: P&I ☐ or P+I ☐ $ _____ No. of Mos. Interest Only _____

Initial Interest Rate: ☐ Fixed _____% ☐ Variable _____ % Initial spread over WSJ Prime _____ % Adjustment Period: Mthly ☐ Qtrly ☐ Other ☐ _____

Life Insurance required? Yes ☐ No ☐ On Whom? _____ How much $ _____ Stand-by Agreements? Yes ☐ No ☐ Amount $ _____

If Start-Up or Purchasing of Existing Business, Amount of Applicant Injection**: Cash $ _____ Assets $_____ Stand-by Debt $ _____ Other $ _____

**Equity in home is not considered injection.

Use of Proceeds:		Collateral:		Market	Existing Lien(s)*		Collateral
Amount	Purpose	Type	Description	Value	Lien holder	Balance	Value
	Acquire/Renovate Real Property						
	Acquire Fixed Assets, Non-RE						
	Impact Current Assets/Liabilities						
	Refinance SBA Debt*						
	Refinance Non-SBA Debt*						
	Purchase Existing Business						
	Other: _____						
	Total						

*If use of proceeds is for debt repayment, Lender must retain copies of refinanced notes. If for participant bank, debt refinancing may not exceed 25% of total loan amount.

H. FINANCIAL STATEMENTS: (Balance Sheet and Current Income Statement must be of the same period)

BALANCE SHEET

☐ Pro Forma ☐ Interim ☐ Year End (As of _____)

ASSETS		LIABILITIES	
Cash Equivalent	_____	Notes Payable	_____
Net Trade Rec.	_____	Trade Payable	_____
Inventory	_____	Current LTD	_____
Other Curr. Assets	_____	Other Curr. Liab.	_____
Total Curr. Assets	_____	Total Curr. Liab.	_____
Net Fixed Assets	_____	Long Term Debt	_____
Other Assets	_____	Other Liabilities	_____
Total Assets	_____	Total Liabilities	_____
		Tangible Net Worth*	_____
		*Including Stand-by debt	

INCOME STATEMENT

No. of Interim Mos. _____
Date _____

		Prior FY	Current	Projected
a)	Net Sales/Revenue	_____	_____	_____
b)	Cost of Sales	_____	_____	_____
c)	Gross Profit	_____	_____	_____
d)	Owner Comp/Drawings	_____	_____	_____
e)	Rent (if applicable)	_____	_____	_____
f)	Depreciation/Amortization	_____	_____	_____
g)	Longterm Debt Int. Exp.	_____	_____	_____
h)	General & Other Exp.	_____	_____	_____
I)	Net Income after "d" above			
A)	Cash Flow (f+g+I)	_____	_____	_____
B)	Term Debt P & I	_____	_____	_____
	Debt Coverage Ratio (A/B)			

I. LENDERS COMMENTS: (Comment on Management's character, and the business' financial strength and repayment ability, including forecast.)

Business Start-Ups and Purchases: Lender **MUST** comment on management qualifications, location, competitive factors and feasibility of business plan.

_____
_____
_____
_____
_____
_____
_____
_____

J. ELIGIBILITY EVALUATION: Refer to program guide. If you have any eligibility questions, please contact the LowDoc Processing Center before submitting an application.

Eligibility Evaluation: To the best of your ability, have you determined that the Borrower meets SBA eligibility requirements as outlined in the "LowDoc Program Guide" and the "Eligibility Checklist?" Yes ☐ No ☐ (Please note, by law, SBA cannot guarantee ineligible loans.)

I submit this application to SBA for approval subject to the terms and conditions outlined above. Without the participation of SBA to the extent applied for we would be willing to make this loan, and in our opinion the financial assistance applied for is not otherwise available on reasonable terms. I certify that none of the Lender's employees, officers, directors, or substantial stockholders (more than 10%) have financial interest in the applicant. I also certify that our institution has at least 20 qualified commercial loans outstanding demonstrating our significant experience lending to small business concerns.

Lender Officer (Print Name) _____

Signature of Lender Officer _____ Title _____ Date _____

SBA*LOWDOC* ELIGIBILITY CHECKLIST

Applicant Name _____ Date _____

This form guides the lender in determining an applicant's eligibility. Do not submit it with the application. Retain in the applicant's file. Any item marked "No" indicates the loan is probably not eligible. Contact your SBALowDoc Processing Center (LDPC) if eligibility is questionable. Please refer to the attached Guidance, the SBALowDoc Program Guide, and SOP 5010 for more information on eligibility requirements.

The products and/or services of the applicant business are available to the general public. ☐ Yes ☐ No

The business or any of its Associates have not been involved in a Federal loan or Federally assisted financing that defaulted and caused a loss to the Federal Government. ☐ Yes ☐ No

Lender has reviewed the Franchise documents and Franchisor does not exercise control to the extent that it restricts Franchisee's right to operate its business independently. ☐ Yes ☐ No

Terms of the Loan

The total gross amount of SBA loans, except disaster loans, to this applicant and its affiliates, including this request, does not exceed $150,000. ☐ Yes ☐ No

Eligible Passive Company (EPC) ☐ Check box if applicable. *If box is checked, provide the following information:*

Name of Operating Company (OC) _____

Nature of OC's Business _____

Legal Form of OC Entity _____

EPC will use loan proceeds to acquire or lease and/or improve or renovate real or personal property (including eligible refinancing) that it leases 100 percent to an OC. ☐ Yes ☐ No

OC is eligible and proposed use of proceeds would be eligible if OC were obtaining the financing directly. ☐ Yes ☐ No

EPC (except eligible trusts) and OC are each small under SBA size standards. ☐ Yes ☐ No

The total amount of all loans, except disaster loans, to the EPC, the OC, and the affiliates, if any, of both does not exceed $150,000. ☐ Yes ☐ No

Neither the EPC nor the OC is a trust or SBA requirements regarding trusts are met. ☐ Yes ☐ No

There is only one OC or multiple OCs have identical ownership, related products and/or services. ☐ Yes ☐ No

OC will be guarantor or co-borrower. Each 20 percent or more owner of EPC and OC will guaranty loan. ☐ Yes ☐ No

Use of Proceeds

Funding or Refinancing a Change of Ownership:

The change will promote sound development or preserve the existence of the business. ☐ Yes ☐ No

Is the change 100 percent of ownership, a repurchase of 100 percent of the interest of one or more owners by the business, or a purchase of 100 percent of the interest of one or more owners by another current owner? ☐ Yes ☐ No

The transaction is arms–length and is supported by an independent third party valuation. ☐ Yes ☐ No

The Buy/Sell Agreement has been reviewed and terms are satisfactory. ☐ Yes ☐ No

SBA Form 2076 (9/98)

...continue on reverse

Debt Refinancing ☐ Check box if applicable:
- The cash flow needed to repay the portion of the loan for refinancing debt is at least 20 percent less than is currently needed to service this debt.
- Loan proceeds to refinance debt owed to the participating lender be 25 percent or less of the total SBA*LowDoc* loan.   ☐ Yes ☐ No
- All debt being refinanced is business debt or personal debt on behalf of the business.   ☐ Yes ☐ No
- The loan will not refund debt owed to an SBIC.   ☐ Yes ☐ No
- Proceeds will **not** pay a creditor in a position to sustain a loss causing a shift to SBA of part or all of that potential loss.   ☐ Yes ☐ No
- The participating lender's loan has never been more than 29 days past due.   ☐ Yes ☐ No
- The loan will not provide or refinance funds for payments, distributions, or loans to Associates of applicant except payment of ordinary compensation for services rendered.   ☐ Yes ☐ No

The loan will not provide floor plan or other revolving line of credit.   ☐ Yes ☐ No

The loan will finance a purpose which will benefit the small business.   ☐ Yes ☐ No

Conflict of Interest

Lender or any Associate of Lender has not accepted funding from a source which restricts, prioritizes, or conditions the types of small businesses that Lender may assist under an SBA program or imposes any conditions or requirements upon recipients of SBA assistance inconsistent with SBA's loan programs or regulations.   ☐ Yes ☐ No

Applicant, an Associate of Applicant, or close relative of Associate of Applicant is not required to invest in Lender.   ☐ Yes ☐ No

Proceeds will not be used to acquire space in project for which Lender has issued a real estate forward commitment.   ☐ Yes ☐ No

Lender has not previously submitted this application to SBA under any of its loan programs, including PLP, CLP, SBA*Express*, and regular 7(a).   ☐ Yes ☐ No

Guidance for Completion of
SBA*LOWDOC* ELIGIBILITY CHECKLIST

Refer to the SBA*LowDoc* Program Guide and SOP 5010 for further guidance on eligibility. This is particularly recommended when a franchise, EPC, debt refinancing, or conflict of interest or potential for such is involved.

Where additional information is needed to support the response to any of the items in the checklist, attach separate sheets of paper. If a section such as EPC or Debt Refinancing does not apply, skip that section.

SBA may not participate in loans to entities which limit access for reasons other than health or safety.

Size
If an applicant has affiliates, the group of affiliates must be small, based on the primary industry of the group, under SBA*LowDoc* size standards and the applicant must also be eligible on the basis of its primary industry.

Franchises
Franchise, license, and dealership agreements must be reviewed to determine whether the business is independent or the franchisor, licensor, etc., exercises control to the extent that the right to operate the business independently and enjoy profits or bear the risks of loss commensurate with ownership are restricted. A "No" response on the franchise item does not render the loan ineligible, but processing time may be extended when SBA has to review franchise documents to determine eligibility.

Terms of the Loan
The applicant and its affiliates, if any, may have one or more loans under SBA*LowDoc* as long the total gross amount of the outstanding loan(s) and the requested loan(s) does not exceed $150,000. Except for disaster loans which are not included, the loan program under which other loans may have been or may be extended does not matter.

Eligible Passive Concerns
Refer to SOP 5010 for information on loans to Eligible Passive Concerns.

Use of Proceeds
Refinancing of existing debt must provide a substantial benefit to and meet a need of the small business applicant. Improving the lien position of the lender is not an acceptable reason. SBA does not want to refinance existing debt that is on reasonable terms or debts where the lender is in a position to sustain a loss that would be transferred to SBA. No more than 5 percent of a SBA*LowDoc* loan may refinance debt owed to the lender participating in the loan. How much of a loan can be used to refinance debts of other lenders is not restricted. All debts being refinanced must be debts of the business or personal debt incurred on behalf of the business for which the applicant can provide documentation. Existing debt on reasonable terms is not eligible for refinancing. Reasonable terms are to be considered on the basis of whether the business can reasonably service all debt, including the loan request under consideration per the lender's proposed structuring.

SBA does not participate in loans for an individual to purchase an interest in a business in which the individual does not already have an interest. Where a loan is for the funding or refinancing of a change of ownership, an independent third party valuation to evidence whether the purchase price is reasonable is necessary. This also establishes that the transaction is arms-length if close relatives are involved. SBA has no objection if the seller is giving a close relative a beneficial price. Our concern is when the price exceeds the value, especially when close relatives are involved.

Financial assistance provided by SBA must be for business purposes. It is not to benefit individuals, either directly or indirectly, other than through the normal course of conducting business.

Floor plans and other lines of credit are not eligible under SBA*LowDoc* because of the complexity of the loan analysis and the processing time required.

SBA financial assistance must be for the benefit of the applicant business. A business may not apply for financial assistance for an affiliate or an Associate or any other party.

Change of Ownership
A loan may not be made to a partner(s) or shareholder(s) to purchase the interest of another partner(s) or shareholder(s). The loan must be to the business (partnership or corporation) to acquire the entire interest of a partner(s) or shareholder(s).

Conflict of Interest

SBA must consider conflicts of interest or any appearance of one very carefully. SOP 5010 specifies who decides whether a conflict of interest or the appearance of one renders an application ineligible.

SBA will not participate in a loan which is the result of a real estate forward commitment by the lender.

It is not appropriate for an application to be submitted under more than one of SBA's loan programs at the same time. In addition, if it has been submitted under another SBA loan program, the lender must inform the LDPC of the type of SBA program under which it was submitted and the SBA office to which it was submitted.

U.S. SMALL BUSINESS ADMINISTRATION
APPLICATION FOR BUSINESS LOAN (UP TO $100,000)
It is not necessary to hire outside assistance for preparation of the application.

rate Name (If any)
Name & Street Address _____

Home Phone (__) _____
Bus. Phone (__) _____

Ownership in any other business? Yes ___ No ___
#Employees (Including Subsidiaries & Affiliates)
Include Owners & Managers

_____ County _____ State ____ Zip _____

Before Loan _____ After Loan _____
Bank of Business Account:

g Address (if different) _____
of Business _____ Date Established _____

IRS Tax ID #

GEMENT (Proprietor, partners, officers, directors owning 20% or more of the company)—Must account for 100% of ownership of the business.

	SOCIAL SECURITY #	Complete Address	% Owned	Y/N	*Military Service From	To	*Race	*Sex

*This data is collected for statistical purposes only. It has no bearing on the credit decision to approve or decline this application. Disclosure is voluntary.

zen? Yes ___ No ___   If no, include a copy of Alien Registration Card (Form I 151 or I 551)   Alien Registration # _____

of the above individuals (a) presently under indictment, on parole or probation, or have they ever been (b) charged for any criminal offense other than a minor vehicle violation, victed, placed on pretrial diversion, or placed on any form of probation including adjudication withheld pending probation for any criminal offense other than a minor vehicle
Yes ___ No ___ If yes, loan request must be submitted under regular 7(a) loan program.

employed anyone to prepare this application? Yes ___ No ___   If yes, how much have you paid? $_____   How much do you owe? $_____

or any officer of your company ever been involved in bankruptcy or insolvency proceedings? Yes ___ No ___ If yes, provide details to bank.
r your business involved in any pending lawsuits? Yes ___ No ___ If yes, provide details to bank.

IBE YOUR BUSINESS OPERATION:

ESS ENGAGED IN EXPORT TRADE? Yes ___ No ___   DO YOU INTEND TO BEGIN EXPORTING AS A RESULT OF THIS LOAN? Yes ___ No ___

ARY OF MANAGEMENT'S BUSINESS EXPERIENCE, EDUCATION, AND TRAINING:

QUEST: HOW MUCH, FOR WHAT, WHY IT IS NEEDED

EDNESS: Furnish information on ALL BUSINESS debts, contracts, notes, and mortgages payable. Indicate by an (*) items to be paid with loan proceeds.

n Payable	Original Amount	Original Date	Present Balance	Rate of Interest	Maturity Date	Monthly Payment	Collateral	Current or Past Due
	$		$			$		
	$		$			$		
	$		$			$		
	$		$			$		

SBA OR OTHER GOVERNMENT FINANCING: If you or any principals or affiliates have ever requested Government Financing complete the following:

Agency	Loan Number	Date Approved	$ Amount	Loan Balance	Status

owingly make a false statement or overvalue a security to obtain a guaranteed loan from SBA you can be fined up to $10,000 or imprisoned for not more than s or both under 18 USC 1001.

certify that all information contained in this document and any attachments is true and correct to the best of my knowledge.

at is a proprietor or general partner, sign here: By: _____ Title _____ Date _____

tion sign below: Corporate Name _____

By: _____   Date: _____   Attested By: _____
Signature of President   Signature of Corporate Secretary

LENDER'S APPLICATION FOR GUARANTY

Name of Lender	Address	Telephone(A/C)	Fax #

Date of Guaranty Agreement (SBA Form 750) _____

Applicant's Trade Name

We request SBA to guarantee _____ % of a loan in the amount of $ _____ for ___ years, with monthly (P&I payments of $ _____ / principal payments of $ _____ plus interest) beginning _____ month(s) from date of note. (If applicable: Interest only payment to begin _____ months from date of note). The interest rate is to be fixed at _____ % OR variable with a base rate of _____ %, spread _____ %, and an adjustment period of _____.

Lender's Experience with Applicant and Assessment of Management's Character and Capability:

CREDIT REPORTS (CR): CR Company _____ Risk Score _____ SIC Code _____ Summary of Business Credit:

OWNERS, GUARANTORS, AND CO-SIGNERS:
Owners of 20% or more of business must guarantee the note. Lender must obtain personal credit reports on all owners, guarantors, and co-signers.
Name (Indicate co-signers with *)   Address   Individual Credit Reports Analysis

Personal F/S: Lender should obtain signed personal financial statements for all owners, guarantors, and co-signers.
Do owners' personal unpledged liquid assets exceed $50,000 (not including IRA, CV Life Insurance, or savings for education)? Yes ___ No ___
Comments on personal resources, including any supplementary or outside sources of income available for debt service or to secure loan:

P&L: Average annual gross sales, including all affiliates, for the last 3 years (if applicable) $ _____
Year end cash flow last 3 years (if applicable)   FY_____, $ _____,   FY_____, $ _____,   FY_____, $ _____
One year projected cash flow after owner's compensation $ _____   Total annual debt service (including interest) after the loan $ _____
Comments on repayment ability:

Pro Forma Balance Sheet: Debt/NW Ratio _____ Current Ratio (CA/CL) _____ Comments on balance sheet:

IF NEW BUSINESS OR FOR PURCHASE OF EXISTING BUSINESS, AMOUNT OF APPLICANT INJECTION - CASH $ _____   OTHER $ _____

Lender's Analysis of Risk (If there are affiliates, submit analysis of financial condition of affiliate and potential impact on applicant business. Affiliates include all businesses owned by applicant or spouse of applicant, even though not in a related business. Comment on bankruptcies and pending lawsuits. Include lien position on collateral.)	Collateral Market Value *	Use of Proceeds:
	Inventory $ _____	Inventory $ _____
	Equipment $ _____	Fixed Assets $ _____
	A/R $ _____	Real Estate $ _____
	R/E ** $ _____	Note Payment $ _____
	_____ $ _____	Working Capital $ _____
	_____ $ _____	SBA Payoff $ _____
		$ _____
	* Value determined by:	$ _____
	Lender ___ Appraisal ___	$ _____
		$ _____
	Other (specify) _____	TOTAL $ _____
	** Furnish Legal Description	

For loans over $50,000 and up to $100,000, the following must be submitted:	IF LOAN IS TO PURCHASE AN EXISTING BUSINESS
1. Lender's internal loan report, including cash flow analysis and pro forma balance sheet	Include copy of terms of sale and F/S on the existing business.
2. Income tax schedule C or front page of corporate returns for past 3 years (if applicable)	Also, comment on any benefit to the business as a result of the change of ownership. Are buyer & seller related? Yes ___ No ___
3. Personal F/S's for all guarantors	State relationship _____

I submit this application to SBA for approval subject to the terms and conditions outlined above. Without the participation of SBA to the extent applied for we would not be willing to make this loan, and in our opinion the financial assistance applied for is not otherwise available on reasonable terms. I certify that none of the Lender's employees, officers, director or substantial stockholders (more than 10%) have a financial interest in the applicant.

Signature of Lender Official: _____   Title _____   Date _____

Loan Number	U.S. SMALL BUSINESS ADMINISTRATION	Loan Submitted As:

U.S. SMALL BUSINESS ADMINISTRATION
LENDER'S APPLICATION FOR GUARANTY
OR PARTICIPATION

Loan Submitted As:
- [ ] Reg 7(a)
- [ ] CLP
- [ ] PLP

...ess Name of Applicant

...e of Lender	Telephone (Inc. A/C)	R.L. Polk's Lender No. (SBA's Use)
...: Address	City	State	ZIP

PROPOSE TO MAKE A (Check One)

	Lender's Share	SBA's Share	Term of Loan	Amount of Loan
Guaranteed Loan	%	%	Years	$ _____

	Lender's Share	SBA's Share	Payment Beginning	Monthly Payment
Immediate Participation Loan (Lender to make and service)	%	%	_____ Months from Date of Note	$ _____

...r's Interest Rate		If Interest Rate is to be Variable	Adjustment Period	Base Rate Source
% Per Annum		Base Rate	Spread	

...NDITIONS OF LENDER (e.g. Insurance requirements, standbys, other conditions. Use additional sheet(s))

...I approve this application to SBA subject to the terms and conditions outlined above. Without the participation of SBA to the extent applied for we would not be willing ...to make this loan, and in our opinion the financial assistance applied for is not otherwise available on reasonable terms. I certify that none of the Lender's employees, ...officers, directors, or substantial stockholders (more than 10%) have a financial interest in the applicant.

...Official (Please Type or Print Name under Signature)	Title	Date

...ON PLP SUBMISSIONS ONLY: I approve and certify that the applicant is a small business according to the standards in 13 CFR 121, the loans proceeds will be used for an eligible purpose, and the owners and managers of the applicant business are of good character.

...ng/Certifying Lender Official (Please Type or Print Name under Signature)	Title	Date

FOR SBA USE ONLY

...ficer's Recommendations

[ ] Approve   [ ] Decline State Reason(s)

...e	Title	Date

...ecommendation if Required

[ ] Approve   [ ] Decline State Reason(s)

...e	Title	Date

THIS BLOCK TO BE COMPLETED BY SBA OFFICIAL TAKING FINAL ACTION

...Approve   [ ] Decline State Reason(s)

...e	Title	Date

INSTRUCTIONS: Lender will complete and enclose as part of this application package, all working papers, support material, and agreements requested herein, specifically including:

1. Balance sheet and ratio analysis - comments on trends, debt to worth, and current ratio.
2. Lender's analysis of repayment ability.

3. Management skill of the applicant.
4. Collateral offered and lien position, and analysis of collateral adequacy.
5. Lender's credit experience with the applicant. Identify weaknesses.

FINANCIAL SPREAD

In Column 1 please show the most recent balance sheet figures of an existing business or the initial equity investment of a start-up business or the purchase of a business. Columns 2 and 3 are to reflect adjusting entries, the use of loan proceeds, and loan repayment. Column 4 is to reflect the balance sheet of the business immediately following loan disbursement. Base the financial analysis on Column 4 figures.

BALANCE SHEET	As of	Fiscal Year Ends	AUDITED ☐	UNAUDITED ☐
		DEBIT	CREDIT	PRO FORMA
Assets				
Cash	$	$	$	$
Accounts Rec.				
Inventory				
Other				
Total Current Assets				
Fixed Assets				
Other Assets				
Total Assets	$	$	$	$
Liabilities & Net Worth				
Accounts Payable	$	$	$	$
Notes Payable				
Taxes				
Other				
SBA				
Total Current Liabilities	$	$	$	$
Notes Payable	$	$	$	$
SBA				
Other				
Total Liabilities	$	$	$	$
Net Worth	$	$	$	$
Total Liab. & Net Worth	$	$	$	$

Profit & Loss	PRIOR THREE YEARS			INTERIM	PROJECTIONS	
Sales	$	$	$	$	$	$
Depreciation						
Income Taxes						
W/D Officer Comp.						
Net Profit after Tax/Deprec.	$	$	$	$	$	$

PRO FORMA SCHEDULE OF FIXED OBLIGATIONS

	YEAR 1	YEAR 2	YEAR 3	YEAR 4
	$	$	$	$

Lender's Analysis:

United States of America

SMALL BUSINESS ADMINISTRATION

STATEMENT OF PERSONAL HISTORY

Please Read Carefully - Print or Type

Each member of the small business concern or the development company requesting assistance must submit this form in TRIPLICATE for filing with the SBA application. This form must be filled out and submitted by:

1. If a sole proprietorship by the proprietor.
2. If a partnership by each partner.
3. If a corporation or a development company, by each officer, director, and additionally by each holder of 20% or more of the voting stock.
4. Any other person including a hired manager, who has authority to speak for and commit the borrower in the management of the business.

e and Address of Applicant (Firm Name)(Street, City, State, and ZIP Code)

SBA District/Disaster Area Office

Amount Applied for: | Loan Case No.

Personal Statement of: (State name in full, if no middle name, state (NMN), or if initial only, indicate initial.) List all former names used, and dates each name was used. Use separate sheet if necessary.

First   Middle   Last

Name and Address of participating bank (when applicable)

2. Date of Birth: (Month, day, and year)

3. Place of Birth: (City & State or Foreign Country)

ive the percentage of ownership or stock wned or to be owned in the small business oncern or the Development Company | Social Security No.

U.S. Citizen ? ☐ YES   ☐ NO
If no, give alien registration number: _____

resent residence address: City   State

om: To: Address:

ome Telephone No. (Include A/C):   Business Telephone No. (Include A/C):

mediate past residence address:

om: To: Address:

URE TO ANSWER THE NEXT 3 QUESTIONS CORRECTLY BECAUSE THEY ARE IMPORTANT.

FACT THAT YOU HAVE AN ARREST OR CONVICTION RECORD WILL NOT NECESSARILY DISQUALIFY YOU. BUT NCORRECT ANSWER WILL PROBABLY CAUSE YOUR APPLICATION TO BE TURNED DOWN.

OU ANSWER "YES" TO 6, 7, OR 8, FURNISH DETAILS IN A SEPARATE EXHIBIT. INCLUDE DATES; LOCATION; S, SENTENCES, ETC.; WHETHER MISDEMEANOR OR FELONY; DATES OF PAROLE/PROBATION; UNPAID FINES PENALTIES; NAMES UNDER WHICH CHARGED; AND ANY OTHER PERTINENT INFORMATION.

you presently under indictment, on parole or probation?
☐ Yes   ☐ No   (If yes, indicate date parole or probation is to expire.)

ve you ever been charged with or arrested for any criminal offense other than a minor motor vehicle violation? Include offenses which have been dismissed, discharged, or e prosequi (All arrests and charges must be disclosed and explained on an attached sheet.)
☐ Yes   ☐ No

ve you **ever** been convicted, placed on pretrial diversion, or placed on any form of probation, including adjudication withheld pending probation, for any criminal offense er than a minor motor vehicle violation?
☐ Yes   ☐ No

☐ Fingerprints Waived
_____ _____
Date   Approving Authority

☐ Fingerprints Required
Date Sent to FBI _____
_____ _____
Date   Approving Authority

10.
☐ Cleared for Processing
_____ _____
Date   Approving Authority

☐ Request a Character Evaluation
_____ _____
Date   Approving Authority

rmation on this form will be used in connection with an investigation of your character. Any information you wish to submit that you feel will expedite this investigation be set forth.

e | Title | Date

sl SBA's policy to provide assistance to persons not of good character and therefore consideration is given to the qualities and personality traits of a person, favorable and unfavorable, relating thereto, behavior, integrity, candor and disposition toward criminal actions. It is also against SBA's policy to provide assistance not in the best interests of the United States, for example, if there is reason to at the effect of such assistance will be to encourage or support, directly or indirectly, activities inimical to the Security of the United States. Anyone concerned with the collection of this information, as to ness, disclosure of routine uses may contact the FOIA Office, 409 3rd St. S.W., and a copy of 9 "Agency Collection of Information" from SOP 40 04 will be provided.

ote: The estimated burden hours for completion of this form is 15 minutes per response. If you have any questions or comments concerning this estimate or any other this information collection please contact, Chief Administrative Information Branch, U.S. Small Business Administration 409 Third Street, S.W. Washington, D.C. 20416 or xman, Clearance Officer, Paperwork Reduction Project (3245-0178), Office of Management and Budget, Washington, D.C. 20503.

PERSONAL FINANCIAL STATEMENT

OMB Approval No. 3245-0188

S. SMALL BUSINESS ADMINISTRATION

As of _____, 19_____

Complete this form for: (1) each proprietor, or (2) each limited partner who owns 20% or more interest and each general partner, or (3) each stockholder owning 20% or more of voting stock, or (4) any person or entity providing a guaranty on the loan.

Name _____ Business Phone ( )

Residence Address _____ Residence Phone ( )

State, & Zip Code _____

Business Name of Applicant/Borrower _____

ASSETS	(Omit Cents)	LIABILITIES	(Omit Cents)
Cash on hands & in Banks . . . . $_____		Accounts Payable . . . . $_____	
Savings Accounts . . . . $_____		Notes Payable to Banks and Others . . . . $_____	
IRA or Other Retirement Account . . . . $_____		(Describe in Section 2)	
Accounts & Notes Receivable . . . . $_____		Installment Account (Auto) . . . . . . $_____	
Life Insurance-Cash Surrender Value Only $_____		Mo. Payments $_____	
(Complete Section 8)		Installment Account (other) . . . . . . $_____	
Stocks and Bonds . . . . $_____		Mo. Payments $_____	
(Describe in Section 3)		Loan on Life Insurance . . . . $_____	
Real Estate . . . . . . $_____		Mortgages on Real Estate . . . . . . $_____	
(Describe in Section 4)		(Describe in Section 4)	
Automobile-Present Value . . . . $_____		Unpaid Taxes . . . . $_____	
Other Personal Property . . . . . . $_____		(Describe in Section 6)	
(Describe in Section 5)		Other Liabilities . . . . $_____	
Other Assets . . . . $_____		(Describe in Section 7)	
(Describe in Section 5)		Total Liabilities . . . . $_____	
		Net Worth . . . . $_____	
Total . . $_____		Total . . $_____	

Section 1. Source of Income		Contingent Liabilities	
Salary . . . . $_____		As Endorser or Co-Maker. . . . . . . $_____	
Net Investment Income . . . . . . $_____		Legal Claims & Judgments . . . . . . $_____	
Real Estate Income . . . . . . $_____		Provision for Federal Income Tax . . . . $_____	
Other Income (Decribe below)* . . . . $_____		Other Special Debt . . . . $_____	

Description of Other Income in Section 1.

_____

_____

_____

*Alimony or child support payments need not be disclosed in "Other Income" unless it is desired to have such payments counted toward total income.

Section 2. Notes Payable to Bank and Others. (Use attachments if necessary. Each attachment must be identified as a part of this statement and signed.).

Name and Address of Noteholder(s)	Original Balance	Current Balance	Payment Amount	Frequency (monthly, etc.)	How Secured or Endorsed Type of Collateral

Form 413 (2-94) Use 5-91 Edition until stock is exhausted. Ref: SOP 50-10 and 50-30

(tumble)

Section 3. Stocks and Bonds. (Use attachments if necessary. Each attachment must be identified as a part of this statement and signed).

Number of Shares	Name of Securities	Cost	Market Value Quotation/Exchange	Date of Quotation/Exchange	Total Value

Section 4. Real Estate Owned. (List each parcel separately. Use attachments if necessary. Each attachment must be identified as a part of this statement and signed).

	Property A	Property B	Property C
Type of Property			
Address			
Date Purchased			
Original Cost			
Present Market Value			
Name & Address of Mortgage Holder			
Mortgage Account Number			
Mortgage Balance			
Amount of Payment per Month/Year			
Status of Mortgage			

Section 5. Other Personal Property and Other Assets. (Describe, and if any is pledged as security, state name and address of lien holder, amount of lien, terms of payment, and if delinquent, describe delinquency).

Section 6. Unpaid Taxes. (Describe in detail, as to type, to whom payable, when due, amount, and to what property, if any, a tax lien attaches).

Section 7. Other Liabilities. (Describe in detail).

Section 8. Life Insurance Held. (Give face amount and cash surrender value of policies – name of insurance company and beneficiaries).

I authorize SBA/Lender to make inquiries as necessary to verify the accuracy of the statements made and to determine my creditworthiness. I certify the above and the statements contained in the attachments are true and accurate as of the stated date(s). These statements are made for the purpose of either obtaining a loan or guaranteeing a loan. I understand FALSE statements may result in forfeiture of benefits and possible prosecution by the U.S. Attorney General (Reference 18 U.S.C. 1001).

Signature: Date: Social Security Number:

Signature: Date: Social Security Number:

PLEASE NOTE: The estimated average burden hours for the completion of this form is 1.5 hours per response. If you have questions or comments concerning this estimate or any other aspect of this information, please contact Chief, Administrative Branch, U.S. Small Business Administration, Washington, D.C. 20416, and Clearance Office, Paper Reduction Project (3245-0188), Office of Management and Budget, Washington, D.C. 20503.

Appendix E

Simplified HyperText Markup Language Coding

HTML is computer programming for the World Wide Web. It's a code that allows Internet browsers to interpret and display text and graphics. The use of the greater than and less than symbols and the characters in between is called a tag. Every web page must contain the following code to begin and end a web page.

```
<HTML>
<HEAD>
<TITLE>Your Title Goes Here; it appears in the title bar on your browser</TITLE>
</HEAD>

<BODY>
```

All text, image files, sound files for your page are placed between the start <BODY> and end </BODY> tags.

```
</BODY>

</HTML>
```

What are html tags? In html a tag tells the browser what to do. When you create an html page, you use tags for many reasons -- to change the appearance of text, to display a graphic, or to create a link to another page. The tags you write are not visible on the browser, but their effects are noticeable.

Tags begin with the symbol < > and end with </ >. Tags usually come in pairs, one to start an action and one that ends it. This tag: <B> causes your text to be bold. This tag: </B> stops the effect of the previous <B> tag, like this bold **bold** . Another example is <i>italics</i> *italics*

The <TITLE> tag is always "nested" in the <HEAD> tag. Be careful when nesting tags, remembering to close them in the proper order. It is the source of many simple but frustrating errors. Nesting is the inserting of pairs of tags within other pairs of tags. It is important to keep the tags in the correct order, or the file will be read incorrectly. The ending tags must be included in the reverse order of the beginning tags
For instance, follow the model of <tag1> <tag2> <tag3> </tag3> </tag2> <tag1>

To control the background color of your web page, your text and your links color you must add a code to your BODY TAG. For example,
<BODY BGCOLOR="#FFFFFF" text="#000000" link="blue" vlink="#999999">

BGCOLOR Specifies the background color for your page.
TEXT Specifies the color for the text on a page.
LINK Specifies the hyperlink color for non-visited links.
VLINK Specifies the color for visited links.

To underline a word or phrase, you simply put <U> before the phrase, and </U> where you want the underline to end.

Headers. There are six commonly used header tags to control the size of headlines. On the left is the HTML code, and the resulting header that gets displayed is on the right.

<h1> Heading 1 size</h1>	# Heading 1 size
<h2> Heading 2 size</h2>	## Heading 2 size
<h3> Heading 3 size</h3>	### Heading 3 size
<h4> Heading 4 size</h4>	Heading 4 size
<h5> Heading 5 size</h5>	Heading 5 size
<h6> Heading 6 size</h6>	Heading 6 size

All tags work in a similar manner, you have to tell a browser by code when to start and stop an action. There are a few exceptions, like <P> the paragraph tag. You don't have to use an stop tag </P>. But, you can and a lot of folks do.   HTML flows all text together eliminating line spaces and paragraph breaks unless tags are inserted. To maintain paragraphing and create lists, special tags are used: paragraph <p> </p>   line break

Lists (ordered, unordered, descriptive)
Here's an unordered list followed by the HTML code to create it:
a   b   c
<ul>   <li>a   <li>b   <li>c   </ul>

Here's an ordered (numbered) list and it's HTML code:
1.line one 2.line two 3.line three
<ol>   <li>line one   <li>line two   <li>line three   </ol>

A descriptive list and its HTML code:
topic 1 definition   topic 2 definition 2
descriptive: <dl>   <dt>topic 1   <dd>definition <dt>topic 2   <dd>definition 2   </dl>

Hyperlinks: You will likely want to make a hypertext link to other pages. This is what makes the web so powerful and fun! To do so, you need to use the following tag:
<a href=" "> </A> The item or page that you want to link to must be within the quotes. The part of your text that you want underlined and linked should be within the tags. To create a link to another page on your web site use a tag like this: **<A HREF="internal.htm">Internal Link</A>** It should look like this on your page:

Internal Link. This is called a relative link.

External Link. To create a link to another page on another Web site use a tag like this: **<A HREF="http://members.xoom.com/myhood/external.html">External Link</A>** It should look like this on your page: External Link. This is called an absolute link.

Image: To display an image file (gif or jpeg) use a tag like this: **<IMG SRC="button.gif">**

Certain characters have special meaning in HTML documents and are reserved and your keyboard does not provide a key for some characters. The ampersand (&) and semicolon (;) are used to create special characters: © displays © " displays " & displays & < displays < > displays >

Sound: To create a link to play a sound file (au, mid or wav) use a tag like this: **<A HREF="song.wav">Play Song</a>** It should look like this on your page: Play Song

Color: To use colored text on your web page make sure you use a browser safe color and use a tag like this: **<FONT COLOR="#008000">COLOR</FONT>**

E-mail: To make a link that sends e-mail use a tag like this: **Please send any comments or suggestions to <A HREF = "mailto:vangreen@texas.net">Me</A>.** It should look like this on your page: Please send any comments or suggestions to Me.

HTML Library program. One tool that is indispensable is The HTML Reference Library. Download it for free at http://www.htmlib.com/where.htm

Aid4 Learning. Need an HTML guide in another language? http://www.y4i.com/htmllanguages.html

HTML 4 Rookies. An extremely easy to understand HTML tutorial for those with little or no webdesign experience. http://www.htmlprimer.com/

HTML: An Interactive Tutorial for Beginners. Teaches you HTML by example. http://www.davesite.com/webstation/html/

HTML Crash Course. An absolute beginner's guide to HTML. Includes all the basics, with clear explanations and lots of examples. http://www.w3-tech.com/crash/

HTML Made Really Easy. Teaches core understanding of HTML. http://www.jmarshall.com/easy/html/

Introduction to HTML. HTML tutorial for people who have never authored hypertext documents before. http://www.cwru.edu/help/introHTML/toc.html

WEB Monkey. Web 101. For examples of most tags you will ever need see the Monkey. http://hotwired.lycos.com/webmonkey/teachingtool/

WebMonkey For Kids. Teaches kids HTML and how to create a Web site. Includes a Planning Guide for parents and teachers.
http://hotwired.lycos.com/webmonkey/kids/lessons/index.html

Webpage Building Tutorial. This tutorial is designed to help you learn how to create a webpage using HTML. There are five lessons arranged in complexity to help you learn the simple art of HTML.
http://www.ccusd.k12.ca.us/httpddoc/high/wayne/stu2/webpage/less1.htm

Writing HTML.. A tutorial for creating www pages. Covers all the basics and more. You can also download this tutorial and learn off-line.
http://www.mcli.dist.maricopa.edu/tut/lessons.html

Be Consistent. To assist you with being consistent in your page layout, develop a page layout that you feel works for your site.

INDEX